Interpretability and Explainability in AI Using Python

Decrypt AI Decision-Making Using Interpretability and Explainability with Python to Build Reliable Machine Learning Systems

Aruna Chakkirala

www.orangeava.com

First Published: April 2025

Published By: Orange Education Pvt Ltd, AVA®

Address: 9, Daryaganj, Delhi, 110002, India

275 New North Road Islington Suite 1314 London,

N1 7AA, United Kingdom

ISBN (PBK): 978-93-48107-57-2

ISBN (E-BOOK): 978-93-48107-74-9

Dedicated To

My Dad, Chandrasekhar:

Who Left This World 30 Years Ago and Yet Has Been a Constant Source of Inner Strength. His Simplicity and Ambition, Despite Numerous Early Hardships, Spoke Volumes and Has Been an Exemplar for Me

About the Author

Aruna Chakkirala, a seasoned technical leader and currently serves as an AI Solutions Architect at Microsoft. She was instrumental in the early adoption of Generative AI and constantly strives to keep pace with the evolving domain. As a Data Scientist, she has built Supervised and Unsupervised models to address cybersecurity problems. She holds a patent for her pioneering work in community detection for DNS querying. Her technical expertise spans multiple domains, including Networks, Security, Cloud, Big Data, and AI. She believes that the success of real-world AI applications increasingly depends on well-defined architectures across all encompassing domains. Her current interests include Generative AI, applications of LLMs and SLMs, Causality, Mechanistic Interpretability, and Explainability tools.

In her two-decade career, she has developed expertise in scale, security, and strategy at various organizations such as Infoblox, Yahoo, Nokia, EFI, and Verisign. Aruna has led highly successful teams and thrives on working with cutting-edge technologies. She is a frequent technical and keynote speaker, panelist, and an active blogger. She contributes to community open groups and serves as a guest faculty member at premier academic institutes. Outside of work, she is an avid reader and enjoys creative writing. A passionate advocate for diversity and inclusion, she is actively involved in GHCI, LeanIn, and WITI communities.

Aruna holds an M.Tech in Software Systems from BITS Pilani and a Master's in Computer Applications from Goa University. She is also an IIMB alumna and has earned certifications in Data Science from IISc Bangalore, Azure Data Science, Azure Data Engineering, and Google Professional Machine Learning Engineer.

About the Technical Reviewer

Nehaa Bansal is a trailblazing thought leader and data scientist with a strong passion for early-stage innovation. Her extensive experience across diverse sectors including banking, finance, telecom, and insurance has honed her expertise in developing impactful predictive models. She graduated with top honors in Computer Science and holds a Master's in Data Science from BITS Pilani, which provided a strong foundation for her career.

Nehaa's professional life is guided by core values of ownership, prioritizing people, and understanding the "why" behind every action. She embraces an agile approach, acting quickly, learning from failures, iterating continuously, and prioritizing fairness. Driven by a passion for solving user problems, Nehaa combines her expertise in analytics, product strategy, and leadership to develop innovative solutions, consistently pushing boundaries and demonstrating unwavering dedication. Nehaa's commitment to continuous learning, inclusivity, and collaboration, combined with her dedication and empathy, makes her an inspiring leader driving positive change in technology and data science.

Acknowledgements

There are a few special people whose unwavering support has meant the world to me during the writing of this book. First and foremost, I would like to thank my mother for encouraging me to spread my wings. I am extremely grateful for the support and motivation provided by my husband Chandrasekhar and daughter Ansha.

My gratitude goes to my organization for providing opportunities to work with the latest technologies and to build influence in the industry. I would like to thank Peter Rizk for the early opportunity in Data Science and Renée Burton, who helped me gain a strong footing in Machine Learning. I was also fortunate to have benefited from the instructive teaching of Prof. Deepak Subramani and Prof. Shashikumaar Ganesan from the Indian Institute of Science. I would like to thank my mentors, colleagues, and industry peers who have guided and shaped my technical perspectives. I would also like to thank my editorial team and technical reviewer, Nehaa Bhansal, for the detailed scrutiny of the content. Lastly, I am extremely grateful to Dr. Rohini Srivathsa for sharing her thoughts in the foreword.

Foreword

– By Dr. Rohini Srivathsa

(Chief Technology Officer – Microsoft India and South Asia)

In today's rapidly evolving technological landscape, the importance of interpretability and explainability in artificial intelligence (AI) cannot be overstated. The transformative power of AI in various industries is undeniable, but with great power comes great responsibility. It is imperative that we ensure our AI systems are transparent, understandable, and trustworthy.

This book is a timely and essential resource for data scientists, machine learning practitioners, and AI enthusiasts. It delves into the critical aspects of interpretability and explainability, providing readers with a comprehensive understanding of these concepts and their practical applications.

The book begins by exploring the fundamentals of interpretability, discussing the differences between white-box and black-box models, and introducing various techniques for explaining AI models. It covers a wide range of topics, from feature effect analysis and post-hoc methods to advanced techniques for interpreting neural networks and transformers. Each chapter is meticulously crafted to provide readers with valuable insights and hands-on experience through Python code snippets.

One of the standout features of this book is its focus on responsible AI. Interpretability is not just about understanding how AI models make decisions; it is also about ensuring that these models are fair, unbiased, and ethical. The book dedicates an entire section to responsible AI, discussing the importance of bias mitigation, causal inference, and adversarial machine learning.

As AI advances, it is crucial to build systems that are not only powerful but also transparent and accountable. This book serves as a guide for achieving that balance, equipping readers with the knowledge and tools needed to develop explainable and trustworthy AI models.

I am confident that this book will be a valuable addition to your library, providing key insights and skills to navigate AI interpretability and explainability. I commend the dedication to this important topic and for creating a resource that will advance responsible AI practices.

Preface

As Machine Learning gains traction in the real-world, Interpretability or Explainability becomes increasingly important. Interpretability is the ability to uncover how a model works or the approach it uses to arrive at a decision. This book unpacks Interpretability for white-box and black-box models through various techniques. White-box models include inherently interpretable models such as Decision Trees and are easier to interpret. On the other hand, Deep Learning models, despite their complexity and black-box characteristics, have techniques for explainability at both the entire model level and for individual decisions.

Explainability in Transformers and LLMs is also gaining traction, given the widespread attention and adoption of LLM models. An entire chapter is dedicated to Explainable Transformers and Large Language Models, touching upon the latest research in this area. Interpretability is also a key component of Responsible AI, ensuring that AI systems are transparent and understandable to users. It encompasses the ability to explain how AI models make decisions, understand the underlying training data, and provide insights into the model's behavior. The focus on interpretability further enables enhanced accountability, trust, and ethical standards in AI development and deployment.

Chapter 1: This chapter starts with a background on Machine Learning and the various supervised and unsupervised modeling techniques. The chapter also reviews deep learning and the facets that add to its complexity. The chapter then introduces Interpretability to gain an intuition on its needs and expectations. Lastly, the chapter describes the various terminology in Interpretability and finally discusses the challenges.

Chapter 2: This chapter details all the model types and the considerations making them Interpretable. The chapter then discusses white-box and black-box models. Finally, the chapter describes model performance metrics and the challenges of improved performance in tandem with Interpretability.

Chapter 3: This chapter extends the previous concept on model types and details the aspects around scope of Interpretability, as well as Interpretability techniques which can be utilized. It also includes a detailed chart of

Interpretability taxonomy and finally discusses Inherently Interpretable models.

Chapter 4: This chapter introduces Model Agnostic Methods, including ICE and PDP plots, which are good visualization tools and provide insights into feature effects in some scenarios. In each of these plots, we focus on the effects of selected features. PDP, or Partial dependence plots, are good for understanding the marginal effect of a feature on the predictions, while ICE plots provide insights of a selected feature's effect on the predictions for every data instance. ALE plots factor in the interaction effects of correlated features and alleviates some of the shortcomings in PDP, making it a useful tool.

Chapter 5: This chapter progresses into Local Model Agnostic methods of LIME and SHAP to understand feature attributions. LIME perturbs the feature of interest and then builds local linear models to explain instances. SHAP identifies the marginal contributions of features and has explainers that leverage LIME techniques. The chapter ends with a hands-on activity to provide a better understanding of these techniques.

Chapter 6: This chapter continues with Model Agnostic explainability methods. Anchors and Counterfactual Explanations are an extension on the LIME and SHAP techniques discussed in the previous chapter. While Anchors provide rules to quantify a local explanation, Counterfactual explanations add additional detail on the changes required in a local instance to get to an alternate outcome.

Chapter 7: This chapter introduces Neural network explainability, starting with computer vision. The previous chapter had examples using LIME & SHAP in deep neural networks, but there are more specific gradient and non-gradient based techniques for integrating explainability and interpretability in Deep Learning.

Chapter 8: This chapter extends on the explainability techniques in Neural Networks. In particular, the chapter focuses on class activation maps as a technique to capture explainability. Lastly, the chapter also discusses the variations of class activation maps for improving explainability.

Chapter 9: This chapter starts with the transformer model and specifically focuses on explainability in large language models. Transformer explainability ranges from leveraging attention, traditional permutation-based methods to more recently researched techniques such as Mechanistic Interpretability. The chapter also reviews the latest Explainability research in Large Language Models and its challenges.

Chapter 10: Interpretability and Explainability is incomplete without a discussion of Responsible AI. This chapter takes a deeper look at Responsible AI, or Ethical AI; identifying and mitigating bias is also an important aspect of Responsible AI. Finally, the chapter concludes with Causal Interpretability, Adversarial attacks in XAI, and the defenses available.

Get a Free eBook

We hope you are enjoying your recently purchased book! Your feedback is incredibly valuable to us, and to all other readers looking for great books.

If you found this book helpful or enjoyable, we would truly appreciate it, if you could take a moment to leave a short review with a 5 star rating on Amazon. It helps us grow, and lets other readers discover our books.

As a thank you, we would love to send you a free digital copy of this book, and a **30%** discount code on your next cart value on our official websites:

www.orangeava.com

www.orangeava.in (For Indian Subcontinent)

☑ **Here's how:**

Leave a review for the book on Amazon.

Take a screenshot of your review, and send an email to **info@orangeava.com** (it can be just the confirmation screen).

Once, we receive your screenshot, we will send you the digital file, within 24 hours.

Thank you so much for your support – it means a lot to us!

Downloading the code bundles and colored images

Please follow the links or scan the QR codes to download the
Code Bundles and Images of the book:

https://github.com/ava-orange-education/Interpretability-and-Explainability-in-AI-Using-Python

The code bundles and images of the book are also hosted on
https://rebrand.ly/bd229f

In case there's an update to the code, it will be updated on the existing GitHub repository.

Errata

We take immense pride in our work at **Orange Education Pvt Ltd**, and follow best practices to ensure the accuracy of our content to provide an indulging reading experience to our subscribers. Our readers are our mirrors, and we use their inputs to reflect and improve upon human errors, if any, that may have occurred during the publishing processes involved. To let us maintain the quality and help us reach out to any readers who might be having difficulties due to any unforeseen errors, please write to us at :

errata@orangeava.com

Your support, suggestions, and feedback are highly appreciated.

DID YOU KNOW

Did you know that Orange Education Pvt Ltd offers eBook versions of every book published, with PDF and ePub files available? You can upgrade to the eBook version at **www.orangeava.com** and as a print book customer, you are entitled to a discount on the eBook copy. Get in touch with us at: **info@orangeava.com** for more details.

At **www.orangeava.com**, you can also read a collection of free technical articles, sign up for a range of free newsletters, and receive exclusive discounts and offers on Print Books and eBooks.

PIRACY

If you come across any illegal copies of our works in any form on the internet, we would be grateful if you would provide us with the location address or website name. Please contact us at **info@orangeava.com** with a link to the material.

ARE YOU INTERESTED IN AUTHORING WITH US?

If there is a topic that you have expertise in, and you are interested in either writing or contributing to a book, please write to us at **business@orangeava.com**. We are on a journey to help developers and tech professionals to gain insights on the present technological advancements and innovations happening across the globe and build a community that believes Knowledge is best acquired by sharing and learning with others. Please reach out to us to learn what our audience demands and how you can be part of this educational reform. We also welcome ideas from tech experts and help them build learning and development content for their domains.

REVIEWS

Please leave a review. Once you have read and used this book, why not leave a review on the site that you purchased it from? Potential readers can then see and use your unbiased opinion to make purchase decisions. We at Orange Education would love to know what you think about our products, and our authors can learn from your feedback. Thank you!

For more information about Orange Education, please visit **www.orangeava.com**.

Table of Contents

CHAPTER 1
Interpreting Interpretable Machine Learning

Introduction

This chapter starts with an overview of Machine Learning and its various types. In the process, we will revisit supervised, unsupervised, and other model types, and explore deep learning along with the factors that add to its complexity. We will then explore Interpretability in Machine Learning, discussing its importance, expectations, and the key terms associated with it. Lastly, we will discuss the challenges and tradeoffs related to Interpretability.

Structure

In this chapter, we will discuss the following topics:

- All Pervasive Machine Learning
- Machine Learning Methods
- Deep Learning
- The Age of the Transformer
- Machine Learning in the Real World
- Interpretability and its Importance
- Challenges and Tradeoffs

All Pervasive Machine Learning

Machine Learning influences our everyday lives in many subtle ways. The buzzing smartphones in our pockets, movies recommended on Netflix, and the discounts offered on our e-commerce purchases are all instances of all-pervasive machine learning. The smartphone that efficiently categorizes our pictures into albums and identifies people in them using vision models. Similarly, the movies recommended to you, which seem very much in line with your taste, are, in fact, a consequence of recommendation systems, which have learned from your previous viewing patterns. Reinforcement learning techniques identify the discounts offered to an end user, which most often results in a purchase to enhance the likelihood of future sales. There are many other instances of machine learning in our vicinity which often go unnoticed and unacknowledged and yet create a positive impact.

Historically, the term Machine Intelligence was coined by Alan Turing in the 1950s marking the start of early Artificial Intelligence. Over the decades, there were years of prolific AI activity while some years witnessed AI winters. In the late 1960s, there were two streams emerging in AI. One camp was working on rules-based systems (also called expert systems or symbolic), while the other group placed their bets on neural networks. The rules-based camp took the lead in the intervening years, primarily because the resources required for neural networks were scarce. Neural networks require relevant data, a strong algorithm, a narrow domain and a concrete goal (source: AI Superpowers - Kai Fu Lee). The availability of data was difficult, and relevant data in particular. A big element of the spurt in Machine Learning was evident when big data came into the fray and data storage became affordable.

There are multiple schools of thought on the definition of Artificial Intelligence and Machine Learning; artificial intelligence is considered all-encompassing and includes machine learning, deep learning among other areas. Recently, the terms Artificial Intelligence and Machine Learning are often used interchangeably. We will continue to use the two terms interchangeably in this book to stick to the prevailing trend.

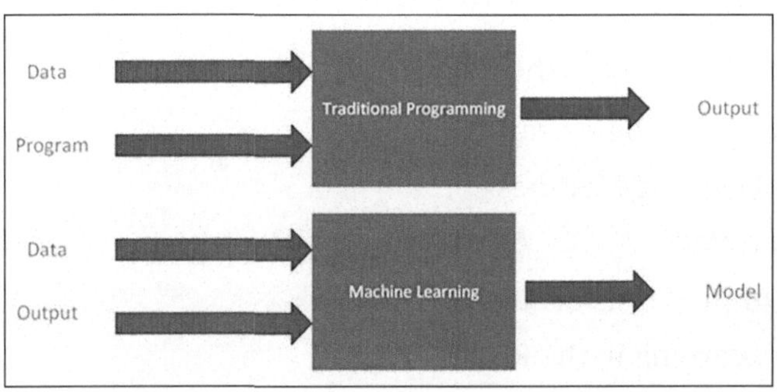

***Figure 1.1**: Machine Learning builds models*

In the past decade, machine learning methods have driven modern data analysis across Industry applications. When we interact with search engines and recommender systems, it is machine learning algorithms under the hood for content recommendation. Similarly, advertisers and financial institutions use machine learning to predict customer behavior, compliance, or risk. Machine learning is termed a general-purpose technology, as it can be used across Industries.

Machine Learning Methods

There are multiple types of machine learning algorithms which are generally divided into four types: Supervised Learning, Unsupervised Learning, Semi-Supervised Learning, and Reinforcement Learning. Deep learning fits into the larger artificial intelligence space and it leverages neural networks at its core. Machine learning algorithms include classification analysis, regression analysis, data clustering, association rule learning, and feature engineering for dimensionality reduction.

In the following machine learning-based classification model, the model is trained from historical data in phase 1, and the outcome is generated in phase 2 for the new test data.

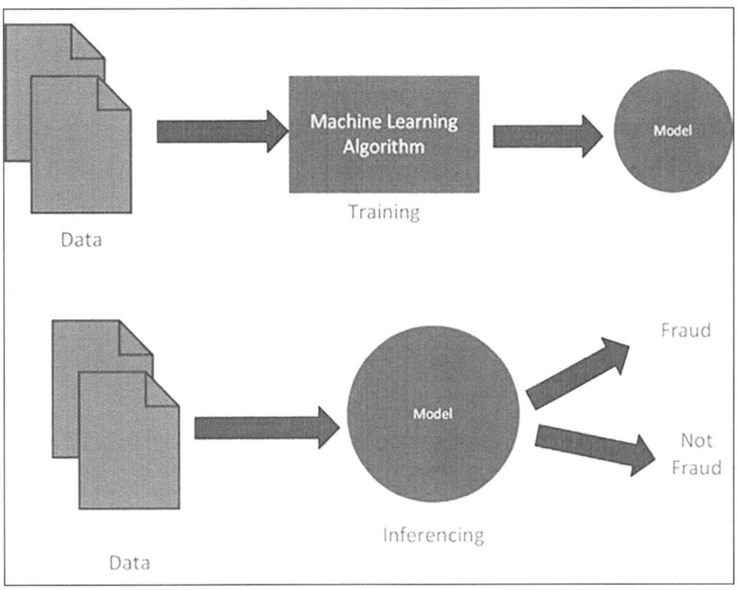

Figure 1.2: *Machine Learning process*

Machine learning algorithms are divided based on the amount and type of supervision provided while training.

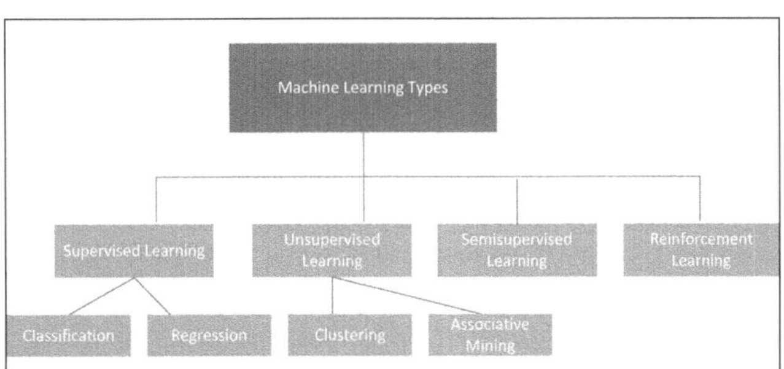

Figure 1.3: *Machine Learning Types*

Supervised Machine Learning

In Supervised Learning, the input includes the training data and the outcomes, also called labels. Supervised Learning can be further divided into Classification and Regression.

Classification

Identifying fraud is a classic example of Classification in supervised learning. Many transactions are provided along with their class (fraud or not fraud), and using this training dataset, the model learns to identify the patterns associated with fraudulent transactions.

Document Classification is another example, where the documents can be classified into multiple classes. For instance, an organization with many departments is regularly classifying the documents based on the content. In this instance, there are as many classes as departments.

Mathematically, it maps a function (*f*) from the input variables (X) to output variables (Y) as a target. The target serves as a label in the training phase and becomes an outcome prediction or category when using the model. Identifying or predicting the class for a data input is a classification problem. For instance, the transaction can be classified as fraud or not fraud.

The following is a list of common types of Classification problems:

- Binary classification is a classification which has two class labels. In the preceding example, spam detection is a binary with the outcome being either spam or not spam.
- Multiclass classification has more than two class labels. The data can be used to predict multiple different classes. Extending our example earlier, the transaction can be classified as fraudulent based on the type of pattern utilized, or a cybersecurity attack can be classified based on the type of attack mechanism utilized. Hence, a network attack can be classified as DDOS (Distributed Denial of Service), U2R (User to Root Attack), R2L (Root to Local Attack), and Probing Attack.
- In machine learning, multi-label classification is an important consideration where an example is associated with several classes or labels. In the preceding document classification, a document can have multiple department labels when the content is relevant across departments. This is unlike traditional classification tasks where class labels are mutually exclusive.

Regression

Regression analysis of machine learning predicts a continuous output based on the value of one or more predictor variables. The difference between classification and regression is that classification is to predict distinct class labels, while in regression, the predicted output is a continuous quantity. Regression models are used in many applications across various fields. For instance, in manufacturing maintenance prediction, marketing, financial forecasting, trend analysis, disease prediction, and many more. There are multiple regression algorithms: linear, polynomial, lasso, ridge regression, and so on.

Note that some regression algorithms can be used for classification as well, and vice versa. For example, Logistic Regression is commonly used for classification, as it can output a value that corresponds to the probability of belonging to a given class (for example, 20% chance of being spam).

Here are some of the most commonly used supervised learning algorithms:

- Linear Regression
- Logistic Regression
- Support Vector Machines (SVMs)
- Decision Trees and Random Forests (Can be used for both Classification and Regression problems)
- k-Nearest Neighbors (Can be used for both Classification and Regression problems)

Unsupervised Learning

As implied in the name, unsupervised learning is devoid of training, which translates to the training phase not having data with the labels, that is, unlabeled data. The model discerns patterns using the features in the data.

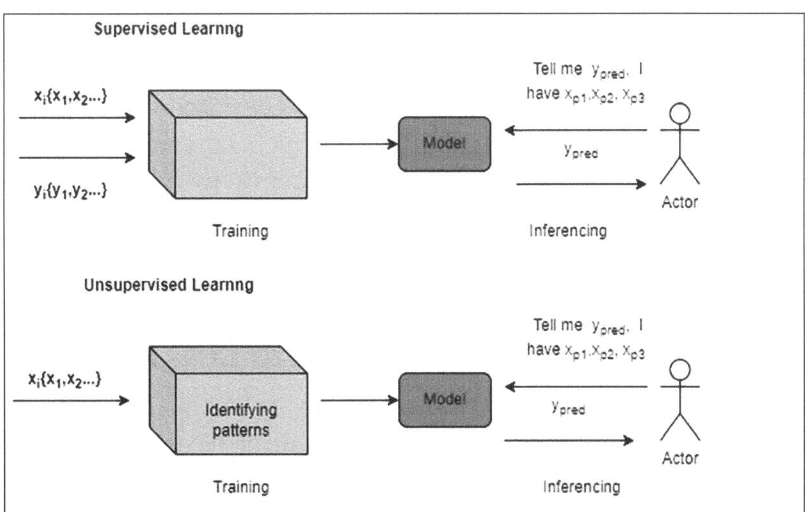

Figure 1.4: *Supervised vs Unsupervised Learning*

For instance, we have a dataset of purchase history on an e-commerce website and want to group customers with similar purchase habits. An algorithm can be used to detect groups with similar habits. At no point do you tell the algorithm which groups to consider and earmark the customers into groups; it finds those connections without your help. It might identify that 40% of the customers are males who love comic books and generally shop on weekends, while 20% are young sci-fi lovers who purchase multiple books periodically, and so on.

Clustering

Cluster analysis, also known as clustering, is an unsupervised machine learning technique that identifies and groups related data points within large datasets. Unlike supervised methods, clustering does not rely on specific outcomes or labels. Instead, it organizes objects into clusters based on their similarity. These clusters reveal interesting trends or patterns, such as consumer behavior groups as mentioned in the example of e-commerce website. Applications of clustering span diverse domains, including cybersecurity, e-commerce, mobile data processing, health analytics, and user modeling.

When employing a hierarchical clustering algorithm, it can further subdivide groups into smaller clusters. This subdivision can be advantageous for targeted communication, such as tailoring posts to specific groups. Consider an example where animals are distinctly separated from vehicles, horses are closely related to deer but distant from birds, and so on.

Clustering visualization algorithms serve as excellent illustrations of unsupervised learning techniques. These algorithms process intricate, unlabeled data and produce 2D or 3D representations that can be easily visualized. Their primary objective is to preserve the inherent structure within the data. By avoiding overlap of clusters in the input space during visualization, these algorithms provide insights into the organization of data and may even reveal unexpected patterns.

Another related task is dimensionality reduction, which aims to simplify data without significant information loss. One approach involves merging correlated features into a single feature. For instance, a car's mileage often correlates with its age. In this case, a dimensionality reduction algorithm would combine these features to represent the overall wear and tear of the car—a process known as feature extraction.

Dimensionality Reduction and Feature Learning

In the realm of machine learning and data science, handling high-dimensional data poses challenges for researchers and developers. Dimensionality reduction, an unsupervised learning technique, plays a crucial role by enhancing human interpretability, reducing computational complexity, and mitigating overfitting and redundancy in models.

Two primary approaches for dimensionality reduction are feature selection and feature extraction. The key distinction lies in their outcomes:

- **Feature Selection**: This method retains a subset of the original features, discarding irrelevant or redundant ones. Before feeding data to another machine learning algorithm (such as a supervised learning model), it is advisable to reduce dimensionality. Doing so results in faster processing, reduced disk and memory usage, and potentially improved performance.
- **Feature Extraction**: Here, entirely new features are created, capturing essential information from the original data. Correlated features can be merged into a single feature. For instance, a car's mileage often correlates with its age. In this case, a dimensionality reduction algorithm would combine these features to represent the overall wear and tear of the car–a process known as feature extraction.

Association Rule Learning

Association Rule Learning is a rule-based machine learning approach that uncovers interesting relationships expressed as "IF-THEN" statements within extensive datasets. For instance, consider the association: If a customer purchases a computer or laptop, they are likely to buy anti-virus software simultaneously.

Association rules are used in various industries for multiple solutions, including behavior analytics, customer purchase patterns, web user behaviors, cybersecurity, medical diagnosis, and others. Unlike sequence mining, association rule learning typically disregards the order of events within or across transactions. To assess the utility of association rules, we rely on parameters such as "support" and "confidence".

Anomaly Detection

Lastly, anomaly detection is a critical unsupervised task. While it is generally classified as unsupervised, it can be a supervised model when the required labeled data of normal and anomalous instances is available. It involves identifying unusual instances, such as detecting fraudulent credit card transactions, catching manufacturing defects, or automatically removing outliers from a dataset before further analysis.

Semi-Supervised Learning

In the realm of machine learning, semi-supervised learning bridges the gap between supervised and unsupervised approaches. Unlike purely supervised learning, where every data point has an associated label, and unsupervised learning, which lacks labeled data, semi-supervised learning operates with a mix of both.

Consider photo-hosting services such as Google Photos as prime examples. When you upload family photos, the system automatically identifies recurring individuals (Person

A in photos 1, 5, and 11, and Person B in photos 2, 5, and 7). This initial recognition is the unsupervised part, achieved through clustering. However, the system still requires your input to assign names to these individuals—just one label per person. This labeling process enhances photo search functionality.

Recently there has been an increase in self-supervised learning, which can be considered as a variation of this method. The key difference is that self-supervised learning does not require labeled data.

Reinforcement Learning

Reinforcement Learning (RL) operates in a distinct manner. In this context, the learning system—referred to as an agent—interacts with its environment, making observations, selecting actions, and receiving rewards (or penalties) in return. The agent's ultimate goal is to discover the optimal strategy, known as a policy, that maximizes cumulative rewards over time. Essentially, a policy guides the agent's actions based on its current situation. The policy also needs to account for the actions repeatedly exploiting one known high-reward action. The explore vs exploit tradeoff means that the agent needs to sometimes explore new actions to understand their rewards/penalties. This is especially important in a dynamic real-world application where the penalties/rewards for certain actions could have changed and periodic revisiting is required to keep learning.

For instance, robots often employ RL algorithms to learn how to walk. Additionally, DeepMind's AlphaGo program serves as a remarkable RL example. In 2016, it gained fame by defeating world champion Lee Sedol in the ancient game of Go. AlphaGo honed its winning policy by analyzing millions of games and even playing against itself.

Deep Learning

Deep Learning gained momentum with growth in data and growth in scale. Machine Learning works well for a lot of scenarios, but as the data increases, counterintuitively the effective impact on the model performance does not increase after a threshold point. On the other hand, Deep Learning models benefit from the increase in data, especially the large neural networks. Deep learning involves layers of neurons in various architectures to process data and simulate human thinking. Some common use cases for deep learning are visual object recognition and understanding human speech. Deep learning uses neural networks composed of multiple layers for processing, such as input, hidden, and output layers, to learn from the data provided.

Deep learning involves a highly diverse set of concepts with deep neural network models of various architectures and modalities, including speech, vision, and text. There are architectures for training deep learning systems, including CNN, RNN, LSTM, Graph Neural Networks, and Transformers. CNNs are typically used for visual data, while more complex tasks in visual data, such as image segmentation, could benefit from Transformers. Similarly, LSTMs work well for time series forecasting since the pattern-matching principles for an image have parallels in time series data. There are, of course, transformer models which are being used in a wide range of activities.

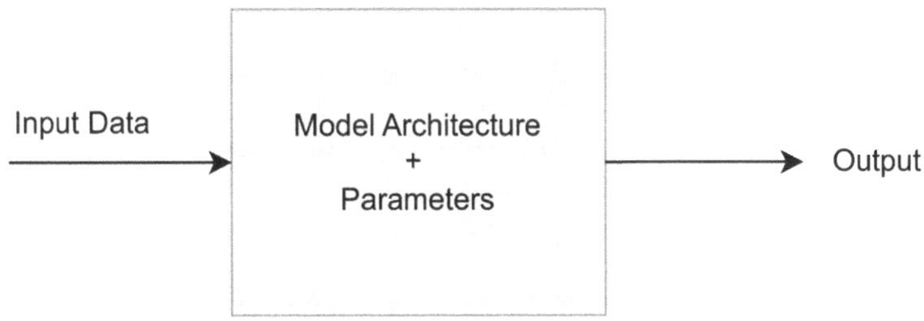

Figure 1.5: *Deep Learning*

Applications in deep learning range across conversation AI, recommendation systems, computer vision, and so on. Conversational AI provides mechanisms to interact using natural language and now also utilize foundational models such as Large Language Models to augment the conversational experience. Conversational AI can also provide a voice-enabled interface to make the user interaction richer and seamless. Recommendation systems offer meaningful and relevant search results and services based on the observed patterns, user interests, and demographics, enriching end-user experiences. Computer vision applications gain knowledge from images and videos and are applicable in many scenarios where image data is highly prominent, such as healthcare.

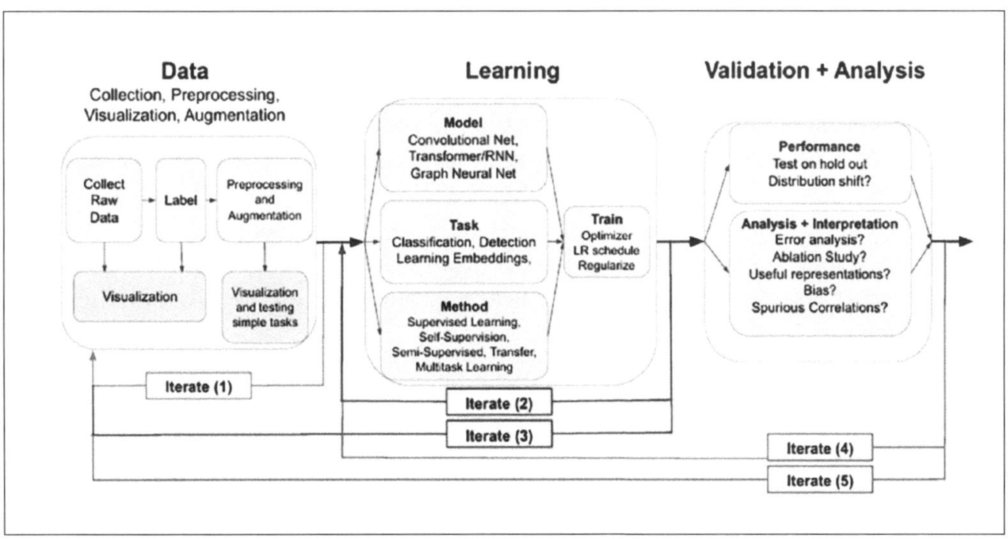

Figure 1.6: *Model Training process*

(Source: A Survey of Deep Learning for Scientific Discovery (2020) Raghu et al)

Deep learning follows a similar machine learning process, but the complexity of the model implies more resource-intensive. Training tasks which originally took days and weeks can now utilize GPU accelerators and deep learning frameworks to speed up training. The deployment of models using GPU-accelerated inference aids in delivering high performance and optimal end-user experience across the cloud, embedded into devices or in edge systems such as cars. The past decade has witnessed many breakthroughs in AI, including DeepMind's AlphaGo, intelligent assistants, and self-driving cars. Now the Transformer has created more ripples with its various models for natural language processing, vision, and other areas.

The Age of the Transformer

The RNNs and LSTMs were an improvement from the previous Deep Learning architectures, but they lacked the ability to handle large sequences and specifically the dependencies. For instance, a sentence to be translated from English to German is as follows:

"Maya likes reading and music, and she is a voracious reader."

The pronoun "she" refers to "Maya" in the sentence. Similarly, the sentence implies Maya is a voracious reader. This is a toy example, but as sentences and paragraphs increase in size, prior context and dependency need to be preserved and ascertained to improve the performance of the model.

In natural language processing, the input is first tokenized, implying the text is tokenized and then converted into vectors understood by the neural network. The input can be a series of tokens with implied dependencies buried across long token sequences; these dependencies are important to capture so as to get a correct output. Recurrent Neural Networks (RNN) processes the input, token by token, and tracking long dependencies is not supported in its inherent design. Attention is a technique which introduces a memory concept by focusing on relevant elements of long sequences. This provides a mechanism to model long-term dependencies in the input to build on selected connections. Self-attention adds an additional element where it focuses on the same sequence, and it is a crucial design element in enhancing the performance for the transformer.

The RNN deficit with memory can be improved with attention techniques, but it still remained slow to train and had inherent optimization challenges with vanishing and exploding gradients. The transformer model addresses these shortcomings with a feedforward neural network which utilizes the self-attention mechanism. Additionally, it also has positional embeddings to track the location aspect of sequential data. The transformer model is based on the exceptionally popular paper, *Attention is all you need*, which has become the basis for many new technologies, including Generative AI.

Generative AI

Generative AI (GenAI), a subset of Artificial Intelligence learns from diverse content–text, images, and audio–to create novel artifacts. Unlike discriminative ML algorithms, which focus on decision boundaries, GenAI produces outputs with a wide spectrum of variety and complexity.

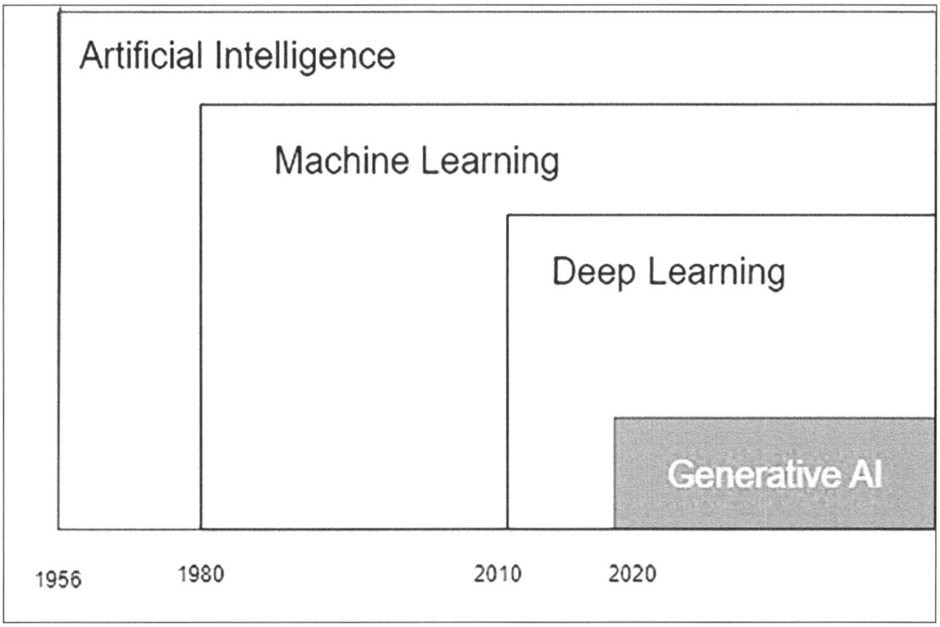

Figure 1.7: *Generative AI in the scheme of things*

A significant recent advancement in GenAI is OpenAI's GPT-3 model. GPT-3 is classified as a Large Language Model, as it has 175 billion parameters. The other remarkable aspect of LLMs is that they are trained on vast volumes of data, leading to a model which is highly adept at many different tasks. Unlike traditional machine learning, where the models are trained for a single task and hence can do a single task, these models can do multiple tasks, such as completion, summarizing, and so on. ChatGPT had witnessed the fastest adoption curve, reaching 100 million users in only a few months. This versatile language model generates remarkably human-like text. These models excel at tasks such as auto-completing code, translating between programming languages and even converting natural language to code.

Additionally, domain-specific generative language models have emerged, addressing areas such as software engineering. The industry has embraced GenAI for software engineering practices, exemplified by tools such as GitHub CoPilot2. Starting from November 2022, after ChatGPT created a *furore*, many large language models have been released. There are also small language models which are geared towards addressing a few tasks well. Small Language Models also have a smaller footprint as they have fewer parameters. Similarly, many multimodal models are now available which can handle media types, such as text, images, speech, videos. Examples include DALL·E, Stable Diffusion, Whisper, and Sora.

A big aspect of using these foundational models is the prompt which is provided. A prompt is the natural language query posed to the model as an input. The model then interprets the prompt and provides a response (technically, it does a completion, which means it is predicting the next set of words iteratively until it satisfies the prompt). Prompting relies on a lot of nuances around precision, grounding and guardrails to ensure that the response is in line with expectations and handles issues like hallucinations and abusive usage appropriately.

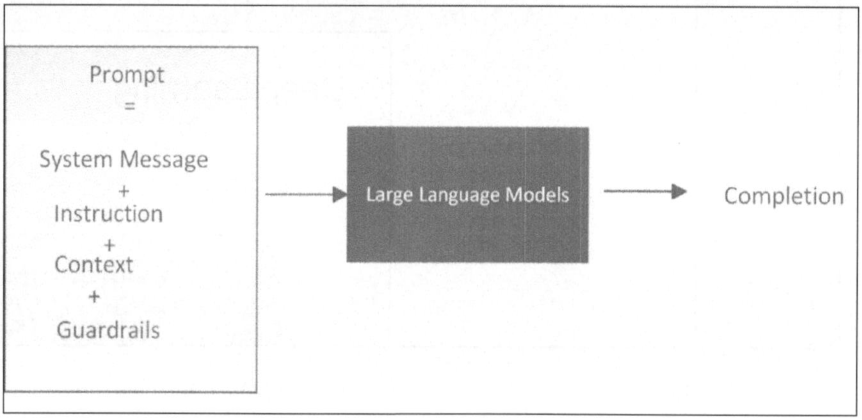

Figure 1.8: *Basics of LLM working*

However, challenges remain. How can we enhance GenAI's accessibility and usage? One critical question centers on explainability: How can users gain a better mental model of GenAI's inner workings?

Machine Learning in the Real World

Every innovation leads to major new trends with the technologies. The era of mobiles and smartphones led to many changes in our lives every day, with technologies such as Uber and Maps easing our movement. Similarly, Artificial Intelligence is geared to make even bigger strides in our lives. Andrew Ng recently termed it as a general-purpose technology akin to electricity, which means it will influence many areas. There are many instances of machine learning around us, and quite a few of those applications are oblivious to humans. Responses to our search keywords, recommended products on Amazon, shortest routes on maps, and many others. There are multiple instances of machine learning in industries across Healthcare, Finance, Retail, Manufacturing, and also in Citizen-centric services.

Some of the often-seen applications of Machine Learning are:

Input (X)	**Output (Y)**	**Application**
User Info, Product Ad	Click (Y/N)	Digital Advertising
Email	Spam (Y/N)	Spam Filtering
DNS Queries	Threat (Y/N)	DNS Security
DNS Queries	Threat Type	DNS Security
Video Streams	Risky activity	Video Surveillance
Customer Purchases	Similar groups	Marketing

Table 1.1: *Applications of Machine Learning*

- **Recommendation Systems:**

  Recommendation engines are widely used in machine learning, including e-commerce websites. The systems analyze user behaviors, including browsing history, past purchases, and shopping cart activity, to identify patterns. Similarly, companies such as **Spotify** and **Netflix** employ similar algorithms to recommend music or TV shows based on users' listening and viewing history.

- **Social Media Connections:**

  Social media platforms (**LinkedIn**, **Instagram**, **Facebook**, and **X**, formerly known as **Twitter**) utilize a similar training algorithm for their **"people you may know"** feature. Evaluating your contacts, comments, likes, and existing connections, the algorithm suggests familiar faces from your real-life network, surfacing potential connections or followers.

- **Virtual Personal Assistants:**
  - **Virtual personal assistants** such as **Amazon's Alexa**, **Google Home**, or **Apple iPhone's Siri,** reside in our homes. The devices utilize **speech recognition technology** and **machine learning** to understand requests and gauge their accuracy. When you start speaking, they listen, interpret your words, and execute commands.
  - For instance, if you ask Siri about the weather, it searches the web for forecasts specific to your location.

- **Conversational AI:**
  - **Chatbots**, a variant of virtual assistants, aim to provide answers to users. They intuitively contextualize responses using **context** and other metadata.
  - Chatbots equipped with **voice** and **natural language interfaces**, powered by **generative AI**, enhance user experience by efficiently delivering the necessary support.

- **Stock Market Predictions:**
    - **Predictive analytics** and **algorithmic trading** find widespread use in industries, such as finance, real estate, and product development.
    - Machine learning **classifies data into groups** and defines them using rules set by data analysts.
    - After classification, analysts calculate the **probability of specific actions**.
    - These methods aid in **predicting stock market performance** based on year-to-year analysis. Analysts can even forecast stock prices for **2025 and beyond**.
- **Credit Card Fraud Detection:**
    - **Predictive analytics** plays a crucial role in determining whether a credit card transaction is **fraudulent or legitimate**.
    - Fraud examiners utilize AI and machine learning to **monitor variables** associated with past fraud incidents.
    - Analyzing these training examples, they assess the **likelihood of specific events** being fraudulent activity.
- **Traffic Predictions:**
    - When using **Google Maps** for navigation, it estimates your arrival time.
    - Google employs **machine learning models** based on historical traffic data to predict trip durations.
    - Considering current traffic conditions, it suggests the optimal route.
- **Image Recognition:**
    - **Machine learning** enables programs to identify objects or people in images.
    - Using pixel intensity, facial recognition systems (such as **Face ID**) enhance security.
    - In law enforcement, databases are filtered to match faces, aiding investigations.
- **Natural Language Processing (NLP):**
    - Language models recognize speech signals and convert them into text.
    - AI-powered software applications can transcribe both recorded and live speech
    - Voice-based technologies can be used in medical applications, such as helping doctors extract important medical terminology from a conversation with a patient.
    - Other speech recognition services provide patients with reminders to "take their medication" as if they have a home health aide by their side.

- **Self-driving car technology:**
    - A frequently used type of machine learning is reinforcement learning, which is used to power self-driving car technology.
    - Self-driving vehicle company Waymo uses machine learning sensors to collect data on the car's surrounding environment in real-time. This data helps guide the car's response in different situations, whether it is a human crossing the street, a red light, or another car on the highway.

Interpretability and its Importance

As machine earning applications become prevalent in many scenarios, building trust in the model becomes important. The machine learning model is focused on predicting outcomes for a given input data. An important question purported by the human user is on the outcomes and the model's rationale in leading to the specific prediction. Trust and transparency are important hallmarks for applying machine learning. The ability to understand how the models work can be an important aspect for building trust in the predictions and hence the model. There are also regulatory requirements for interpretability in industries, such as finance and healthcare, which make this a necessity.

Defining Interpretability

In the context of ML systems, Interpretability is the ability to explain or make it understandable for a human. In models, Interpretability provides a mechanism to evaluate decisions with additional information. This information serves the purpose of explaining the system and the reasoning for the decisions; we can then verify whether the reasoning sounds plausible.

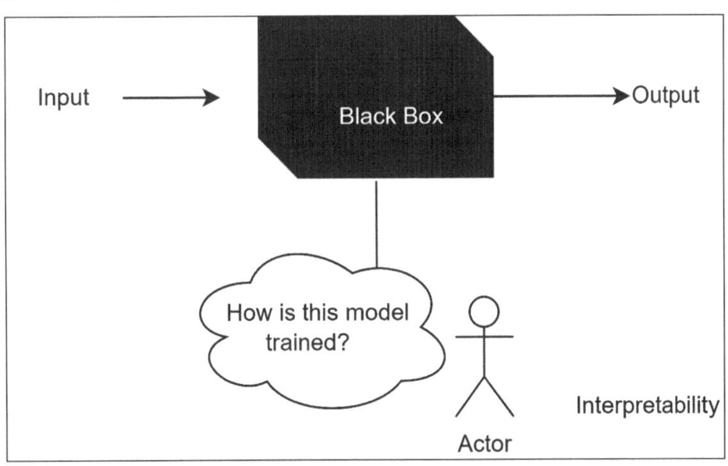

***Figure 1.9**: Models and Interpretability concerns*

Explainable AI

XAI is defined as the extent to which AI outcomes are insightful for the general public. The primary difference cited between Interpretability and Explainability is in the scope applied to a model and its predictions. Interpretability deals with the model as a whole, while Explainability refers to the ability to explain individual outcomes. Considering the scope of Interpretability across the model and all its behaviors, Explainability is considered as a sub section of interpretability. In many papers, XAI is considered synonymous with Interpretability, and we will stick to this definition in this book primarily since Interpretability is often achieved through explainability techniques.

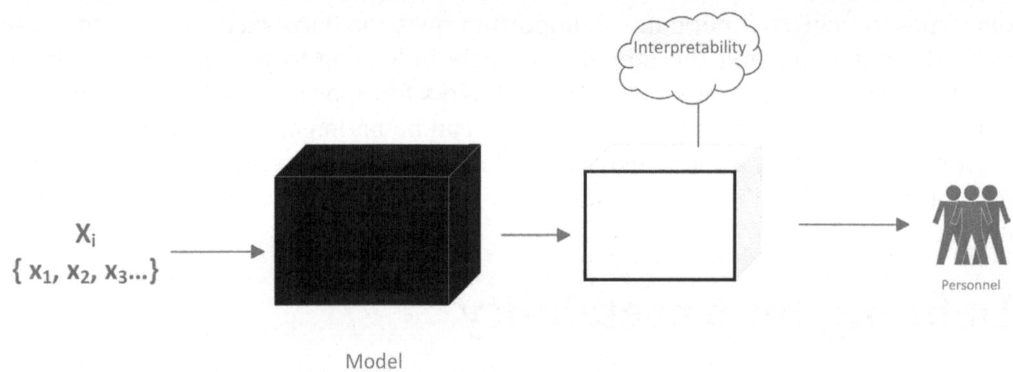

***Figure 1.10**: Interpretability in Machine Learning*

Interpretability and explainability fit into the larger umbrella of Responsible AI. As Artificial intelligence (AI) becomes a mainstay in various industries with the potential to revolutionize fields from healthcare to finance, there is an increasing callout for transparency and trust. In other applications, we see an increased emphasis on adopting strong measures for controlling fairness, bias and reliability in AI. Responsible AI places importance on developing trustworthy AI systems that reduce bias and provide security and privacy. This essentially enhances transparency and accountability. Explainable AI (XA) is sometimes considered as a basis or a tool for enabling Responsible AI (RAI) by improving transparency.

Interpretability or XAI is indeed a powerful tool for answering critical How and Why questions of models and their decisions. A decision to buy a house based on a couple of factors or features such as the size and amenities could be easily accomplished with a Linear Regression model. And given the nature of the model, it is possible to interpret the behavior of the features which impacted the outcome. The complexity increases when many features are involved and the increased dimensionality renders the model difficult to interpret by a human. The interpretability gap is further exacerbated in deep learning models.

Consider a model which takes as input an amino acid sequence and outputs the predicted protein properties. Training the model would mean a neural network involving many layers and complex architectures. We would like to understand how the amino acid sequence resulted in a specific protein function. Interpretability techniques can be used to answer such questions. Interpretability methods are often believed to be a fully understandable, step-by-step explanation of the model's decision process. Such a detailed insight may not be a possibility, especially for complex deep neural network models. To address such situations, Interpretability focuses on a wider set of techniques to provide insights ranging from feature importance and feature attributions (determining what input features matter the most) to model inspection (determining what causes certain neurons in the network to fire).

Need for Interpretability

Machine learning models are built and trained with the aim of optimizing an objective function such as an accuracy metric. Such object functions are not sufficient measurements in capturing the real-world implications of a model's decisions. Implications on fairness and bias are also difficult to discern from the objective function, making it difficult to quantify the cost of an unfair or biased decision.

Interpretability is needed to augment the model metrics. It also gives us the ability to understand what the model is learning, decision justifications, and other information enabling us to enhance the trust and transparency of the real-world problem we are trying to solve.

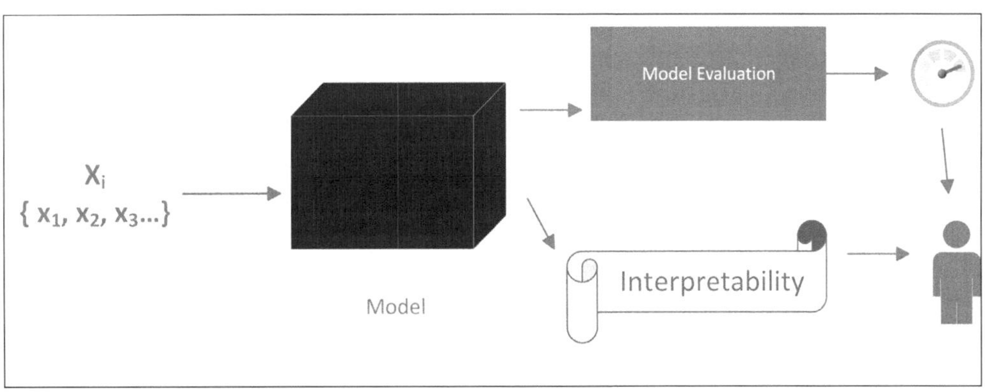

Figure 1.11: *Integrated Interpretability into Machine Learning Lifecycle*

The models where the inner workings are not visible or known is a black box as they consume an input and produce an output prediction, but the process of arriving at the specific prediction is not understood. This raises questions about the predictions and decisions. Can the predictions be trusted? What is the rationale leading to the prediction? To address these questions, machine learning interpretability has emerged as an important area to provide insights into the model decisions. The research is also now expanding into newer interesting areas: interpretability in large language models and reverse engineering deep learning models.

Interpretability Expectations

Questions of this nature are indicative of interpretability:

- How does this model work?
- Why is the prediction 'y' for my data?
- What caused the prediction to be 'y'?
- What do I need to fix in my input to have a different outcome?
- Can I trust this model and its predictions?

The needs and requirements of explainability vary across personas:

- **A Data scientist** wants to build models with high accuracy. Their prerogative is to understand the underlying features and algorithms to find out how they can pick the best model and improve it. Additionally, they want to get insights from the model, as they are required to communicate their findings to their target audience.
- **End users** primarily are keen to understand the rationale for the prediction given by a model. They want to be assured that they are being treated fairly and want to build trust when they are shopping online or doing other activities on the web. They want to know how they will be affected by those decisions and also whether they need to object to any decision.
- **Regulators** and lawmakers are primarily concerned with protecting consumers. They also want to make the system fair and transparent.

While each persona has specific needs leading to interpretability, the collective goal of interpretability methods and needs is to address the following requirements:

- **Trust and Transparency:** Transparent models enable users to trust the decisions made by AI, increasing the adoption of machine learning in various industries. Interpretability, just like trust, is difficult to define. Trust can be a factor in the comfort we have in deploying a model into a real-world scenario, while interpretability can often be a precursor to building trust. A model that is better understood makes it easier to be deployed, especially in high-stakes environments such as financial or medical applications where the implications of an incorrect decision have consequences. This comfort on the model is not indicative of the model's effectiveness or accuracy. But relies more on the understanding and the mechanics of arriving at individual predictions. It becomes especially imperative to build trust when the deployment environment diverges from the training environment.

- **Compliance and Regulations**: Many industries, such as finance and healthcare, require explanations for AI-based decisions, necessitating interpretable models. The regulatory requirements are created with the consumers' best interests so that every decision involving the consumer is backed by an understandable reasoning for the outcomes. Non-compliance with regulations can lead to monetary penalties, and hence, organizations are proactively seeking interpretability and explainability. The AI decisions in healthcare are also viewed with more rigor, as they directly impact a human. The ethical and regulatory requirements imply a need for explainability.
- **Causality:** Supervised machine learning models learn some patterns and associations between input variables and outcomes, leading to hypotheses. These associations can be further tested to verify the associations. For instance, when we learn a relationship between sale of ice-creams and hot weather or an association between COVID-19 and long-term COVID-19, clinical tests can be conducted to determine if there is a cause effect relationship in the latter.
- **Debugging and Improvemen**t: Understanding how a model makes decisions helps to identify potential issues and improve model performance.
- **Transferability:**

  The ability to generalize is a lot easier for humans in comparison to machine learning models. Model interpretability provides a mechanism to determine the model's performance in the real-world setup. The model may need to be monitored to understand its performance on deployment. An instance where the model is unable to generalize is adversarial attacks. In the following figure, we see a fast-adversarial example on ImageNet which leads the image of a panda to be misinterpreted as a gibbon. While adversarial training can help in such scenarios, the point under consideration is the model's inability to generalize. Understanding the models working helps to identify such potential problems and accordingly use appropriate measures.

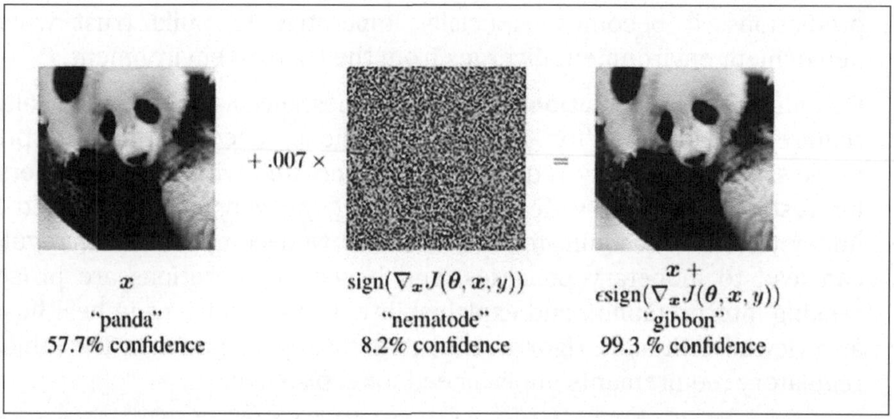

***Figure 1.12**: Adding a vector leads to incorrect "gibbon" prediction*
(Source: EXPLAINING AND HARNESSING ADVERSARIAL EXAMPLES(2015) Goodfellow et al)

- **Informativeness:**

  The model is optimizing for an objective which is often insufficient in providing useful information to decision-makers. The objective provides some form of guidance to the models. The intermediate features while training the convolutional neural network or the magnitude of the variables in a linear regression model are a few examples.

- **Fair and Ethical Decision Making:**

  Interpretability of results provides a means to verify that AI models are not biased, discriminatory, or making unfair decisions. This is important for all models to provide the required information to decision-makers. There are also regulatory requirements which require explainability. For instance, the European Union regulations require that individuals impacted by model decisions have a right to an explanation. This means that model decisions must be explainable when challenged with the option to modify when required.

Challenges and Tradeoffs

Increasingly, as we have decisions being made by Artificial Intelligence, the need for trust in the models increases. In a more recent paper, the lack of consensus around terminology and formulation of interpretable machine learning properties has been described as a challenge.

The Complexity of Explainable (XAI) in Practice

There are multiple examples of the implications of AI-based decisions; we will look at three instances which are illustrative of the different failures to explain AI-based decisions.

In 2019, a credit card customer, the creator of Ruby, tweeted that his wife was given a substantially lower credit limit. The tweet went viral, with many others saying the same thing, including Apple co-founder Steve Wozniak. Just three days later, the New York State Department of Financial Services announced a legal investigation. One year later, if you search for Goldman Sachs women and credit, or Apple women and credit, the searches are full of allegations of discrimination. Thus, the incident brought a significant reputational, legal, and financial cost for both companies.

During the COVID-19 pandemic, schools were deliberating on appropriate methods to grade students as the final examinations could not be conducted. In the UK, the students finishing their A-Levels in the summer of 2020 were similarly impacted, with tests canceled and teaching halted. The Office of Qualifications and Examinations Regulation (Ofqual) consulted on the way forward for awarding grades and decided on utilizing an algorithm to moderate the grades awarded by teachers, known as teacher assessed grades (TAGs). The algorithm used historic data of students to determine individual grades, it was also designed to weed out bias and inflated grades creeping in through teacher assessed grades. Ironically, the standardization process that was used to uncover bias caused a controversy, as it appeared to disadvantage students from deprived areas. This resulted in high-achieving students from low-achieving institutes being penalized, while lower achieving students from high-achieving institutes had inflated grades.

The beauty industry has been experimenting with AI to provide tools for its consumers to find the right products suitable for each individual. This led to a lot of revelations around its inadequacy to address the needs of colored women.

In all three cases, we are aiming to reduce bias and unfairness to make more objective decisions with data and algorithms. In the first two cases, the workings of the algorithms could be explained to an extent, and yet the AI outcomes may result in not meeting public values of non-discrimination, equal treatment and independence. The third case was less easy to explain out of the box and required using additional tools to introduce interpretability. The accuracy in predicting outcomes should also be a factor of adhering to societal and ethical aspects. Additionally, it can be observed that despite the ability to explain, distrust can persist, and results can be contested.

Machine Learning Challenges: Traditional Interpretability Practices Do Not Measure Up

Frameworks for managing model risk often incorporate an element of interpretability. However, the methods typically employed for traditional software may not be robust enough to effectively control risk when used with machine learning (ML) models. Here are some of the difficulties encountered when applying standard interpretability techniques to machine learning:

- **Interpreting the overall behavior of the model:** Comprehensive knowledge and comprehension of a traditional model's structure, assumptions, and limitations might be enough to confidently understand how it functions. However, in machine learning, model outputs are derived from conditional interactions between dependent and independent variables, often making the model's operation too intricate to explain by simply referring to a set of rules. Many machine learning models lack explicit coefficients and statistical significance tests for a specific feature, making it extremely hard to ascertain the weights assigned to a feature as it appears in various calculations during model operation. This restricts the depth of understanding one can have of a model by merely knowing its design.
- **Interpretability of features:** A complete understanding of each feature, that is, each individual characteristic or independent variable used as input in a system, can help in developing a comprehensive understanding of how the model works. However, automated feature engineering is becoming more common. For example, generative models can generate their own inputs. As this trend continues, it may become increasingly difficult to fully understand features, and use that understanding to illuminate how the model works.
- **Transparency of the solution:** Traditionally, designing a model's technical details to be transparent can assist in understanding how a model arrives at its output. In machine learning, these details might include the number of layers in a neural network or the nodes and splits of a decision tree. Unfortunately, merely knowing these details does not necessarily provide enough insight into how specific predictions are made.
- **Consistency:** The ability to consistently reproduce a model's results using the same inputs is one way to understand how a model function. However, for machine learning, factors such as model complexity, hardware variability, and computational cost can make it challenging to reproduce a model's results and also expensive.

It is evident that satisfying the interpretability requirements for machine learning model governance will necessitate the development of new techniques.

Ambiguities and Uncertainties Related to ML Interpretability

In the absence of standards, several challenges hinder the development and integration of meaningful interpretability practices into governance. Awareness of each of these challenges is vital for organizations trying to define their interpretability requirements and methods. The main challenges can be grouped into four categories:

- Challenges specific to the industry

- Challenges related to goals and objectives
- Challenges related to model complexity, and
- Technique related challenges

The following tables outline concerns in each category, describing challenges, their implications, and their potential impacts on customers or end users.

Industry Challenges

Different industries will have different explainability requirements. An industry where most applications are low-stakes, such as workforce scheduling, may not need strict interpretability standards, as the risk of harm or unintended consequences is relatively low. However, interpretability standards are not just about reducing harm but also about enhancing trust in machine learning. The extent to which this needs to be done likely requires discussion and negotiation by organizations and their stakeholders on a case-by-case basis.

The following table outlines some of the main industry-level challenges companies should be aware of when considering how interpretability will be incorporated into the governance of their use of machine learning models:

Challenges	Description
Non-standard definition of interpretability	No standard definition of interpretability means it cannot be systematically measured or adhered to
Skill Gap	There is a higher level of skill required for analyzing and interpreting models
Contested Predictions	The human subjective element can creep into the predictions, leading to contested predictions
Dynamic Data	Changes in data and patterns can impact the explanations
Contextual Influence	The impact of context on the outcomes may not always be apparent.
Algorithmic Influence	Collecting and processing data from different sources as well as variances in algorithms can impact the decisions.

***Table 1.2**: Challenges in Interpretability requirements*

There are additional issues that may impact the approach to interpretability. One is the degree to which organizations feel comfortable relying on 'explainable machine learning' services, which are advertised as being able to provide full accounts of how black-box models operate. These should be approached with a healthy skepticism. The consequence of misplaced trust in such a service may be that a model use case in which interpretability should be prioritized is not due to overconfidence in an explainable machine learning service. A second issue is the potential for nefarious activities, including manipulation and malicious attacks, to impact model output. If the possibility is high or consequential, it may tip the balance toward greater prioritization of interpretability over performance.

- **Interpretability Challenges**: Organizations may be hesitant to depend on 'explainable machine learning' services that claim to demystify complex models. Caution is advised, as non-reliance could lead to neglecting interpretability where it is crucial. Additionally, the risk of malicious activities affecting model outputs might necessitate prioritizing interpretability over performance.
- **Public Understanding and XAI**: Explainable Artificial Intelligence (XAI) aims to make solutions clear to the public, assuming a level of expertise that many may not have. This can lead to oversimplified explanations that deviate from actual decision-making processes. Moreover, while individual decisions can be justified, the collective impact may remain unexplained.
- **Neutrality in Explanation**: Explaining AI decisions is not impartial. Omitting sensitive data to prevent bias can lead to other variables indirectly reflecting those characteristics. The simplification required for public understanding can introduce bias, and explanations may vary based on the interpreter's perspective.
- **Algorithm Dynamics**: Algorithms are not static; they evolve by learning from new data and past decisions. This dynamic nature challenges XAI, as explanations can quickly become outdated, and even experts may struggle to pinpoint changes.
- **Interactions and Bias**: Algorithms can influence each other, leading to decisions affected by biased data and other algorithms. The reliance on tacit knowledge, which algorithms cannot process, further complicates explainability.
- **Context-Dependent Decisions**: Algorithmic decisions vary per individual, making generalized explanations difficult. Transparency is limited if decisions significantly impact personal lives. While equal treatment is valued, individualized explanations reveal the complexity and variability inherent in AI decisions. Segmentation based on societal or economic factors can be contentious, as seen in critiques of AI applications that differentiate between rich and poor.

Trust in Explainable AI

XAI is often viewed as a means to build trust and hence societal acceptance of AI based decisions. The goal is that XAI creates transparency which in turn leads to decision making which is bereft of ambiguity and hence results in a trust on the decisions. The ideal expectation being unbiased decisions and hence a trust in the decisions being fair and effective. Paradoxically, transparency might influence trust in a manner that consumers do not purchase, shareholders do not invest, or agencies are not trusted. This leads to situations where even the best XAI might not result in the desired trust. It can be further aggravated when people with limited knowledge of how AI works will have lower confidence in AI decisions and hence will not use or approve of its outcomes.

In addition to these challenges of XAI, there is a societal aspect when AI models are used. This context can have a major impact on the explainability of AI. This possible societal impact can also influence the explainability. The context and impact can be used for classifying the situations for deploying XAI, as shown in the following figure.

- The context of using algorithms might be less or more subjective. Subjectivity refers to a higher instance of diverse objectives leading to possible conflict and the chance of having contested outcomes. Contested outcomes refer to issues in which the public have opposing opinions, like immigration or judgements, often dependent on individual perspectives.
- AI-based decisions might have high or low impact. For example, certain decisions can be high impact in areas such as law enforcement, while others may be low impact, such as a fine for speeding.

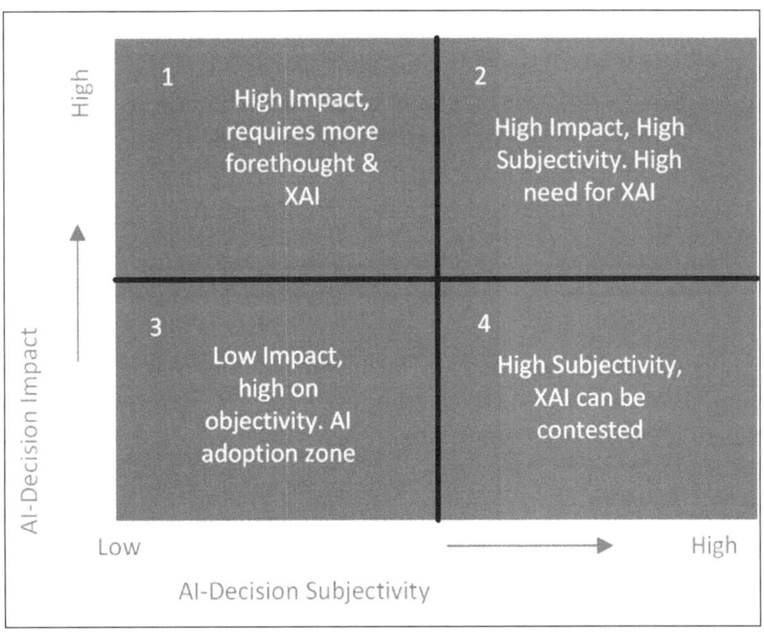

Figure 1.13: *Model Decisions and impact*

Quadrant 2 is when the decisions are high on subjectivity and also have a high impact; this begets a high need for explainability but also rife for criticism from the public. This means that XAI will have groups with different views on what constitutes a right decision and whether a decision can be viewed as fair.

Quadrant 3 is the opposite with a low level of politics and low impact. These decisions might also be relatively simple, not requiring black-boxed AI solutions. Simpler models such as rule-based systems might be suitable and not require Explainable AI. Additionally, the stakeholder may not be interested in explanations of the model decisions given the limited consequences. Although a divergent thought could be to use such instances to test the reliability of XAI methods in the field while building trust in low-impact areas while slowly taking it forward into more impactful scenarios.

In quadrant 4, there is high subjectivity, where even an AI-based decision with a low impact can be perceived as problematic. This could mean every decision is viewed through a lens of suspicion. The decisions may be contested more often, causing a higher interest for the public. Despite being low impact, the conflicting views can deepen the distrust in AI decisions.

The last quadrant, the quadrant 1 is the high impact zone with more objectivity. These scenarios will benefit from XAI and will have higher acceptance of the decisions. The objective nature of the decisions means that the explainability of the outcomes is easier to comprehend and project.

Conclusion

In this chapter, we start with an introduction of Machine Learning and Deep Learning. There are multiple approaches which have become common practices for incorporating AI in applications. The chapter also introduces Transformers which have become prominent with Large Language Models. Interpretability and Explainability have an important role in impactful decision-making scenarios, and we looked at the various reasons leading up to this need. They are also pivotal in building trust and transparency in numerous instances, especially when the outcomes are high impact or bound by regulations.

In the following chapter, we will gain an intuition on model factors which aid in Interpretability. We will also look at the multiple Interpretability types and the properties which make models white box or black box.

References

1. Book: AI Superpowers (Kai Fu Lee)
2. A Survey of Deep Learning for Scientific Discovery (2020) Raghu et al https://arxiv.org/pdf/2003.11755.pdf
3. Attention-Based Models for Speech Recognition (2015) Chorowski et al https://arxiv.org/abs/1506.07503
4. Towards A Rigorous Science of Interpretable Machine Learning (2017) Doshi-Velez et al https://arxiv.org/abs/1702.08608

5. The perils and pitfalls of explainable AI: Strategies for explaining algorithmic decision-making (2021) Bruijn et al https://doi.org/10.1016/j.giq.2021.101666
6. Explainable AI is Responsible AI: How Explainability Creates Trustworthy and Socially Responsible Artificial Intelligence (2023) Baker et al https://arxiv.org/pdf/2312.01555.pdf
7. What Makes a Good Explanation?: A Harmonized View of Properties of Explanations (2022) Chen et al https://openreview.net/pdf?id=YDyLZWwpBK2
8. The impact of COVID-19 on A-Levels since 2020 https://blogs.lse.ac.uk/politicsandpolicy/impact-of-covid19-on-a-levels/
9. Black Loans Matter: Fighting Bias for AI Fairness in Lending https://mitibmwatsonailab.mit.edu/research/blog/black-loans-matter-fighting-bias-for-ai-fairness-in-lending
10. AI bias tests gloss over a crucial aspect of skin color https://www.theverge.com/2023/10/4/23902728/ai-bias-skin-tone-hue-sony-research-artificial-intelligence-ethics
11. Machine Learning Interpretability: New Challenges and Approaches (2022) Jonathan Woods https://vectorinstitute.ai/machine-learning-interpretability-new-challenges-and-approaches/
12. EXPLAINING AND HARNESSING ADVERSARIAL EXAMPLES(2015) Goodfellow et al : https://arxiv.org/pdf/1412.6572)

Chapter 2
Model Types and Interpretability Techniques

Introduction

In this chapter, we will look at the factor considerations that make models Interpretable. We will then understand white box and black box models. We will also look at model performance metrics and the challenges of having expected performance in tandem with Interpretability.

Structure

In this chapter, we will cover the following topics:

- Interpretability in Models
- White Box Models
- Black Box Models
- Machine Learning Lifecycle
- Performance Interpretability Conundrum

Interpretability in Models

In *Chapter 1, Interpreting Machine Learning*, we reviewed a wide range of machine learning model algorithms. There are models which are designed for certain data, such as classification models for predicting discrete outcomes and regression models for continuous data. There are also models in the deep learning domain which are preferred for their higher accuracy. We will now delve into the mechanics of training models and evaluate them to achieve desirable outcomes.

Model Mechanics

A Supervised Machine Learning model can be a Regression or a Classification. When we are dealing with continuous data such as for predicting the housing prices, we have a Regression problem. On the other hand, a banking department identifying the likelihood of loan defaults before disbursing a loan will be a Classification model. A decision tree could be a good algorithm for predicting loan defaulters if we have historical data on individuals and their past performance on loan defaults. Some models, such as decision trees, are easy to visualize and understand the mechanics.

A decision tree is an example of a white box model. The visual of the decision tree makes it immediately apparent on the decision-making path. A white box model essentially exposes the model's internal working without any additional tools or techniques.

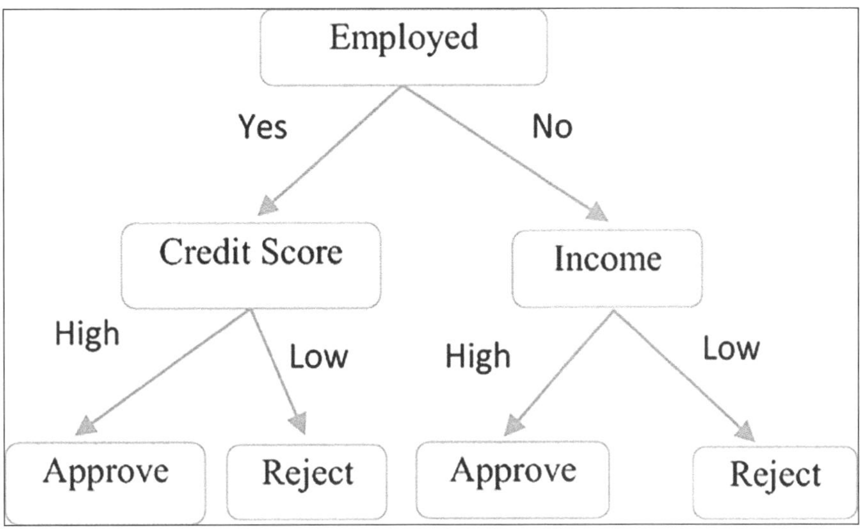

Figure 2.1: *Sample Decision Tree*

A refusal of loan disbursal can be traced to the underlying tree and the features which influenced the decision. The processing of a white box model is transparent which aids in the interpretability of the model.

White Box Models

In this section we will take a closer look at white box models and the models which fit into this category.

Introduction to White Box Model

White box models are models that provide transparency and explainability in the decision-making process. These models allow users to understand how predictions are made by revealing the internal mechanisms and features used for classification or regression tasks.

Here are some key characteristics of white box models:

- **Understandable Features**: The features used by the model should be understandable.
- **Transparent Process**: The machine learning process should be transparent.

Interpretability in White Box Models

Linear Regression:

In its simplest form, a regression model can be expressed as a linear model with a single feature impacting the outcomes.

Consider a tutor who is keen to motivate her students to put in more study hours. She builds a simple model with data on the number of study hours per week and grades achieved.

Do note that this is a toy example to understand the Interpretability concept in a simple model. There are multiple other conditions that could impact the grades, and the data points at hand will not be doing complete justice. This is only an illustrative example.

The historical data is as follows:

No. of Study Hours	Grades
8	45
10	49
6	38
7	47
3	25
8	49
7	35

Table 2.1: *Student data on grades and hours of study per week*

This fits into the scheme of a regression model where we have continuous data like grades, which have to be predicted. A linear regression model can be expressed as the following:

$$\mathbf{Y = m * x + c}$$

Where c is the intercept (or error) and m is the coefficient (or weight) for x. We will be using the linear regression model from scikit-learn to train the model. The sklearn library abstracts out the underlying workings and trains the models. For the code, any IDE with support for Jupyter Notebooks can be used to run the notebooks. There is also a GitHub link with the notebooks for all chapters.

Step 1: Import the following libraries:

```
# Importing Standard Libraries
import numpy as np
import matplotlib.pyplot as plt

# Importing sklearn Libraries
from sklearn.model_selection import train_test_split, learning_
curve
from sklearn.linear_model import LinearRegression
#from sklearn import linear_model
from sklearn.metrics import mean_absolute_error, mean_squared_
error, r2_score
```

Step 2: Initialize the training features:

```
 # x is the feature, number of study hours
 # y is the target, grade obtained
x = np.array([8,10,6,7,4,8,7]).reshape(-1,1)
y = [37,49,35,38,30,45,37]
```

Step 3:

```
 # Instantiating LinearRegression() Model
lr = LinearRegression()
 # Training/Fitting the Model
model = lr.fit(x, y)
```

Step 4:

The trained model can be used for predicting new values:

```
 # create 10 points between 0 and 10
xfit = np.linspace(0, 10, 10)
 # predict the values for dependent variable
yfit = model.predict(xfit[:, np.newaxis])
```

Step 5:

Plotting the graph of the predicted values with the trained values gives a visual understanding of the error from the linear equation derived from the training.

```
plt.title('Linear Regression decision line for predicting grades')
plt.xlabel('Hours of Study per week')
plt.ylabel('Grades')
```

```
plt.scatter(x, y, c='b')
plt.plot(xfit, yfit, 'k');
```

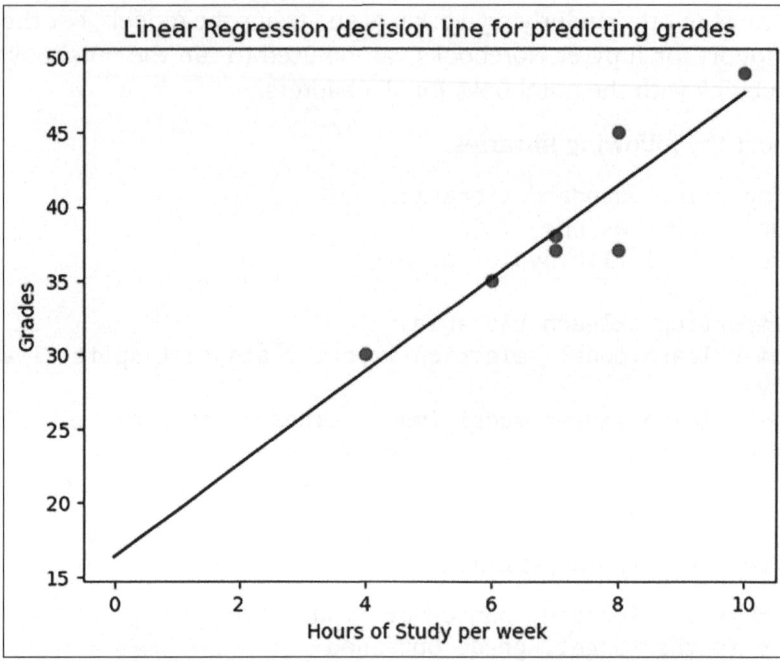

***Figure 2.2**: Regression line plotted with hours of study*

Step 6:

Printing the coefficients gives us the following:

```
print("y=",np.round(model.intercept_,3),"+",np.round(model.coef_
[0],3),"*x")
y= 3.13 *x + 16.356
```

The coefficient of x is 3.13 which is the weight that the feature hours of study have on the final outcome. The coefficient is the slope of the regression line which indicates the average change in the outcome for every unit change of the feature 'x'. A negative coefficient indicates an inverse relation, which means that the value will reduce, while a positive value means an increase in the input value x. In the preceding example, the positive coefficient indicates that the independent variable 'hours of study' is directly proportional to the resulting grades. Additionally, we can also understand that any predicted grade would be within an error of +16.356 or -16.356. This is a lot of information to interpret and understand how a feature is influencing the outcome.

The preceding example trivializes the complexity of predicting grades, as multiple other conditions, such as a students' behavioral and emotional state on a specific day, could also influence the outcome. This example is primarily used as a toy model to understand the interpretability concept in a simple model.

Regression:

When explaining the outcome of a model **f**, we are interested in how each feature (or possibly groups of features) affects the prediction of the instance being explained. For a linear model, it is easy to identify the importance and influence of each feature, where the prediction for an instance x is:

$$\mathbf{f(x) = w_0 + w_1x_1 + \cdots + w_n\, x_n}$$

Multiple Regression:

Consider the Diabetes dataset in scikit-learn. The dataset has 10 features:

1. age in years
2. sex
3. bmi body mass index
4. bp average blood pressure
5. s1 tc, total serum cholesterol
6. s2 ldl, low-density lipoproteins
7. s3 hdl, high-density lipoproteins
8. s4 tch, total cholesterol / HDL
9. s5 ltg, possibly log of serum triglycerides level
10. s6 glu, blood sugar level

The target is a quantitative measure of disease progression one year after baseline. We first build a Linear regression similar to our first example. There are 10 features in this dataset, unlike the first example.

We load the required libraries, load the dataset, and train and test the model.

```
# Import the necessary libraries
from sklearn.datasets import load_diabetes
import pandas as pd
import numpy as np
from sklearn.model_selection import train_test_split
from sklearn.linear_model import LinearRegression

from sklearn.metrics import r2_score, mean_absolute_error

# Load the diabetes dataset
diabetes = load_diabetes()

# Create a pandas DataFrame from the dataset
```

```
df = pd.DataFrame(data=np.c_[diabetes['data'], diabetes['target']],
                  columns=diabetes['feature_names'] + ['target'])

# Train-test split
X = df.drop('target', axis=1)
y = df['target']


# Train-test split
X = df.drop(['target','s2'], axis=1)
y = df['target']


X_train, X_test, y_train, y_test = train_test_split(X, y, test_
size=0.2, random_state=42)

# Train the model
model = LinearRegression()
model.fit(X_train, y_train)

# Make predictions on the test set
y_pred = model.predict(X_test)


# Calculate the mean squared error
mse = mean_squared_error(y_test, y_pred)

# Print the mean squared error
print("Mean Squared Error: %.3f" % mse)

# Calculate the mean absolute error
mae = mean_absolute_error(y_test, y_pred)

# Print the mean absolute error
print("Mean Absolute Error: %.3f" % mae)

#Calculate the R2 score
r2score = r2_score(y_test, y_pred)

#Print the R2 score
print("R2 score: %.3f" % r2score)
```

The model gives us a mean absolute error of 42.880

Mean Squared Error: 2900.254

Mean Absolute Error: 42.880

R2 score: 0.453

We use the model to get the linear model intercept and coefficients. The linear equation is printed with the following code:

```
print("y=",np.round(model.intercept_),end =" ")
k=0
for i in model.coef_:
    k+=1
    symb = "-" if i<0 else "+"
    print("%s %.3f b%d" % (symb, np.absolute(i), k),end =" ")
#     print(symb,str(np.abs(np.round(i,3))),"b",str(k),end =" ")
    if k ==5:
        print("\n")

y= 151.0 + 43.181*b1 - 241.376*b2 + 555.710*b3 + 344.647*b4 -
316.745*b5 - 81.326*b6 + 241.184*b7 + 492.772*b8 + 53.003*b9
```

This model has many features, and the linear equation is also exhibiting this complexity. We will then use Lasso Regression to check for any overfitting, and see if it gives us the same performance.

```
# Import the necessary libraries
from sklearn.datasets import load_diabetes
import pandas as pd
import numpy as np
from sklearn.model_selection import train_test_split
from sklearn.linear_model import Lasso
from sklearn.metrics import mean_absolute_error,r2_score

# Load the diabetes dataset
diabetes = load_diabetes()

# Create a pandas DataFrame from the dataset
df = pd.DataFrame(data=np.c_[diabetes['data'], diabetes
['target']],
                  columns=diabetes['feature_names'] + ['target'])

# Train-test split
X = df.drop(['target','s2'], axis=1)
y = df['target']
X_train, X_test, y_train, y_test = train_test_split(X, y, test_
size=0.2, random_state=42)


# Train the model
model = Lasso()
model.fit(X_train, y_train)

# Make predictions on the test set
```

```
y_pred = model.predict(X_test)


# Calculate the mean squared error
mse = mean_squared_error(y_test, y_pred)

# Print the mean squared error
print("Mean Squared Error: %.3f" % mse)

# Calculate the mean absolute error
mae = mean_absolute_error(y_test, y_pred)

# Print the mean absolute error
print("Mean Absolute Error: %.3f" % mae)

#Calculate the R2 score
r2score = r2_score(y_test, y_pred)

#Print the R2 score
print("R2 score: %.3f" % r2score)
```

Mean Squared Error: 3403.576

Mean Absolute Error: 49.730

R2 score: 0.358

The lasso regression, while handling the overfitting, reduced the dimensionality of our problem, although it does not yield an improved R2 score over linear regression.

```
print("y=",np.round(model.intercept_),end =" ")
k=0
for i in model.coef_:
    k+=1
    symb = "-" if i<0 else "+"
    print("%s %.3f b%d" % (symb, np.absolute(i), k),end =" ")
#     print(symb,str(np.abs(np.round(i,3))),"b",str(k),end =" ")
    if k ==5:
        print("\n")


y= 153.0 + 0.000*b1 + 0.000*b2 + 413.432*b3 + 34.831*b4 +
0.000*b5 + 0.000*b6 + 0.000*b7 + 258.153*b8 + 0.000*b9
```

Lasso regression is a regularization method that applies a penalty for preventing overfitting and enhancing accuracy. We find that some of the coefficients are close to zero; hence, reducing the impact of those features on the model's predictions. While the primary purpose of the L1 regularization is to reduce overfitting, an added benefit is in clarifying the features with the most impact and hence providing the ability to interpret the model.

We use the same diabetes dataset to run a classification model. This dataset has a continuous value as its label (or target); we convert it into a classification label by computing the median value and using that as a measure to determine boundaries to get one of the two classes.

Decision Tree:

```
# Import the necessary libraries
from sklearn.datasets import load_diabetes
import pandas as pd
import numpy as np
from sklearn.model_selection import train_test_split
from sklearn.tree import DecisionTreeClassifier
from sklearn.metrics import accuracy_score, confusion_matrix
from sklearn.tree import plot_tree
import matplotlib.pyplot as plt

# Load the diabetes dataset
diabetes = load_diabetes()

# Create a pandas DataFrame from the dataset
df = pd.DataFrame(data=np.c_[diabetes['data'], diabetes
['target']],
                  columns=diabetes['feature_names'] + ['target'])

# Convert the target variable into a binary variable
median_value = df['target'].median()
df['target'] = (df['target'] >= median_value).astype(int)

# Train-test split
X = df.drop('target', axis=1)
y = df['target']
X_train, X_test, y_train, y_test = train_test_split(X, y, test_
size=0.2, random_state=42)

# Train the model
model = DecisionTreeClassifier()
model.fit(X_train, y_train)

# Make predictions on the test set
y_pred = model.predict(X_test)
```

Accuracy: 0.685

Confusion Matrix:

[[36 13]

[15 25]]

Please note that the accuracy can vary slightly across model runs and hence should be understood accordingly.

In a Decision Tree model, feature importance is calculated as the decrease in node impurity weighted by the probability of reaching that node. The node probability can be calculated as the number of samples that reach the node, divided by the total number of samples. The higher the value the more important the feature.

We print the feature importance values from the scikit learn **DecisionTree** library and plot a bar graph with the values.

```
# Print the feature importance
feature_importance = pd.DataFrame({"Feature": X.columns,
"Importance": model.feature_importances_})
feature_importance = feature_importance.sort_values
(by="Importance", ascending=False)
print(feature_importance)
```

	Feature	Importance
2	bmi	0.324180
8	s5	0.170917
3	bp	0.122341
5	s2	0.083766
6	s3	0.071293
9	s6	0.070988
0	age	0.066997
4	s1	0.038495
7	s4	0.032896
1	sex	0.018128

***Figure 2.3**: Feature Importance*

```
feature_names = diabetes['feature_names']
importance = decisiontree.feature_importances_
tree_importances = pd.Series(importance, index=feature_names)

fig, ax = plt.subplots()
tree_importances.plot.bar(ax=ax)
ax.set_title("Feature importances using MDI")
ax.set_ylabel("Mean decrease in impurity")
fig.tight_layout()
```

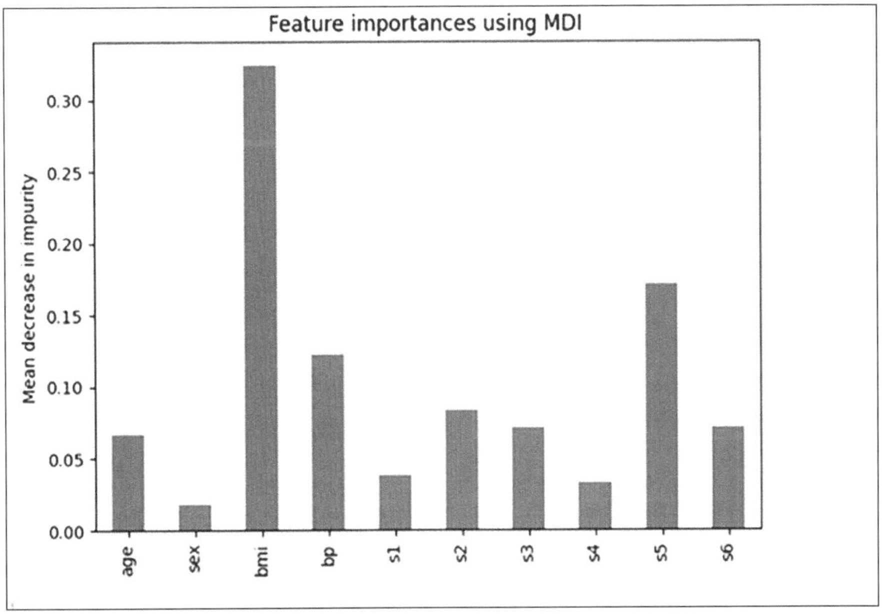

Figure 2.4: *Plotted Feature Importance*

The preceding values are indicative and can change slightly across model runs.

Let us also look at the tree structure created by our model.

```
# Plot the decision tree
plt.figure(figsize=(20,10))
plot_tree(model, filled=True, feature_names=X.columns.tolist(),
class_names=['0', '1'], proportion=True)
plt.show()
```

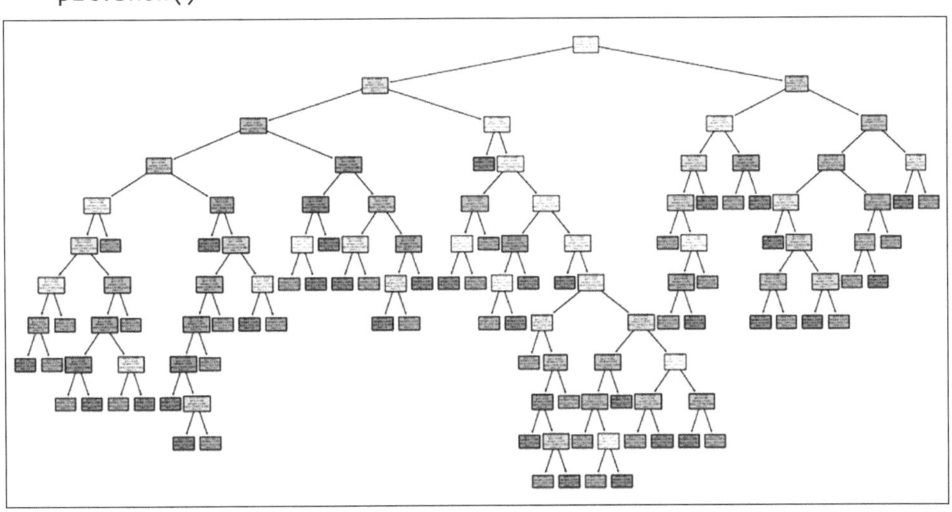

Figure 2.5: *Decision Tree visualized*

The tree structure is a lot more complex to visualize quickly, as we had more features in this dataset. We could still use the feature importance exposed by the model to understand the features which are higher up in the chain.

When we zoom into the first three layers of the tree, we see the root of the node and the decision paths which can be used to manually traverse to explain a prediction.

```
# Plot the decision tree
plt.figure(figsize=(20,10))
plot_tree(model, max_depth= 2, feature_names=X.columns.tolist(),
class_names=['0', '1'], proportion=True)
plt.show()
```

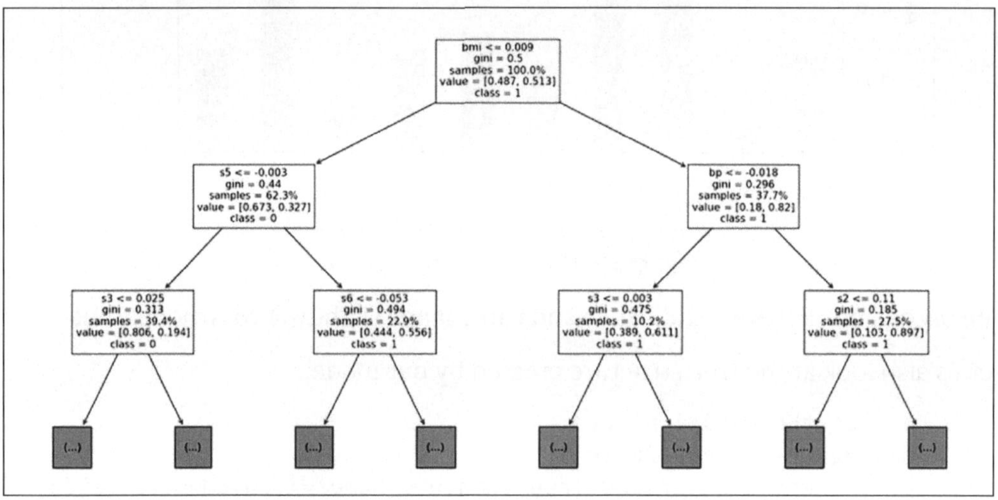

***Figure 2.6**: Decision Tree visualized for two layers*

The decision tree model run here gave an accuracy of 0.685, and in the next model, we will use a random forest to improve the accuracy. Please note that the values can change slightly across model runs, and you may get a different value.

```
# Calculate the accuracy and confusion matrix
accuracy = accuracy_score(y_test, y_pred)
cm = confusion_matrix(y_test, y_pred)

# Print the accuracy metrics
print("Accuracy:", np.round(accuracy,3))
print("Confusion Matrix:\n", cm)
```

Accuracy: 0.685

Confusion Matrix:

[[36 13]

[15 25]]

The Decision Tree in the sklearn also exposes a feature importance parameter. In the further chapters, we will be exploring feature importance in more detail.

Feature importance measures the importance of elements based on the distribution under a qualification threshold. Feature importance can also be described as the contribution of each feature to a high-accuracy space.

```
# Print the feature importance
feature_importance = pd.DataFrame({"Feature": X.columns,
"Importance": model.feature_importances_})
feature_importance = feature_importance.sort_values
(by="Importance", ascending=False)
print(feature_importance)
```

Feature Importance

2 bmi 0.324180

8 s5 0.170917

3 bp 0.122341

5 s2 0.083766

6 s3 0.071293

9 s6 0.070988

0 age 0.066997

4 s1 0.038495

7 s4 0.032896

1 sex 0.018128

In the **sklearn** function for a Decision Tree, the importance of a feature is the Gini importance based on the reduction. It is the total reduction in the impurity criterion brought by that feature. Such impurity-based feature importance can be misleading for high cardinality features where there are many unique values.

Plotting the feature importance as follows, we see that features, such as bmi are the most important.

```
fig, ax = plt.subplots()
tree_importances.plot.bar(ax=ax)
ax.set_title("Feature importances using MDI")
ax.set_ylabel("Mean decrease in impurity")
fig.tight_layout()
```

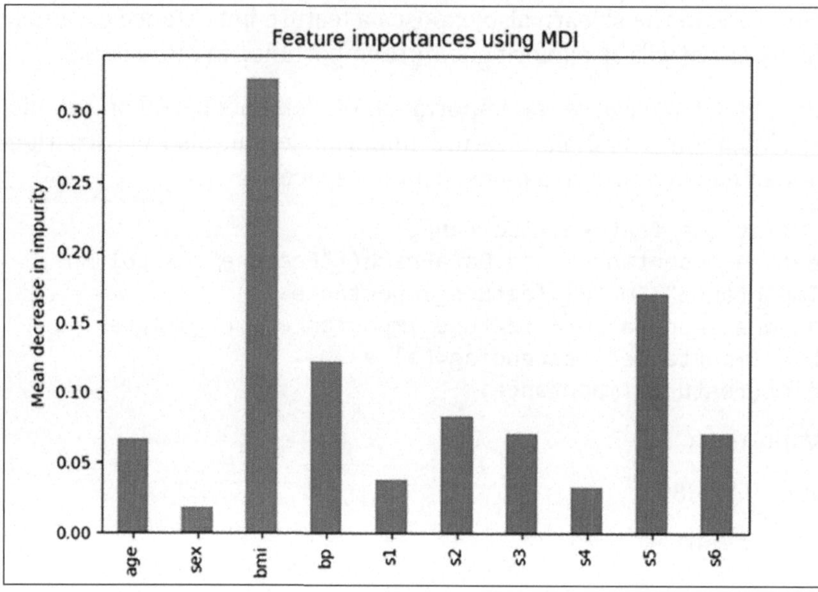

***Figure** 2.7: Decision Tree Feature Importance plotted*

We will next look at permutation feature importance using the native feature importance function in sklearn. The input to the estimator function **permutation_importance** can be from the training dataset or the test dataset. The permutation importance of a feature is calculated by permutating or changing a specific feature while keeping other feature values the same. The permutation importance is the difference between the baseline metric and metric from permutating the feature column. In the next chapter, we will cover the feature importance and the different techniques in detail.

```
from sklearn.inspection import permutation_importance

result = permutation_importance(
    model, X_test, y_test, n_repeats=10, random_state=42, n_
jobs=2
)

DT_importances = pd.Series(result.importances_mean,
index=X.columns)
print(DT_importances)
```

Plot the permutation feature importance.

```
import matplotlib.pyplot as plt


fig, ax = plt.subplots()
DT_importances.plot.bar(yerr=result.importances_std, ax=ax)
```

```
ax.set_title("Feature importances using permutation on full model")
ax.set_ylabel("Mean accuracy decrease")
fig.tight_layout()
plt.show()
```

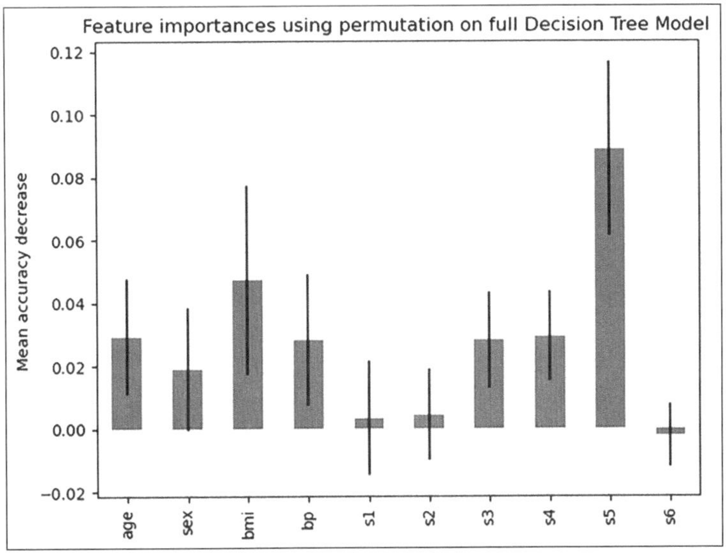

Figure 2.8: *Decision Tree Permutation Feature Importance*

Random Forest:

We will next try the same dataset with a Random Forest model.

```
from sklearn.ensemble import RandomForestClassifier
from sklearn.model_selection import cross_val_score,Repeated-
StratifiedKFold, train_test_split
from sklearn.datasets import load_diabetes
import pandas as pd
import numpy as np

from sklearn.preprocessing import StandardScaler
from sklearn.metrics import accuracy_score, confusion_matrix

# Load the diabetes dataset
diabetes = load_diabetes()

# Create a pandas DataFrame from the dataset
df = pd.DataFrame(data=np.c_[diabetes['data'], diabetes
['target']],
                  columns=diabetes['feature_names'] + ['target'])

# Convert the target variable into a binary variable
median_value = df['target'].median()
```

```
df['target'] = (df['target'] >= median_value).astype(int)

X = df.drop('target', axis=1)
y = df['target']

# Split the data into training and testing sets
X_train, X_test, y_train, y_test = train_test_split(X, y, test_
size=0.2, random_state=42)

# Create a Random Forest Classifier
forest = RandomForestClassifier(n_estimators=50, random_state=42)

# Train the model
forest.fit(X_train, y_train)


y_pred = forest.predict(X_test)
# Calculate the accuracy and confusion matrix
accuracy = accuracy_score(y_test, y_pred)
cm = confusion_matrix(y_test, y_pred)

# Print the accuracy metrics
print("Accuracy: %.3f" % accuracy)
print("Confusion Matrix:\n", cm)
```

The preceding code is training a Random Forest model on the diabetes dataset. The model's accuracy increases this time to 0.742.

Accuracy: 0.742

Confusion Matrix:

[[38 11]

[12 28]]

Let us look at the importance.

```
# Print the feature importance
feature_importance = pd.DataFrame({"Feature": X.columns,
"Importance": forest.feature_importances_})
feature_importance = feature_importance.sort_values
(by="Importance", ascending=False)
print(feature_importance)
```

Feature Importance

2 bmi 0.218705

8 s5 0.149231

3 bp 0.129069

5 s2 0.100357

6 s3 0.088594

0 age 0.078156

9 s6 0.077821

4 s1 0.077379

7 s4 0.062547

1 sex 0.018140

Plotting the Random Forest feature importance.

```
import matplotlib.pyplot as plt

fig, ax = plt.subplots()
feature_importance.plot.bar(ax=ax)
ax.set_title("Feature importances on full model")
ax.set_ylabel("Mean accuracy decrease")
fig.tight_layout()
plt.show()
```

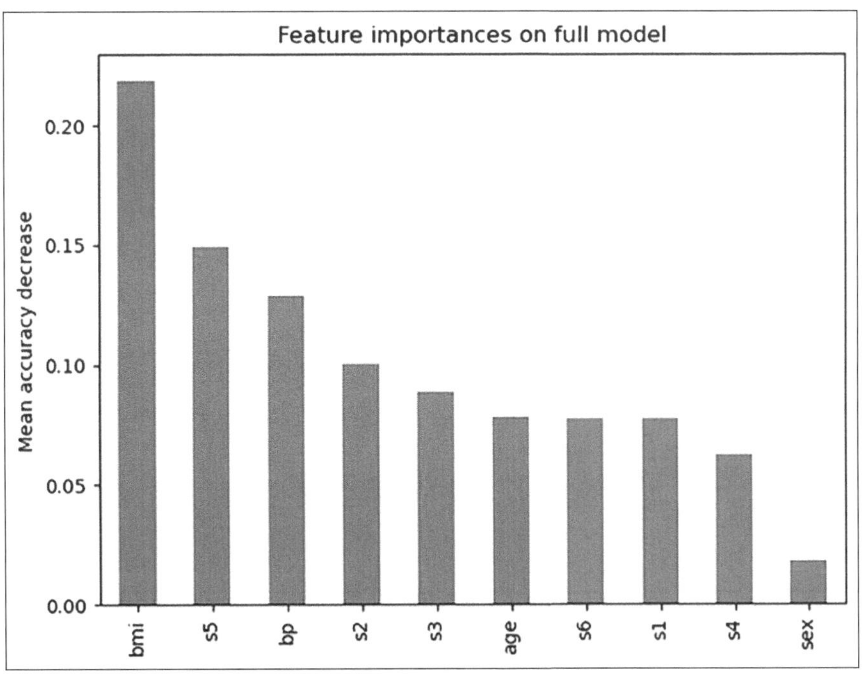

***Figure 2.9**: Random Forest Feature Importance*

Next, let us look at its permutation feature importance.

```
from sklearn.inspection import permutation_importance


result = permutation_importance(
    forest, X_test, y_test, n_repeats=10, random_state=42, n_
jobs=2
)


forest_importances = pd.Series(result.importances_mean, index=X.
columns)
print(forest_importances)
```

age -0.002247

sex 0.015730

bmi 0.047191

bp 0.011236

s1 -0.005618

s2 0.015730

s3 0.013483

s4 0.011236

s5 0.046067

s6 0.002247

dtype: float64

```
import matplotlib.pyplot as plt

fig, ax = plt.subplots()
forest_importances.plot.bar(yerr=result.importances_std, ax=ax)
ax.set_title("Feature importances using permutation on full model")
ax.set_ylabel("Mean accuracy decrease")
fig.tight_layout()
plt.show()
```

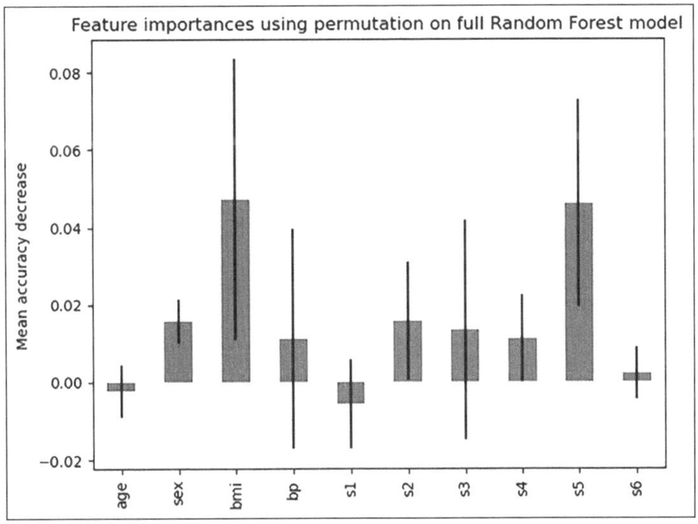

Figure 2.10: *Random Forest Permutation Feature Importance*

Comparing the Permutation Feature Importance of Decision Tree and Random Forest:

We see that both the Decision Tree (*Figure* 2.8) and Random Forest (*Figure* 2.10) have rated bmi, s5 (Serum Triglycerides level), as the top two important features. The one surprising detail between the two charts is the increased importance of s4 in the random forest model. The feature s4 is total cholesterol or HDL and in the random forest, it identifies that the feature has a positive impact on label 0.

Black Box Models

Transparency in the model working is a property which determines whether it will be labeled as a white box. Models which do not exhibit this property are clubbed as black box models since their internal working is not directly understood.

Consider building a model to do image recognition, which is a classification problem. An image of resolution 100 * 100 pixels has many features, as every pixel is considered a feature. A deep learning model such as a CNN works best at identifying the images, given the scale and complexity of an image.

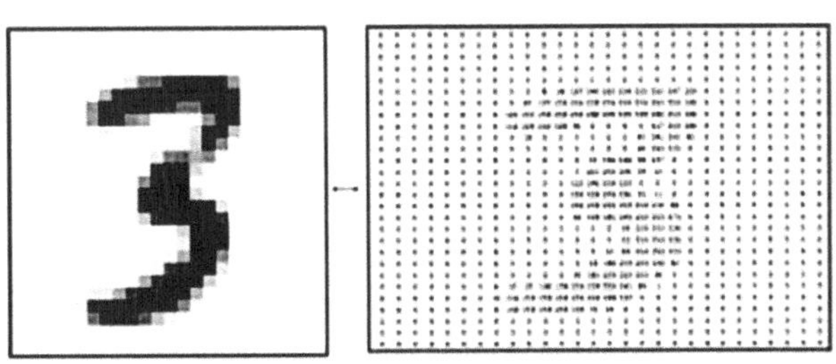

Figure 2.11: *Image for classification*

In the preceding images, the trained CNN model can classify the images as number 3 or not.

Convolutional neural networks (CNNs) emerged from the study of the brain's visual cortex, and they have been used in image recognition since the 1980s. CNNs have managed to achieve superhuman performance on some complex visual tasks. They power image search services, self-driving cars, automatic video classification systems, and more. Moreover, CNNs are not restricted to visual perception: they are also successful at other tasks, such as voice recognition or natural language processing (NLP); however, we will focus on visual applications for now.

The most important building block of a CNN is the convolutional layer: 6 neurons in the first convolutional layer are not connected to every single pixel in the input image but only to pixels in their receptive fields. In turn, each neuron in the second convolutional layer is connected only to neurons located within a small rectangle in the first layer. This architecture allows the network to concentrate on low-level features in the first hidden layer, then assemble them into higher-level features in the next hidden layer, and so on. This hierarchical structure is common in real-world images, which is one of the reasons why CNNs work so well for image recognition.

CNN is a neural network with multiple hidden layers and many parameters. A typical CNN architecture is shown in the following figure:

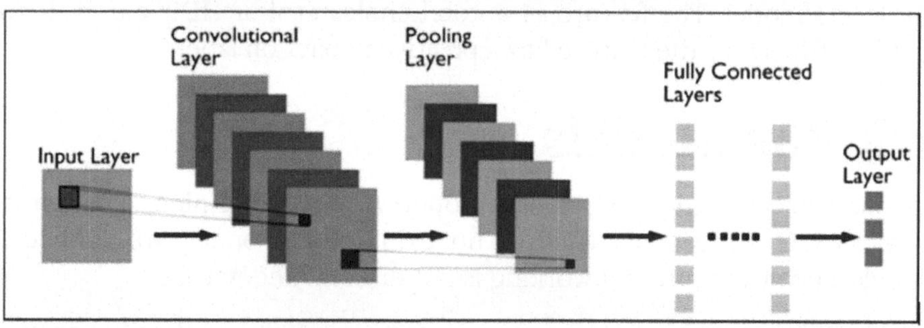

Figure 2.12: CNN Architecture

As evident from the CNN architecture the neural network has many layers. Each layer in turn has complexity. Black box models are also called opaque to indicate the lack of transparency. The complexity and size of the model imply that it is not directly interpretable, and hence labelled as a black box model.

Black Box Pros:

- Essential for speech recognition, image recognition, natural language processing, recommendation systems, and fraud detection
- High predictive accuracy

- Can train models with complex relationships in large datasets more effectively as they can handle large amounts of data

Black Box Cons:

- Low algorithm interpretability
- Difficult to explain Black Box decisions to internal or external stakeholders
- Results may not be perfectly reproducible

Machine Learning Lifecycle

The first stage in training a model is data preparation. The machine learning lifecycle is iterative in nature. The data preparation stage is followed by model selection. A machine learning life cycle describes the steps a team (or person) should use to create a predictive machine learning model. The general rationale is to start with a basic model which can serve the purpose and provide the required kind of performance.

Models are built on training data which is expected to be a reflection of the real world. An important next step is model performance. Evaluation typically deals with the model's performance in terms of its closeness to the real-world data.

This is a simplification of the Machine Learning lifecycle, primarily focusing on the five stages. We will see in *Chapter 10, Explainability and Responsible AI*, aspects influencing the explainability and hence the evaluations.

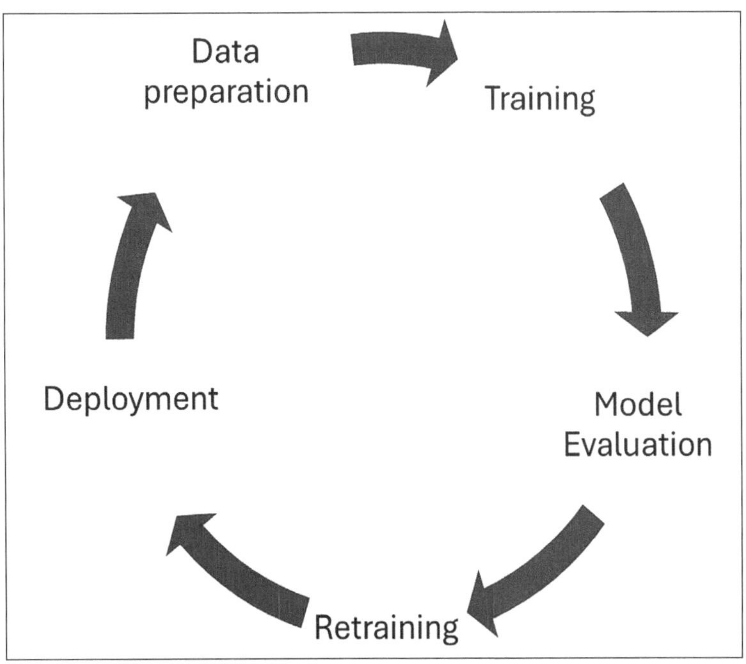

Figure 2.13: *Simplified Machine Learning Lifecycle*

Model Metrics

A trained model undergoes a rigorous evaluation phase where metrics such as accuracy and RMSE are probed. In a quest to achieve expected accuracies, a model will go through multiple iterations to arrive at the right algorithm and appropriate parameters. The models which provide the higher accuracies are not always interpretable such as in a black box model.

Evaluating a model is part of the machine learning lifecycle. In this stage, the model is evaluated using different metrics. These evaluation metrics measure the machine learning model's performance. Model evaluation is important in assessing the model efficacy in the initial phases and iterating the training process as required until the desired performance is achieved.

Classification:

In classification, performance can be measured using multiple metrics. The most popular metrics for measuring classification performance include accuracy, precision, recall, confusion matrix, log-loss, and AUC (area under the ROC curve).

- Accuracy is a measure of the number of correct predictions by the model; it is the ratio between the number of correct predictions and the total number of predictions.
- Precision is a measure of the proportion of predicted Positives which are truly Positive. It is a good choice of evaluation metrics when you want to be very sure of your positive predictions. For example, if you are building a system to predict whether to decrease the credit limit on an account, then you want to be very sure about the prediction or it may result in customer dissatisfaction.
- Recall is a measure of the number of positive instances that have been correctly identified. It is an important measure when trying to reduce false negatives.
- A confusion matrix (or confusion table) is a breakdown of the correct and incorrect classifications for each class. A confusion matrix is useful to understand the distinction between classes, particularly when the cost of misclassification might differ for the two classes, or you have a lot more test data on one class than the other. For example, the consequences of making a false positive or false negative in a cancer diagnosis are very different.
- Log-loss (logarithmic loss) is used when the output of the classifier is a numeric probability instead of a class label. The probability can be understood as a gauge of confidence, as it is a measurement of accuracy.
- AUC (Area Under the ROC Curve) is a measurement for classification problems at various threshold settings. It tells a model's capability to distinguish between classes. A higher AUC signifies a better model at predicting that a 0 is actually a 0 and a 1 is actually a 1. Translated to a use case, it implies that a higher AUC,

that is, the model is better at distinguishing between patients with a disease and no disease.

Regression:

R Square represents the proportion of the variance for a dependent variable that is explained by an independent variable

Adjusted R Square is a corrected goodness-of-fit (model accuracy) measure for linear models. It identifies the percentage of variance in the target field that is explained by the input or inputs.

Mean Squared Error (MSE) measures how close a regression line is to a set of data points. It measures the average squared difference between the predicted and the actual target values within a dataset. MSE is used to check how close estimates or forecasts are to actual values. The lower the MSE, the closer the forecast is to the actual. This is used as a model evaluation measure for regression models, and the lower value indicates a better fit.

Root Mean Squared Error (RMSE) is the root of the mean squared error. It is computationally simple and easily differentiable, which many optimizations algorithms desire. RMSE does not penalize the errors as much as MSE does due to the square root.

Mean Absolute Error (MAE) is the average variance between the significant values in the dataset and the projected values in the same dataset.

The Performance Interpretability Conundrum

Accuracy vs. Explainability Tradeoff:

The **accuracy-explainability tradeoff** refers to the balance between the performance of a machine learning model and its level of explainability.

In many scenarios, you can either have:

- A **simpler but less accurate model**, which is more interpretable.
- A **more accurate but less interpretable model**, often considered a “black box” due to its complex internal structure.

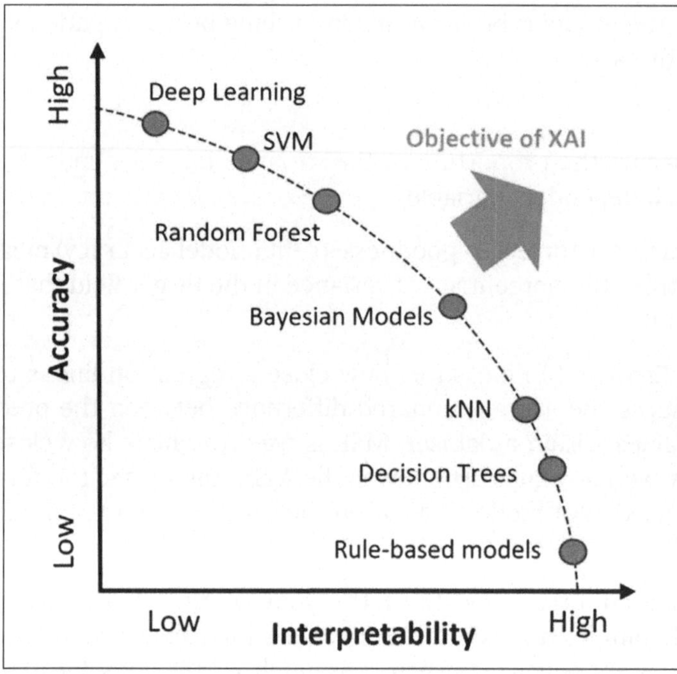

Figure 2.14: *Illustrative Accuracy vs. Interpretability graph*

Performance metrics such as accuracy and RMSE are top priorities for data scientists when evaluating model effectiveness. The next phase of the cycle involves evaluating the metric. If the accuracy is not within the expected range, several paths can be followed to improve the model's performance. Assuming the data provided for training is good, the data scientist will move on to the next model in the chain to improve the accuracy. Most competitions focus on improved performance in terms of accuracy or other such scores. This builds a notion of performance metrics indicative of accuracy and not the correctness of the algorithm, interpretability of the model, and explainability of the data points.

As machine learning has gradually entered into ever more sectors of public and private life, there has been a growing demand for algorithmic explainability. How can we make the predictions of complex statistical models more intelligible to end users?

The general tendency is for humans to be reticent in adopting algorithms or techniques that are not directly interpretable, tractable, and trustworthy. An increasing emphasis on ethical AI is also another reason for the focus on interpretability. It is customary to think that by focusing solely on performance, the systems will be increasingly opaque. This is true in the sense that there is a trade-off between the performance of a model and its transparency. However, an improvement in the understanding of a system can lead to the correction of its deficiencies. When developing an ML model, the consideration of interpretability as an additional design driver can improve its implementability for three reasons:

- Interpretability helps in bringing impartiality to decision-making by detecting bias in the training dataset and providing opportunities to correct the bias.
- Interpretability highlights any potential adversarial perturbations that could change the prediction. thus providing robustness.
- Interpretability helps in ensuring that only meaningful variables infer the output. The underlying causality is thus rooted in the reality of the model reasoning.

All of these mean that the interpretation of the system should, in order to be considered practical, provide either an understanding of the model mechanisms predictions or a visualization.

Explainability has taken on more urgency within banks, a result of the growing complexity in AI algorithms, which is happening at a breakneck pace, thanks to greater computing power, the explosion of big data, and advances in modeling techniques, such as neural networks and deep learning. Regulatory bound Industries such as banking establish special task forces for explainability initiatives in coordination with AI teams and business units. Regions or countries are also bound by regulatory requirements like GDPR, requiring a right to transparency on decision-making.

Simpler models are typically more transparent but lack predictive power and accuracy. More complex models such as deep neural networks score on accuracy and are desirable for building solutions in vision and speech. This is exacerbated by the fact that high-performance models are typically opaque, making it difficult to understand the logic for individual predictions. The simpler models also get more difficult to interpret with increasing scale.

Explainable AI can help in bridging this gap between model complexity and intuitiveness to enable users the benefit of increased performance along with the desired levels of explanations.

Conclusion

In this chapter, we understood the concept of White Box models and the properties which make them interpretable. We also looked at the various perspectives of Interpretability and models which fit into each of these buckets. We also looked at Interpretability while training models in Regression and Classification. We also discuss the properties of Black Box models and their performance benefits while getting less interpretable.

In the next chapter, we will look at the properties of Interpretable models. We also look at white box models, also called Intrinsically Interpretable models, in more detail and models which are specifically designed with an interpretability perspective. These models are sometimes differentiated and labeled as glass-box models.

References

- Explainable Artificial Intelligence (XAI): Concepts, Taxonomies, Opportunities and Challenges toward Responsible AI (2020) Arrieta et al https://doi.org/10.1016/j.inffus.2019.12.012
- The Mythos of Model Interpretability (2017) Lipton et al https://arxiv.org/pdf/1606.03490
- Hands-On Machine Learning with scikit-learn and TensorFlow, Geron

CHAPTER 3
Interpretability Taxonomy and Techniques

Introduction

This chapter extends the previous concept on model types and details the aspects around the scope of Interpretability and techniques that can be utilized. It also provides a detailed understanding of the taxonomy and commonly used terms.

Structure

In this chapter, we will cover the following topics:

- Interpretable Machine Learning
- Inherently Interpretable Models
- Other Intrinsically Interpretable Models

Interpretable Models

Interpretable models can be viewed as models with certain characteristics. These factors influence the model's ability to be labeled as interpretable.

Properties

Models exhibit certain properties that make them interpretable. The properties can be viewed from two perspectives:

- Transparency
- Post-hoc explanations

The first relates to transparency; that is, how does the model work? The second consists of post-hoc explanations, that is, what else can the model tell me?

Transparency

The word transparency means the ability to see through something. In a machine learning context, model transparency means that the model's inner mechanics or workings. In our Decision Tree example in *Chapter 2, Model Types and Interpretability Techniques*, there is transparency on how the tree makes decisions. We are essentially answering questions of the form, What is model mechanics? How does it work?

The model's transparency can be based on three aspects:

Simultability

From a transparency perspective, Simultability means that the entire model can be understood. It basically implies that using the input data, the entire model can be worked out by using the model's weights and parameters, and in a reasonable time, arrive at the prediction provided by the model. This indicates that the model's internal workings can be visualized, and the model exposes the weights and parameters. We can look at Simultability from the size of the model or the number of computations to be done to arrive at the predictions. In our previous example of the Decision Tree, we can infer the result by working through the tree. But this does not scale on the simultability front as the Decision Tree grows in depth and nodes. Similarly, we will see how transparency from a Simultability perspective is hindered in Linear Regression as the number of coefficients, which translates to the number of features, increases. Instead, models such as Lasso Regression perform better, as they can lead to sparse regression with variable selection and limiting the number of non-zero coefficients. There is a subjective element in determining what is a reasonable number of features or layers. But this is clearly tied to the limits of human cognition and what is too many to fathom. From this perspective, we can argue that neither linear models, rule-based, or decision trees are interpretable. We can suffice to say that with higher dimensionality, and deep decision trees we are not able to comprehend and hence interpret the model, thus making the models less transparent at that scale and magnitude.

Decomposability

Each part of the model, the calculations, the parameters, and the data points can be understood intuitively. This is another interpretation of transparency. In our decision tree example, every node has a clear explanation of its decision point which can be intuitively understood. The coefficients of a linear model can be interpreted as representing the strengths of the feature and the impact it is having on the result.

The underlying presumption here is that the features are themselves individually interpretable, and there is no ambiguity on the feature, the data source, and its interpretation. Similarly, a node labeled bmi < 0.009 is understood by the reader and aids in interpreting the model. One important factor to note is the fragility associated with feature selection, the preprocessing and the impact that it has on the model and hence the interpretations we derive. For example, the associations between flu risk and vaccination might be positive or negative depending on whether the feature set includes indicators of old age, infancy, or immunodeficiency.

Algorithmic Transparency

Algorithmic Transparency is applied at the level of learning the algorithm itself. In linear models, we can understand the error surface because of the manner in which the training is done. In the training phase, we can prove that the model can converge to a solution even on unseen datasets. This contrasts with the deep learning models which are black box in nature and do not have any algorithmic transparency. The heuristic techniques employed in the back propagations and forward pass phases make it more powerful but does not aid our understanding of how the model is working hence lacking transparency.

Post-hoc Interpretability

This property of the Interpretable model applies after the model is built, post-hoc. In this method, we use techniques on the trained model to extract information. Visualizations of the models and the learned representations, explanations in natural language and even explanations by example are methods used in post-hoc interpretability. Similar techniques are often employed in human interactions to explain situations by comparing similar-looking scans or through visualizations. While post-hoc interpretability does not clearly provide a means of understanding the model mechanics, it provides sufficient information and adds value to the users. The explanations can be for the overall model or for individual data points, both of which provide value for the practitioners in interpretations. The prime advantage is that it provides a mechanism to interpret opaque models after the fact, although they are not inherently interpretable. Since this is post facto, after the model is trained, it is also not sacrificing the predictive performance of the model.

Taxonomy

A model's ability to be interpretable depends on the properties it exhibits. The following classification is a summary of all the different factors aiding interpretability in models.

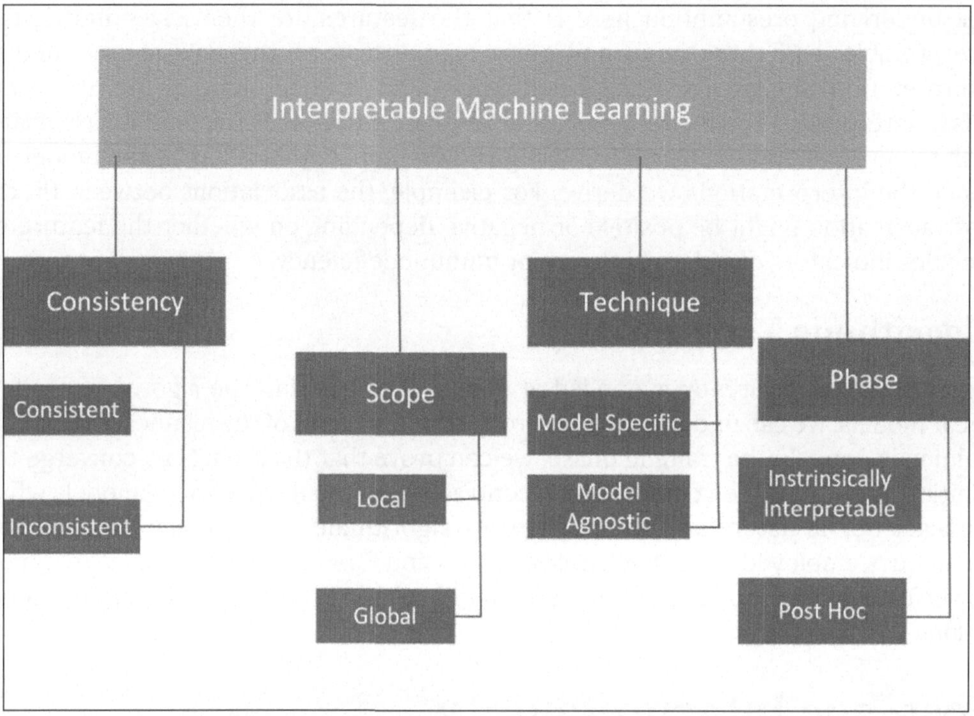

***Figure 3.1**: Taxonomy for Interpretable Machine Learning*

Consistency

Consistency is the similarity of explanations for a model prediction on similar data. It can also be termed as the stability of the model in arriving at predictions and hence in the explainability of the outcomes. For instance, a model identifies two COVID-19 patients as COVID-19 positive. The typical symptoms of COVID are similar to flu. An explanation is often needed after detecting a COVID-19 patient. In the preceding case, consistency measurement determines the similarities of two patients' symptoms and dissimilarities with flu patients.

Based on the consistency measurement, IML methods are divided into two classes:

- **Consistent**: An IML model is treated as a consistent model if it generates consistent explanations for similar data instances. In other words, the explanation for a certain type of data instance is said to be consistent when the explanation is similar to the same type of data and dissimilar to different types of data.
- **Inconsistent**: On the other hand, when the explanations for similar types of data instances are varied, the IML model that is used for these explanations is inconsistent no matter what happens with different types of data.

Scope

The scope refers to the explanation coverage. For a given data instance, the explanation can be visualized from a localized perspective or from the overall model workings.

Depending on the scope of influence, IML methods can be classified into two categories:

- **Global**: Explainability has a global scope when the relationship is between the input variables and the full model based on the target variable. This type of interpretation is often highly presumptive but provides an insight into the larger model.
- **Local**: In a local scope, we get a local explanation of how the machine learning model makes individual predictions. Local model explainability is beneficial for understanding the individual feature points that influence a particular choice. This is extremely critical for regulatory requirements. For instance, a loan request refused by the model could be challenged on its outcome. In such scenarios, local explainability identifies the elements which influenced the outcome. In some instances, the local explainability can also serve as a feedback for improving the outcome. Although some organizations may be wary of always disclosing detailed explanations as the information may be misused in gaming the models.

Model Interpretability Techniques

The techniques for model interpretability can be classified into the following IML methods. There are two types of model interpretability techniques.

- **Model Specific**: IML techniques designed to apply only for a type or class of algorithms are termed model specific.
- **Model Agnostic**: These techniques can be applied in various types of machine learning models and are not specific to classes of models, as in the case of model specific.

Phase

Phase here refers to the point at which Interpretability is applicable. There are two phases in which a model can be Interpreted:

- **Intrinsically Interpretable Models:**

  The model is inherently interpretable without the need for additional layers or methods. These are also called white box models or Inherently Interpretable models. In *Chapter 2, Model Types and Interpretability Techniques*, we looked at white box models at length and understood the factors that make them easy to interpret. In the case of a linear regression, the linear equation gives an indication of the features' influence in the outcomes. Similarly, CART models such as Decision Tree also have an inherent algorithmic transparency for the outcomes.

The caveat is that the complexity of a linear regression could easily go out of bounds as the number of features increases. In our previous discussion on Interpretable model properties, we highlighted these outlier scenarios when scale becomes a hindrance to transparency in being human readable.

- **Post Hoc Methods:**

  These are methods which can be applied to a trained model to provide explanations of the outcomes, these methods employ the property of post-hoc interpretability. These methods are not dependent on a model group or type and hence are more widely applicable in Interpretability.

Terms and Definitions

We will decrypt some of the terms commonly used in Interpretable machine learning to provide a high-level perspective. All these concepts will be discussed in greater detail in the upcoming chapters.

Global and Local Interpretability

As previously mentioned, Global Interpretability gives a global insight about the model and its working, but cannot explain the prediction for a specific data point. Alternatively, Local Interpretability focuses on each data point, providing explanations for a specific data point and its predictions. This could be in terms of feature contribution or proximity measures.

Intrinsically/Inherently vs. Post-Hoc Methods

Inherently Interpretable models could provide accurate and undistorted explanations but may sacrifice prediction performance to some extent. The post-hoc ones are limited in their approximate nature while keeping the underlying model accuracy intact.

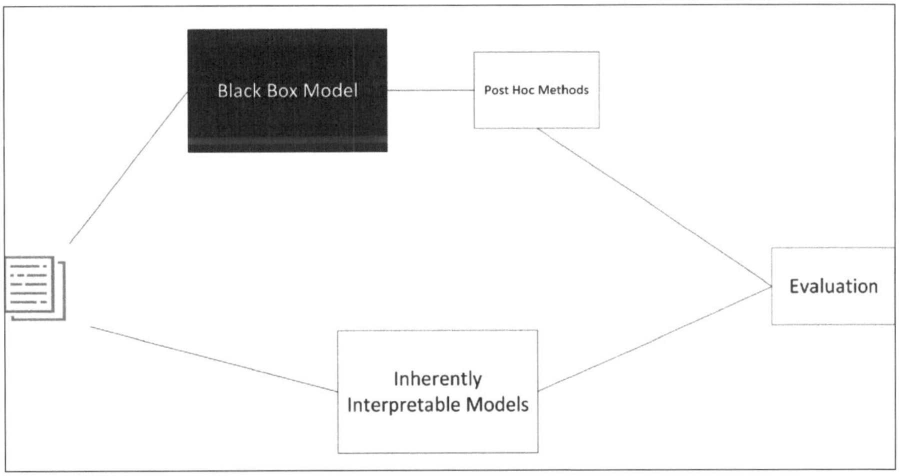

Figure 3.2: *Phases of applying Interpretability*

Model Specific versus Model Agnostic

Model-specific interpretation tools are specific to a single model or group of models. Model Agnostic methods, on the other hand, are flexible and can be applied for many models. For instance, a number of the post methods are Model Agnostic as they are applied post the model training.

Base Concepts

In the previous chapter, we used the feature importance functions provided by the scikit-learn package in analyzing the models. We will look to understand Feature Selection methods, including Feature Importance. This is an important base concept, and often the feature selection techniques provide a good starting point in understanding features importance and influence on the models. We will discuss more advanced techniques for feature interpretability in the upcoming chapters.

Feature Selection

Feature selection is an important step in reducing model noise, handling overfitting, improving performance, and enhancing interpretability. The most informative features can be selected by leveraging domain knowledge or data-driven algorithmic approaches. A naive viewpoint is that more features mean more information. More features need not always mean a better model. As the number of features starts to increase, we encounter situations such as overfitting and the curse of dimensionality. The curse of dimensionality is a term used to describe the impact of redundant, irrelevant, and too many features on a model's performance. Similarly, overfitting is also not desired, as it does not guarantee the desired performance or accuracies on real-world data. Feature Selection or Feature Extraction are two methods used to handle these impacts, reducing dimensionality and hence simplifying models. Feature Extraction uses techniques such as PCA and manifold learning, and it can produce lower-dimension projections. Feature Extraction may work better than Feature Selection, but the interpretability of the Feature Extraction model depends on the interpretability of the extracted features.

There are three classes of Feature Selection methods:

- Filters
- Wrappers
- Embedded methods

Filters

Filters can be used to identify the relevance of features using statistical properties with target variables, primarily using the feature properties. Feature Selection methods construct a measure that quantifies the dependency between features and the target variable. A numerical score is calculated for each feature $x_{j,}$ and the features are ranked accordingly.

Feature Selection using filters includes techniques like:

- Correlation
- Multicollinearity
- Variance Threshold
- Information Gain

Correlation

Correlation is a key statistical concept used in analyzing data and their connections. The connection between two or more variables is called correlation. Correlation is the degree to which variables change together. It helps to understand the relationship between variables. Looking at one variable and examining how it increases or decreases independently is not enough. Simultaneous fluctuations in both or all variables measured are examined in correlation. A high correlation indicates the variables tend to move in tandem. A low correlation means the variables are not closely associated with their fluctuations.

Highly correlated features provide redundant information, and feature selection removes uninformative features to simplify models. Redundant features are identified by analyzing graphs for correlations. Reducing the features to the meaningful minimal set also helps in preventing overfitting, improving the model's ability to generalize.

Analyzing feature correlations can also help in detecting multicollinearity.

Multicollinearity is when two or more variables in a model are linearly correlated with each other. There can be a negative impact on the models, as multicollinearity increases the variance, making it difficult to determine the effect of individual variables.

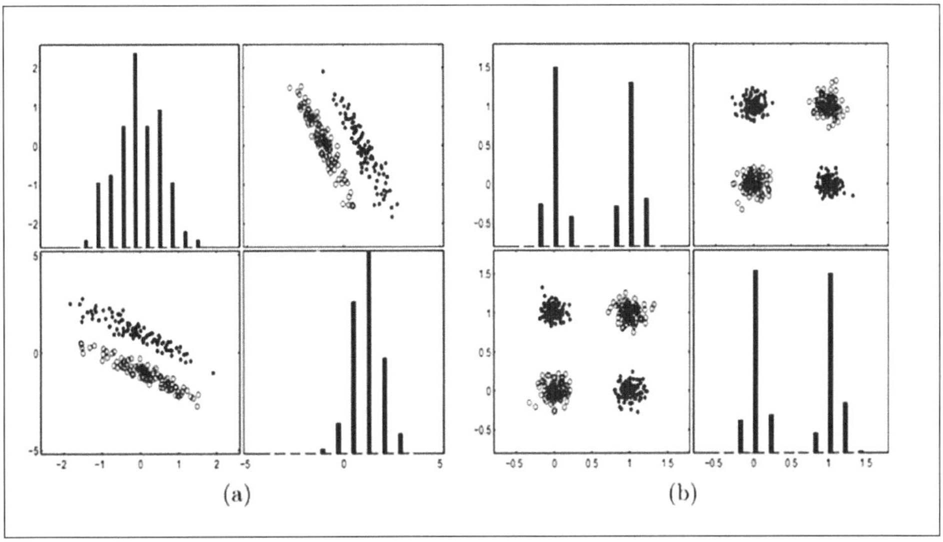

***Figure 3.3**: Correlation in data. (Source - An introduction to variable and feature selection (2003) Guyon et al)*

The preceding figure is a graph of two features along with their labels. The graphs in part a, show that the two features are highly correlated in the scatter plot. While the bar plot captures the spread of the two features, the scatter plot graphs in part b do not show any correlation.

Similar to correlated features, parameters with high multicollinearity provide redundant information. Multicollinearity leads to inflated standard errors which makes the estimated coefficients less reliable. Multiple techniques such as principal component analysis can be applied to the input features for improving the model's stability.

Interpretability

Correlations help in interpreting machine learning models. As a model's complexity increases, it gets increasingly difficult to explain all the interacting variables; it can be difficult to explain why a model makes certain predictions. Analyzing the correlation between the features and the labels gives an insight into the variables with the strongest impact on the models' predictions.

Some of the commonly used measures of correlation include:

- Pearson's correlation coefficient
- Spearman's correlation coefficient

The Limitations of Correlation:

Correlation analysis is useful for identifying relationships between variables, but correlation does not necessarily imply causation. Two factors varying together based on the available data does not imply that one factor is causing the other. Causation is an important effect, and we will delve into the details of causality for Interpretability in further chapters.

Embedded Methods

Embedded methods integrate Feature Selection directly into the specific model using techniques, such as CART, L0, L1. In *Chapter 2, Model Types and Interpretability Techniques*, we looked at Decision Trees (CART techniques) and Lasso Regression (L1 regularization).

Feature Importance

Feature Importance refers to techniques that assign a score to input features based on their influence in predicting a target variable. In *Chapter 2, Model Types and Interpretability Techniques*, we used the out-of-box scikit-learn function for feature importance in the decision tree and random forest. Impurity reduction techniques such as Gini measures and entropy are used in feature selection. The features are selected based on their feature Importance.

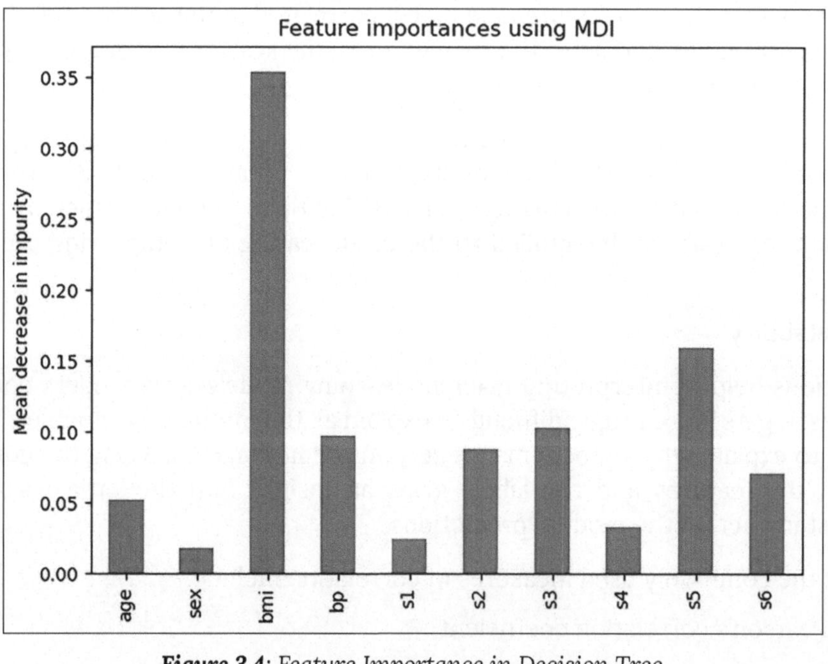

Figure 3.4: *Feature Importance in Decision Tree*

Wrapper Methods

These methods use a model to evaluate subsets of features. There are multiple wrapper methods, including permutation feature importance, sequential feature selection and others. We will understand the permutation feature importance method which was used in *Chapter 2, Model Types and Interpretability Techniques*.

Permutation Feature Importance

Permutation feature importance measures the reduction in model's accuracy or the increased error rates after a feature value is permuted or shuffled. The intuition is straightforward, and it can be easily implemented. Permuting the values of a feature x_j changes its explanatory power as it breaks the association to the outcome variable y. If the model was relying on the feature x_j, the prediction error of the model should increase when predicting with the "permuted feature" in the dataset. On the other hand, an increase in the prediction error is tied to the importance of feature x_j. The average of the errors in prediction is used to understand the feature importance. A feature is considered important if the increase in the prediction error was large and vice versa.

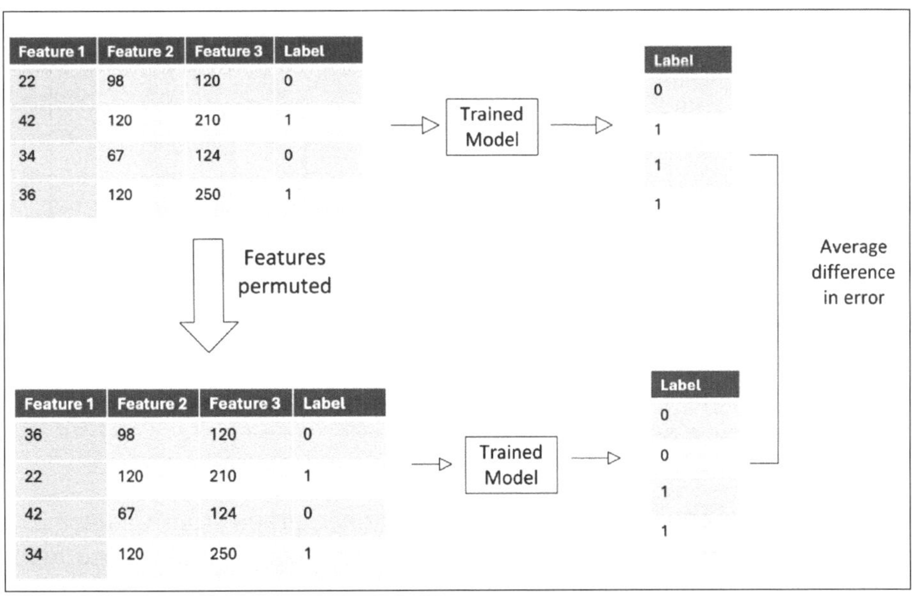

***Figure 3.5**: Permutation Feature Importance*

The Permutation Feature Importance algorithm does the following:

For an input set of features and output y:

1. Train the model on dataset, and score the model (model performance) on a test dataset to get the original error

2. For each feature x_i where i = 1...n
    a. Permute or shuffle the feature column
    b. Score the model using the permuted feature
    c. Calculate the difference between the permuted model prediction score and the original model score as the feature importance
    d. Repeat the preceding three steps for all features or for the number of steps mentioned
3. Compute the average difference as the final feature importance
4. Sort features in descending order

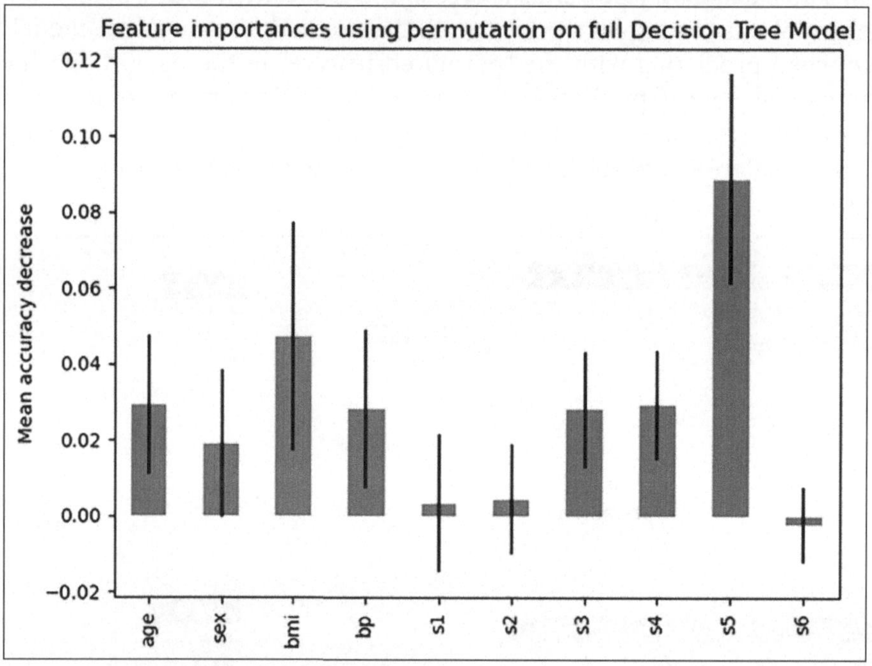

***Figure 3.6**: Permutation Feature Importance for Decision Tree*

Let us relook at the permutation feature importance graph from *Chapter 2, Model Types and Interpretability Techniques*. The permuted feature importance highlights a different feature than the plain vanilla feature importance technique. In PFI, the permuting of features with the change in error has provided a different perspective in identifying the impactful features.

Inherently Interpretable Models

Let us look at all the different types of Inherently Interpretable models:

Rule Based Models

Rule-based systems is a model using a set of prewritten or preidentified rules to make decisions based on an event or precedent.

Bayesian Rule Lists:

These models are in the form of sparse decision lists with a series of if. . . then. . . statements. The 'if' statements enclose a set of features and the 'then' blocks correspond to the predicted outcome of interest. The traditional construction methods such as classification and regression trees (CART) or C5.0 are greedy techniques. Though they are not very computationally demanding, this greediness impacts the solution quality, both in terms of accuracy and interpretability. Given this context, Bayesian Rule Lists provides a balance between accuracy, interpretability, and computation.

if male **and** adult **then** *survival probability* 21% (19%–23%)
else if 3rd class **then** *survival probability* 44% (38%–51%)
else if 1st class **then** *survival probability* 96% (92%–99%)
else *survival probability* 88% (82%–94%)

***Figure* 3.7**: *Bayesian Rule Lists. (Source:* INTERPRETABLE CLASSIFIERS USING RULES AND BAYESIAN ANALYSIS: BUILDING A BETTER STROKE PREDICTION MODEL (2015) *Letham et al)*

Decision trees are constructed in a top-down greedy manner. Each split in the tree is chosen with the objective of maximizing information gain or minimizing impurity at the node. Optimizing a decision tree over the full space of all possible splits is not a tractable problem. Bayes Rule Lists strikes a balance between these extremes, in that its solutions are not constructed in a greedy way involving splitting and pruning, yet it can solve problems at the scale required to have an impact on real problems in science or society, including modern healthcare. A major source of BRL's practical feasibility is the fact that it uses premined rules, which reduces the model space to that of permutations of rules as opposed to all possible sets of splits. The complexity of the problem then depends on the number of pre-mined rules rather than on the full space of feature combinations; in a sense, this algorithm scales with the sparsity of the data set rather than the number of features. As long as the premined set of rules is sufficiently expressive, an accurate decision list can be found. An additional advantage to using premined rules is that each rule is independently both interpretable and informative about the data. Bayesian rule lists can be used to build naturally interpretable models through rule extraction.

Interpretable Decision Sets:

Collections of Decision sets are if-then rules and can be considered in any order. A data point not covered by any rule is assigned a default class label. The non-hierarchical Decision sets aids in interpretability. In the absence of an if-then structure to identify narrow cases, a single rule in the decision set must also be an accurate predictor in isolation. An observer can read the decision sets and understand the workings of each rule, one at a time.

The simplicity of Decision set implies that they are naturally interpretable. Although, there is a bound on the extended complexity of the model beyond which it may not be easy to comprehend and will be above human cognition. The interpretability of a decision set is defined by four natural metrics: size, length, cover, and overlap. A small size implies decision sets with a small number of rules. Interpretable rules can be short and succinct by minimizing the length metric. The cover metric denotes the number of data points that satisfy the itemset of a rule; this is required for defining the other metrics. Lastly, reducing cover is indicative of each rule covering independent parts of the feature space. Essentially, Decision sets are optimized for various metrics, such as recall, precision, distinctness, parsimony, and class coverage. For instance, classes with lesser representation are also surfaced and represented.

Risk Scores

Risk scores are simple classification models which work by adding and subtracting points. The model is a set of lists where points are assigned for each condition. The points are accumulated based on the various conditions, leading to a risk score. These models provide calibrated risk estimates.

1.	Married	3 points	...
2.	Reported Capital Gains	2 points	+ ...
3.	Age 22 to 29	-1 point	+ ...
4.	Highest Level of Education is High School Diploma	-2 points	+ ...
5.	No High School Diploma	-3 points	+
		SCORE	=

SCORE	-4 to -1	0	1	2	3	4	5
RISK	< 5.0%	11.9%	26.9%	50.0%	73.1%	88.1%	95.3%

Figure 3.8: *Risk Score. (Source: Learning Optimized Risk Scores (2019) Ustun et al)*

Risk scores are widely used in multiple industries. The conditions and points are traditionally picked by domain experts, and models were, until recently, manually created. These models can also be learnt from data using statistical techniques and are popular in medicine, finance, and criminal justice.

Generalized Additive Models (GAM)

Generalized Additive Models (GAMs) allow modeling of non-linear data while maintaining explainability.

Poisson Regression, Logistic Regression are examples of a broader kind of models which are also called as Generalized Linear Model (GLM). Generalized Additive Models (GAMs) are different from GLM, as they are more flexible in blending parametric and non-parametric techniques. GAMs introduce flexibility to linear regression models and express "almost linear" behavior. In GAMs, the coefficients are expressed as functions, making it possible to capture non-linearity.

GAMs aid Interpretability through the additive function. In an additive model, the interpretation of the impact of a single variable does not depend on the values of the other variables in the model. We can make simple statements about the effects of the predictive variables by simply looking at the output of the model.

Model	Form	Interpretable	Accuracy
Linear Model	$y= \beta_0 + \beta_1 x_1 + \beta_2 x_2 + \ldots \beta_n x_n$	+++	+
Generalized Linear Model	$g(y)= \beta_0 + \beta_1 x_1 + \beta_2 x_2 + \ldots \beta_n x_n$	+++	+
Additive Model	$y= f_1(x_1)+f_2(x_2)+\ldots f_n(x_n)$	++	++
Generalized Additive Model	$g(y)= f_1(x_1)+f_2(x_2)+\ldots f_n(x_n)$	++	++
GA2M (Interactions GAMs)	$g(y) = \sum f_i(x_i) + \sum f_{ij}(x_i x_j)$	++	++
Full Complexity Model	$Y=f(x_1 \ldots x_n)$	+	+++

***Figure* 3.9**: *GAM and GA2M*

In the preceding figure, we start with a Linear model, which is high on Intelligibility but low on accuracy as well. The model with the highest accuracy, Full Complexity Model could be a deep learning model which maximizes accuracy in most scenarios but also exhibits a black box effect by not being Interpretable.

As a side note, the main difference between Linear Models and Generalized Linear Models is that the linear model residuals follow a conditionally normal distribution. GLM loosens this assumption, allowing for a variety of other residual distributions from the exponential family. A similar difference applies between the Additive Models and GAMs.

Let us consider Generalized Additive Models of form

$$g(y)=f_1(x_1) + f_2(x_2)+\ldots f_n(x_n)$$

where f_i are functions, y_i is the output or label, x_i, and j are input observations needed in function j. (where i=1,2,3......n)

Each feature is expressed as its own function to handle nonlinear problems, and this adds to its interpretability.

GA2M (Interaction Terms)

GAM or Generative Additive models were added to augment the accuracy of GAM's, GA2M was proposed and is also more commonly referred as Interactive GAM.

$$g(y)=\Sigma f_i(x_i)+\Sigma f_{i,j}(x_i,x_j)$$

This equation is quite similar to the GAM equation from the previous section, except it adds functions that can account for two feature variables at once, that is, interaction terms. An example of a model which uses GA2M is Explainable Boosting Machine developed by Microsoft Research.

Explainable Boosting Machine (EBM)

Explainable Boosting Machine (EBM) is a boosting model which uses a tree-based, cyclic gradient boosting Generalized Additive Model with automatic interaction detection. EBMs are often as accurate as other models while also having the advantage of being interpretable.

EBM is a glassbox model, designed to have accuracy comparable to state-of-the-art machine learning methods such as Random Forest and Boosted Trees while being highly intelligible and explainable. EBM is a generalized additive model (GAM) of the form:

$$g(E[y])=\beta 0+\Sigma fj(xj)$$

where *g* is the link function that adapts the GAM to different settings such as regression or classification.

EBM has a few major improvements over traditional GAMs. First, EBM learns each feature function using modern machine-learning techniques, such as bagging and gradient boosting. The boosting procedure is carefully restricted to training on one feature at a time in the round-robin fashion using a very low learning rate so that feature order does not matter. The round-robin cycles through features to mitigate the effects of collinearity and to learn the best feature function for each feature to show how each feature contributes to the model's prediction for the problem. Second, EBM can automatically detect and include pairwise interaction terms of the form

$$g(E[y])=\beta 0+\Sigma fi(xi)+\Sigma fi,j(xi,xj)$$

which further increases accuracy while maintaining intelligibility. EBM is a fast implementation of the GA2M algorithm. EBMs are highly intelligible because the contribution of each feature to a final prediction can be visualized and understood in plotting. As an additive mode, each feature contributes to predictions in a modular way, which makes it easy to reason about the contribution of each feature to the prediction.

To make individual predictions, each function acts as a lookup table per feature and returns a term contribution. These term contributions are simply added up and passed through the link function to compute the final prediction. Because of the modularity (additivity), term contributions can be sorted and visualized to show which features had the most impact on any individual prediction. To keep the individual terms additive, EBM pays an additional training cost, making it somewhat slower than similar methods. However, because making predictions involves simple additions and lookups inside of the feature functions, EBMs are one of the fastest models to execute at prediction time. EBM's light memory usage and fast prediction times make it particularly attractive for model deployment in production.

Explainable Boosting Machine (EBM) is part of the InterpretML framework and can be implemented using the package.

Step 1:

Install the **`Interpretml`** library. Install the **`datasets`** package from huggingface if not already present.

```
!pip install datasets
!pip install interpret
```

Step 2:

Load a huggingface dataset and train the model:

```
# Import necessary libraries
from datasets import load_dataset
from sklearn.model_selection import train_test_split
from interpret.glassbox import ExplainableBoostingClassifier
import pandas as pd

# Load the dataset
#If loading fails, use "https://huggingface.co/datasets"
dataset = load_dataset('imodels/credit-card')
df = pd.DataFrame(dataset['train'])

# Split the dataset into features (X) and target (y)
X = df.drop(columns='default.payment.next.month')
y = df['default.payment.next.month'].values

# Split the data into training and testing sets
X_train, X_test, y_train, y_test = train_test_split(X, y, test_
size=0.2, random_state=42)

# Create an EBM classifier
```

```
ebm = ExplainableBoostingClassifier(random_state=42)

# Train the classifier
ebm.fit(X_train, y_train)
```

Step 3:

Let us check the accuracy score and Area Under the Curve (AUC) for the EBMClassifier:

```
from sklearn.metrics import roc_auc_score, accuracy_score

auc = roc_auc_score(y_test, ebm.predict_proba(X_test)[:, 1])
accuracy = accuracy_score(y_test, y_pred)
print("AUC: {:.3f}".format(auc))
print("Accuracy: {:.3f}".format(accuracy))
```

AUC: 0.779

Accuracy: 0.815

Step 4:

Next we look at the global explanations of the model:

```
from interpret import show

show(ebm.explain_global())
```

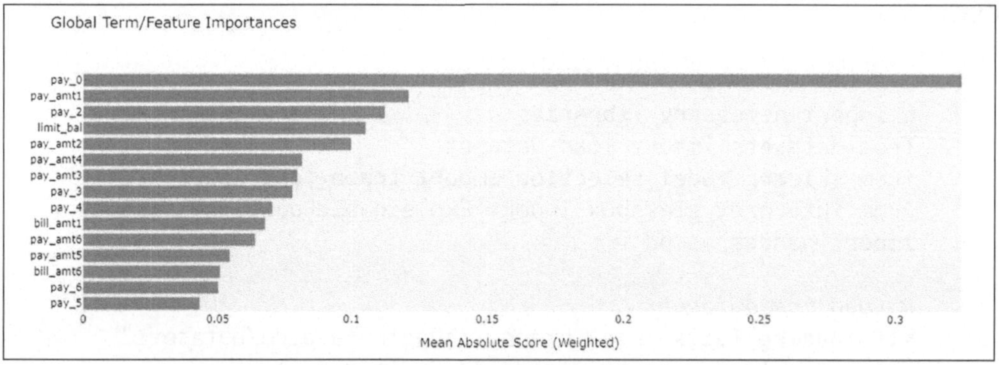

Figure 3.10: *EBMClassifier Global Feature Importance*

In the preceding graph, we see that **`pay_0`** (the first payment) has the highest impact on the model followed by the first payment amount and other features. The first payment is clearly the biggest influencer on the model.

Step 5:

We can also look at individual features and see the local explanations of the individual features.

```
show(ebm.explain_local(X_test[:5], y_test[:5]), 0)
```

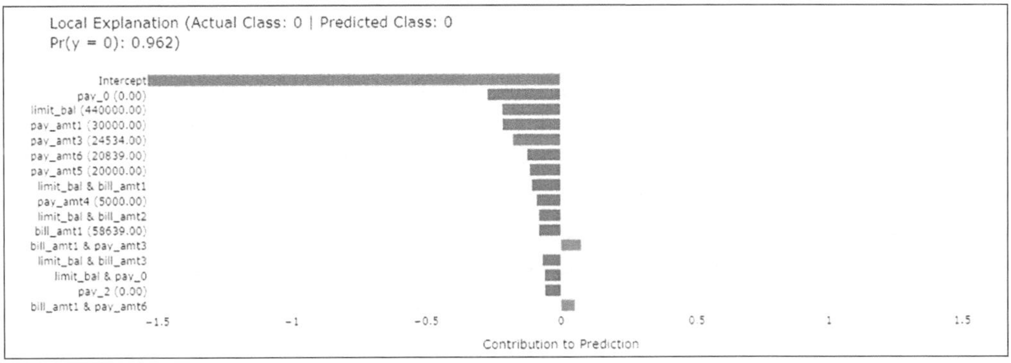

***Figure 3.11**: EBMClassifier Local Explanations*

When we look at the local explainability of individual predictions, we can see the features impacting the individual predictions. We see that **`pay_am2`** and the first payment (done or not) influences the prediction. The prediction probability for this data point was also high at 0.962, with the prediction being that the individual will not default. Let us next look at a few other predictions, including a predicted defaulter.

Step 6:

When we look at the local explainability of individual predictions, we can see the features impacting the individual predictions. We see that **`pay_am2`** and the first payment (done or not) has an influence on the prediction. The prediction probability for this data point was also high at 0.939, with the prediction being that the individual will not default. Although the actual class was a defaulter, this could mean we do not have enough class coverage and need to add more data.

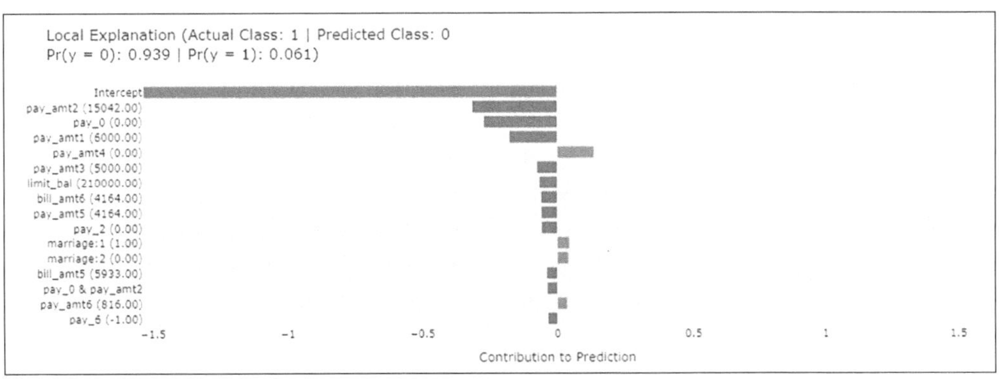

***Figure 3.12**: EBMClassifier Local Explanations on data point with class 1*

This datapoint instance has a low prediction probability.

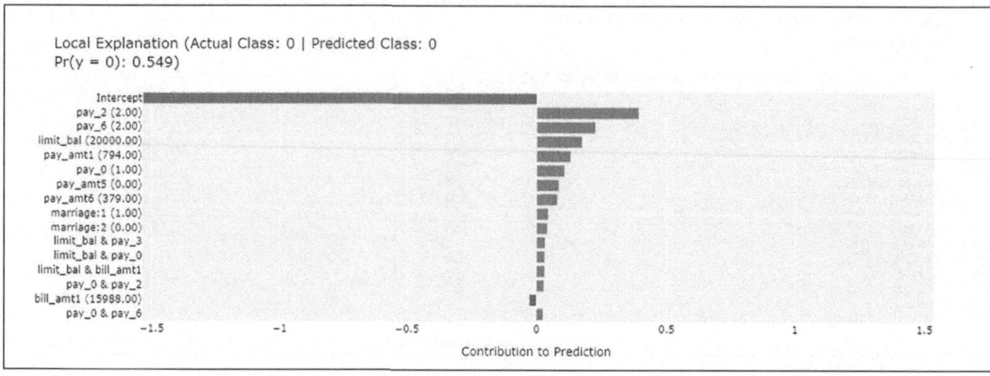

***Figure 3.13**: EBMClassifier Local Explanations on data point with class 0*

Prototype Based Models

Prototype-based models are a commonly utilized set of approaches in both supervised and unsupervised learning. Observations are stored in terms of typical representatives. Combined with a suitable measure of similarity, the models can be used in the unsupervised and supervised analysis of potentially high-dimensional, complex datasets.

Prototype based models have several advantages: the extraction of information from previously observed data into prototypes is transparent and intuitive. In the next phase, the novel data are compared with the prototypes using suitable (dis-)similarity or distance measures. Prototype systems are frequently used in unsupervised analysis of complex data sets to identify underlying structures, such as clusters. In supervised machine learning, the models are being used for classification problems or for continuous target values in regression tasks. The similarity or distance measure is an important element of the model; most frequently, standard Euclidean distance is employed as a distance measure.

kNN

kNearest Neighbor:

kNN is a Prototype based model. kNearest Neighbor uses a distance measure to arrange the variables in the model. The underlying intuition for Nearest Neighbor Classification is straightforward; examples are classified based on the class of their nearest neighbors. More than one neighbor is taken into account as it is often useful, and hence the technique is called k-Nearest Neighbor (k-NN) Classification, where k is the number of nearest neighbors used in determining the class. It is termed a Lazy Learning technique as induction is delayed until run time. The training examples are needed at run-time, and they need to be in memory at run-time; hence, it is sometimes also called Memory-Based Classification.

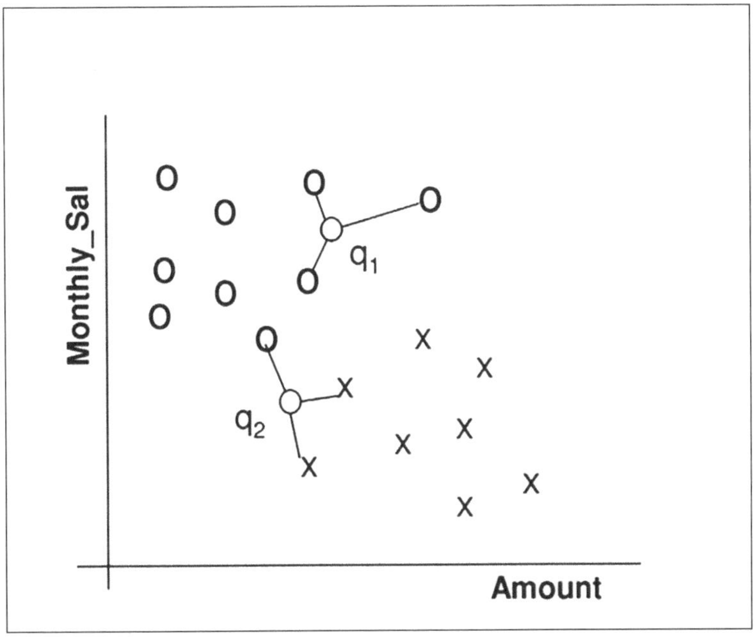

Figure 3.14: *3-Nearest Neighbor Classification in a 2D feature space*

The k nearest neighbors are selected based on this distance metric. Then there are a variety of ways in which the k nearest neighbors can be used to determine the class of q. The most straightforward approach is to assign the majority class among the k nearest neighbors to the query.

Step 1:

Install the required packages.

Step 2:

Load the dataset and build the KNN model.

```
# Import necessary libraries
from datasets import load_dataset
from sklearn.datasets import load_iris
from sklearn.neighbors import KNeighborsClassifier
import matplotlib.pyplot as plt
import pandas as pd
from mlxtend.plotting import plot_decision_regions

# Load the dataset
iris_data = load_iris()

X = iris_data.data[:,[0,2]]
y = iris_data.target
```

```
k=2

# Create a KNN classifier
knn = KNeighborsClassifier(n_neighbors=k)

# Train the classifier
knn.fit(X, y)
```

Step 3:

Plot the decision boundary to see the class distinctions for the data points.

```
from mlxtend.plotting import plot_decision_regions
import numpy as np

# Plotting decision region
plot_decision_regions(X, y, clf=knn, legend=2)
# Adding axes annotations
plt.xlabel('Sepal Length [cm]')
plt.ylabel('Petal Length [cm]')
plt.title('Knn with K='+ str(k))
plt.show()
```

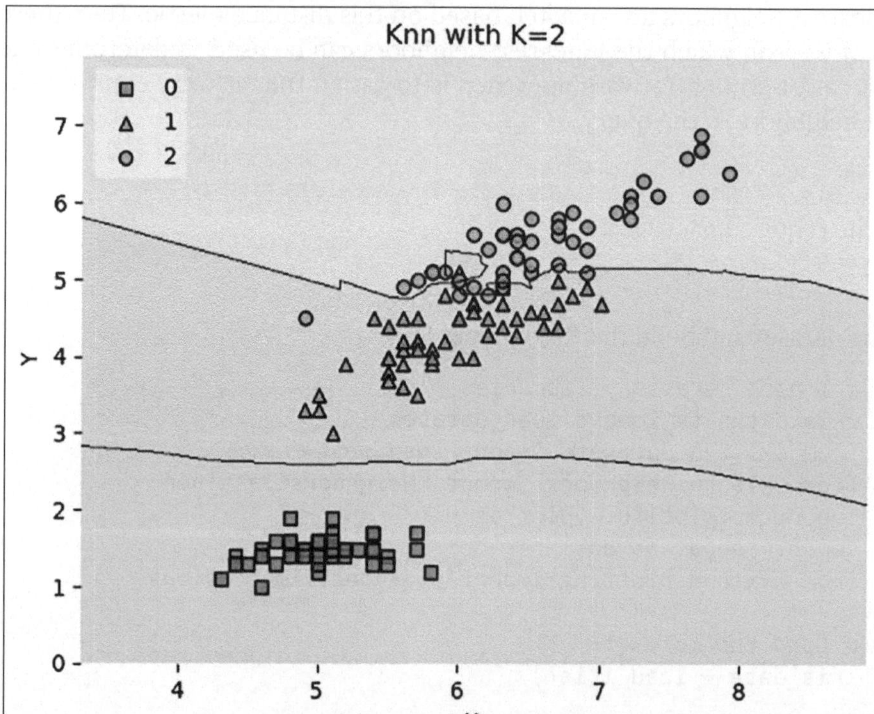

***Figure 3.15**: kNearest Neighbor classification*

Other Intrinsically Interpretable Models

Naive Bayes is a probabilistic machine learning algorithm based on the Bayes Theorem with the naive assumption of conditional independence between pairs of features. Naive Bayes does not learn which features are most important to differentiate between classes.

Applying Bayes rule, we see that P(Y = yi |X) can be represented as,

$$P(y|X)= P(X|y)\ P(y)\ /\ P(X)$$

where, y is class variable and X is a dependent feature vector (of size n) where:

$$X=(x1,x2,x3,.....,xn)$$

Naive Bayes is an interpretable model because of the independence assumption. It can be interpreted on the modular level. It is very clear for each feature how much it contributes towards a certain class prediction since we can interpret the conditional probability.

Conclusion

In this chapter, we covered the various interpretability techniques and concepts. Interpretability can be achieved through models that are inherently interpretable. Alternatively, models can use post hoc methods which is a good option being model agnostic, meaning they would work for all kinds of models. On the other hand, there are also post hoc methods that are specific to types of models. We also understood the various methods of using features to gain an understanding of the model's workings. A key factor to note is that there are certain properties which lend a model to be interpretable, and the ability to determine our interpretability requirements will help us make clear decisions on the techniques needed.

In the last section, we reviewed all the different techniques in Inherently Interpretable models. Rule based models and Risk scores are easy to understand the rationale behind the decisions. Similarly, GAM's, which includes Linear regression is also a popular model that also benefits from the interpretability perspective. Prototype based models such as k Nearest Neighbor (kNN) have a spatial aspect, which makes it easy to understand details such as proximity with other points to compare the decisions. We also understood GA2M and specifically Explainable Boosting Machine (EBM), a model-specific interpretability method.

In the next chapter, we will understand visual methods to understand feature effects and hence augment our interpretability of models. We will look at Partial Dependence Plots (PDP), Individual Conditional Expectations (ICE), and Accumulated Local Effect (ALE), which cover both Local Interpretability and Global Interpretability methods.

References

1. The Mythos of Model Interpretability (2017) Lipton et al https://arxiv.org/abs/1606.03490
2. Stanford Seminar - ML Explainability Part 2 I Inherently Interpretable Models https://www.youtube.com/watch?v=9Th86_3Ea7o
3. Taxonomy and Survey of Interpretable Machine Learning Method (2020) Das et al https://www.academia.edu/88956836/Taxonomy_and_Survey_of_Interpretable_Machine_Learning_Method?uc-sb-sw=44448081
4. The Elements of Statistical Learning (Book)
5. Accurate Intelligible Models with Pairwise Interactions (2013) Lou et al
6. https://www.cs.cornell.edu/~yinlou/papers/lou-kdd13.pdf
7. Interpretable Decision Sets: A Joint Framework for Description and Prediction (2016) Lakkaraju et al https://cs.stanford.edu/people/jure/pubs/interpretable-kdd16.pdf
8. RANDOM FORESTS (2001) Leo Breiman https://www.stat.berkeley.edu/~breiman/randomforest2001.pdf
9. An introduction to variable and feature selection (2003) Guyon et al https://dl.acm.org/doi/10.5555/944919.944968
10. Prototype-based Models for the Supervised Learning of Classification Schemes (2016) Biehl et al https://doi.org/10.1017/S1743921316012928
11. All Models are Wrong, but Many are Useful: Learning a Variable's Importance by Studying an Entire Class of Prediction Models Simultaneously (2019) Fisher et al https://arxiv.org/abs/1801.01489
12. ON BAYESIAN GENERALIZED ADDITIVE MODELS (2023) Solonen et al https://arxiv.org/pdf/2303.02626
13. k-Nearest Neighbour Classifiers 2nd Edition (with Python examples) (2020) Cunningham et al https://arxiv.org/pdf/2004.04523
14. INTERPRETABLE CLASSIFIERS USING RULES AND BAYESIAN ANALYSIS: BUILDING A BETTER STROKE PREDICTION MODEL (2015) Letham et al https://arxiv.org/pdf/1511.01644
15. Learning Optimized Risk Scores (2019) Ustun et al https://jmlr.org/papers/volume20/18-615/18-615.pdf

CHAPTER 4
Feature Effects Analysis with Plots

Introduction

In this chapter, we look at introductory Model Agnostic Methods. ICE and PDP plots are good visualization tools and provide insights into feature effects in some scenarios. In each of these plots, we focus on the effects of selected features. PDP or Partial dependence plots are good for understanding the marginal effect of a feature on the predictions while ICE plots provide insights into a selected feature's effect on the predictions for every data instance. ALE plots factor in the interaction effects of correlated features and alleviate some of the shortcomings in PDP making it a useful tool.

Structure

In this chapter, the following topics will be covered:

- Feature Effects
- Individual Conditional Expectation (ICE)
- Partial Dependence Plots
- ICE and PDP Plots
- Accumulated Local Effects (ALE)

Feature Effects

A powerful interpretation tool is visualization. The marginal contribution of a feature of interest to the prediction is the feature effect and can be visualized in a graph. Regression coefficients are one mechanism for analyzing feature effects.

In a Linear Model without interaction independent features:

$$f(x) = w_0 + w_1x_1$$

w_0 is a linear effect of feature x_i which applies globally to all observations. In the Model equation $\mathbf{f(x) = w_0 + w_1x_1}$ where x_1 describes a global effect. In a Linear Model without interaction, the assumption is that the effect of each feature on the dependent variable is independent of the other features.

Local feature effect methods analyze the effect from individual observations while global effects are computed by aggregating local effects.

We will look at multiple methods to analyze feature effects on the predictions, namely Individual Conditional Expectation, Partial Dependence Plots, and Accumulated Local Effect.

Individual Conditional Expectation (ICE)

In Individual Conditional Expectation, we observe the prediction impact from modifying the feature of interest with all observed values. The observed predictions give a sense of the feature effects.

Consider an observation *x*, where x_s is the feature of interest and the remaining features x_{-s} as shown in the following figure:

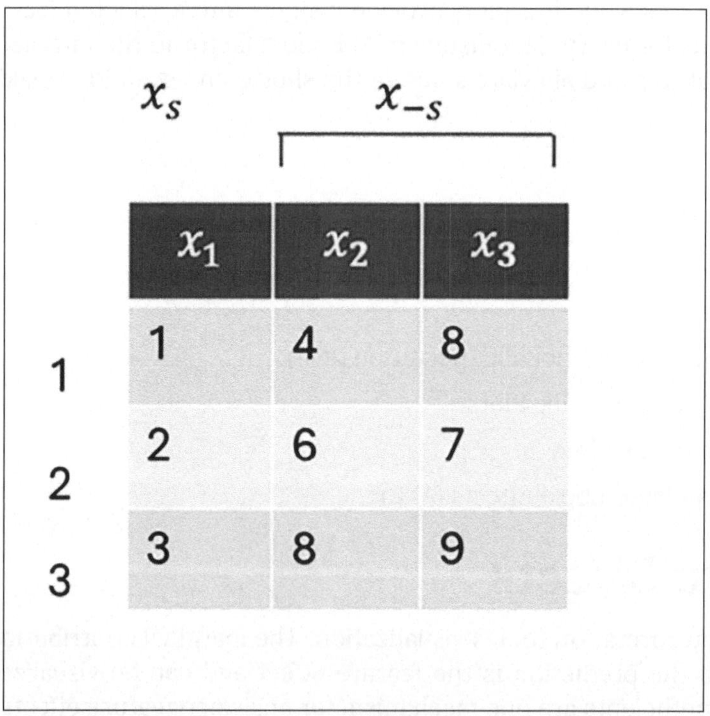

Figure 4.1: *Feature Dataset with a Feature of Interest*

The feature of interest in this instance is x_1. The value of x_1 is modified in the *i*th instance and monitored for its impact on the prediction.

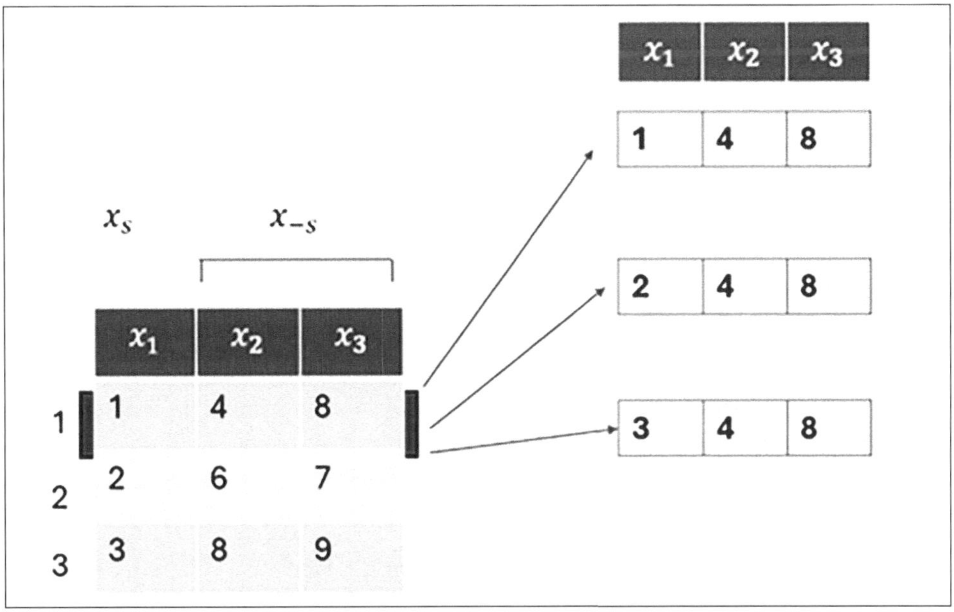

Figure 4.2: *Feature Modification for First Instance*

The first instance of the input is used for the model prediction with the feature of interest x_1 changed across the instances.

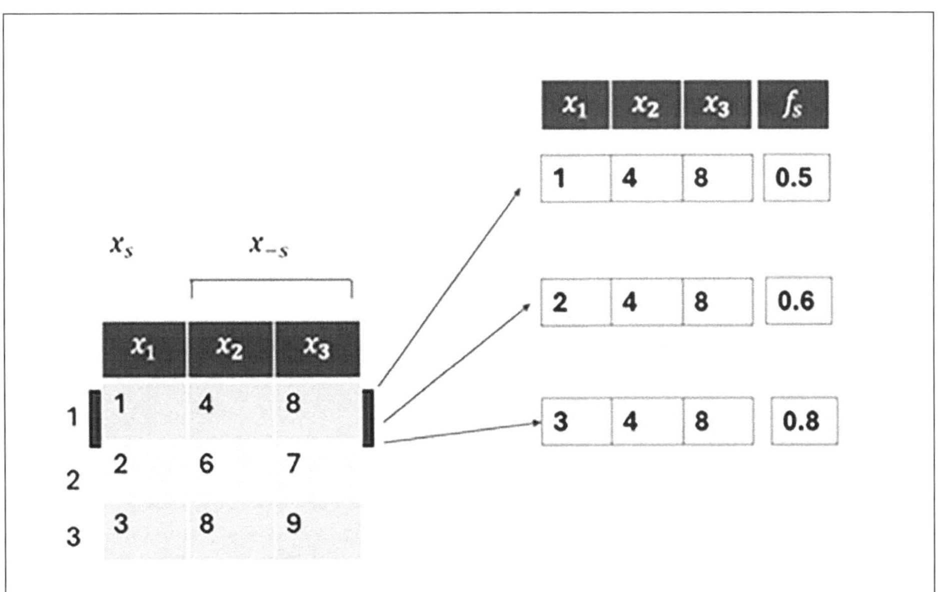

Figure 4.3: *Predictions for the Features*

The graph of instance i, where i=1 is plotted as follows:

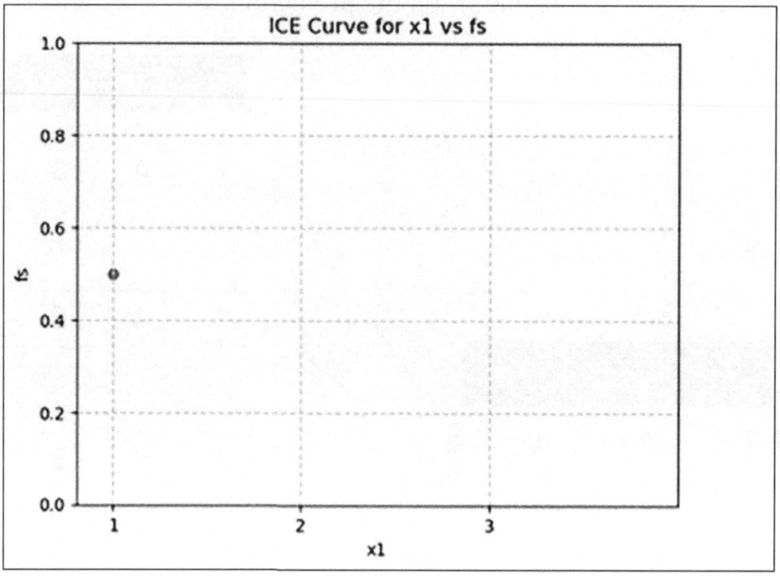

Figure 4.4: *First Datapoint ICE Plot*

The second instance of the input is used for the model prediction with the feature of interest x1 changed across the instances. The following plot has all the predictions for the modified data points:

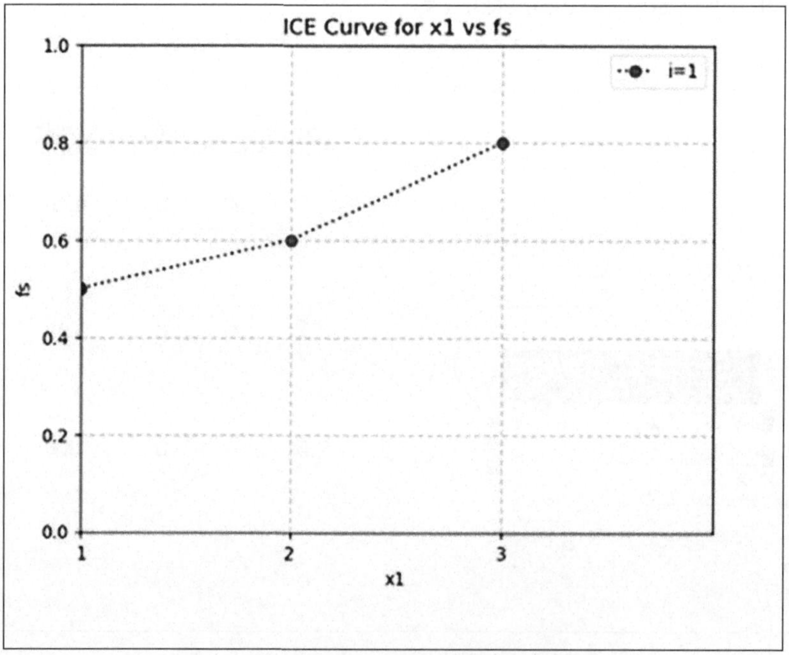

Figure 4.5: *ICE Curve for First Datapoint*

Similarly, we graph instance i where i=2 as follows:

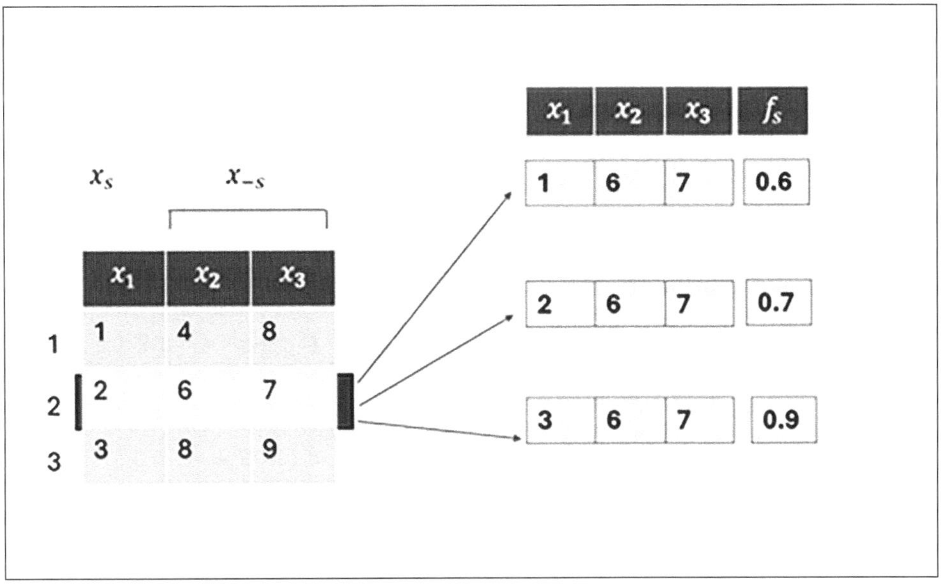

***Figure 4.6**: Feature Modification for Second Instance*

The third instance of the input is used for the model prediction with the feature of interest x1 changed across the instances.

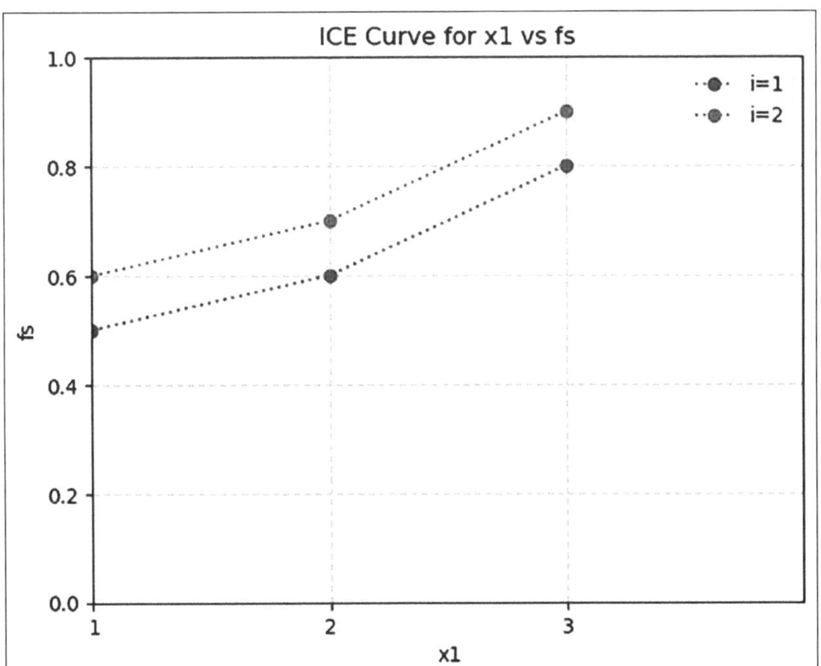

***Figure 4.7**: Plot for the First Two Instances*

Feature modification for i=3:

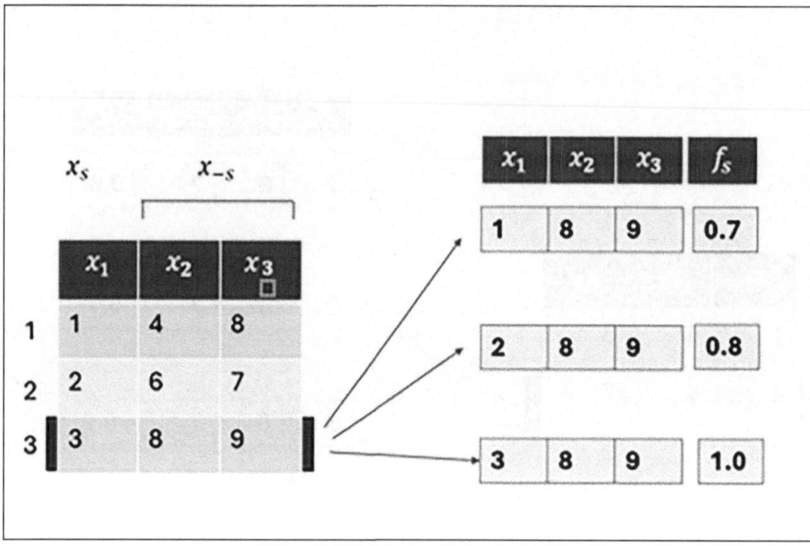

Figure 4.8: *Feature Modification for Third Instance*

Here is the plot for all the 3 modified instances:

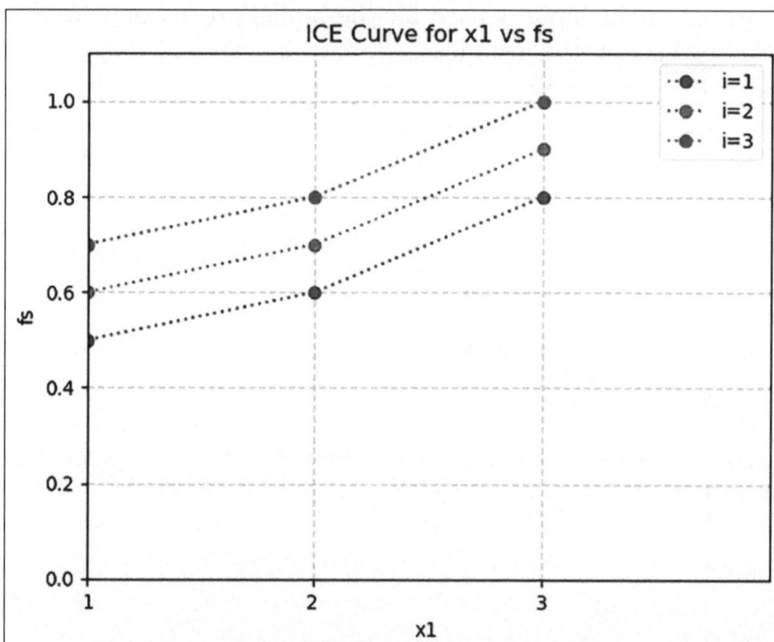

Figure 4.9: *Plot for All the Three Instances*

Feature modification table with predictions for all instances:

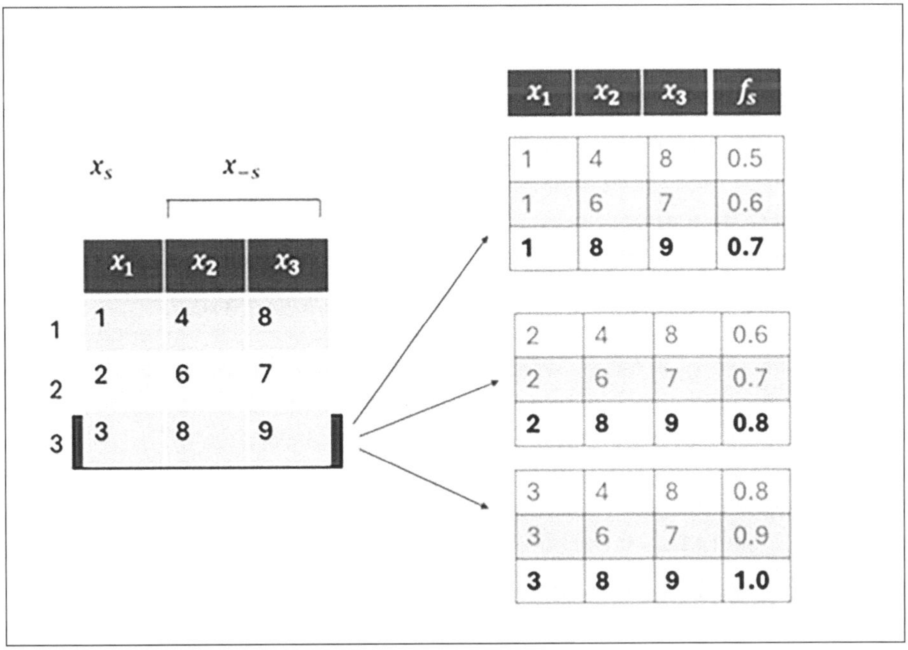

***Figure 4.10**: Table with All Feature Changes*

An ICE plot visualizes the dependence of the prediction on a feature for each instance separately, resulting in one line per instance, compared to one line overall in partial dependence plots. ICE plots highlight the variation in the fitted values across the range of a covariate, giving indications of the heterogeneities within the values.

Visually, ICE plots disaggregate the output of classical PDPs. Rather than plot the target covariates' average partial effect on the predicted response, we instead plot the N estimated conditional expectation curves, each reflecting the predicted response as a function of covariate x_S, conditional on an observed x_{-s}.

Partial Dependence Plots (PDP)

Partial Dependence Plots (PDPs) provide a mechanism to understand and visualize the dependence of the target on a set of features. In particular, PDP focuses on the average partial relation between the target and a feature of interest. When there are interaction effects for the features, the PDP which is an average curve can obscure the complexity of the modeled relationship. ICE plots on the other hand refine the partial dependence plot by graphing the functional relationship between the predicted response and the feature for individual observations.

The average effect from the plotted ICE curves is computed as shown in the following image:

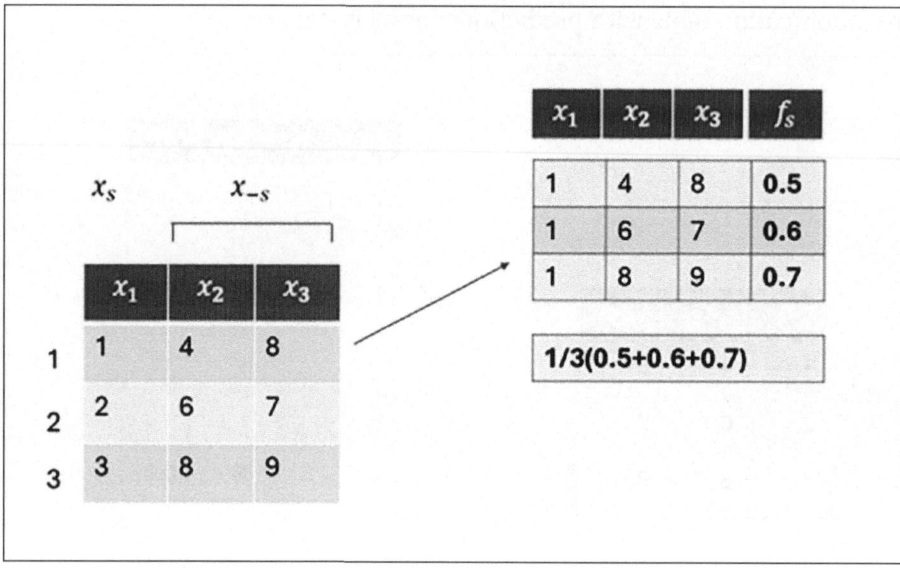

Figure 4.11: *Average Effect of Predictions for the First Instance*

This is done for every single instance of the data points.

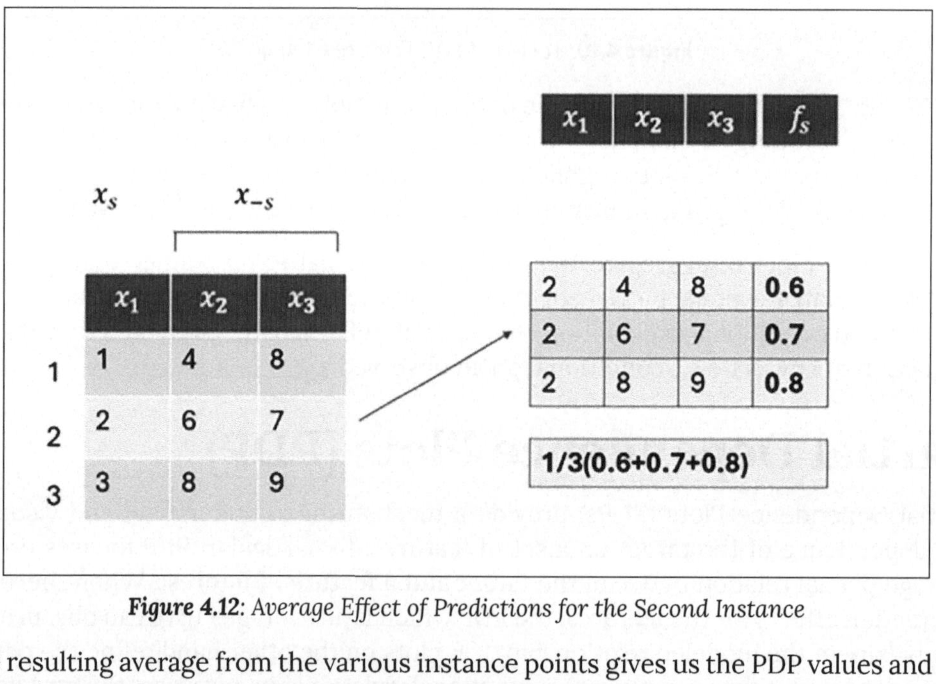

Figure 4.12: *Average Effect of Predictions for the Second Instance*

The resulting average from the various instance points gives us the PDP values and the plotted graph shows us the ICE curves along with the PDP.

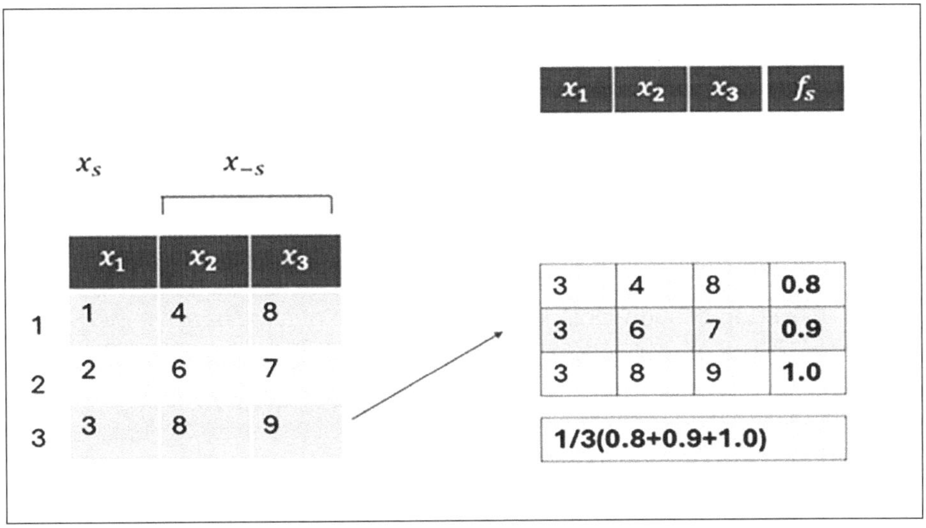

Figure 4.13: *Average Effect of Predictions for the Third Instance*

Following is the plot for ICE and the PDP:

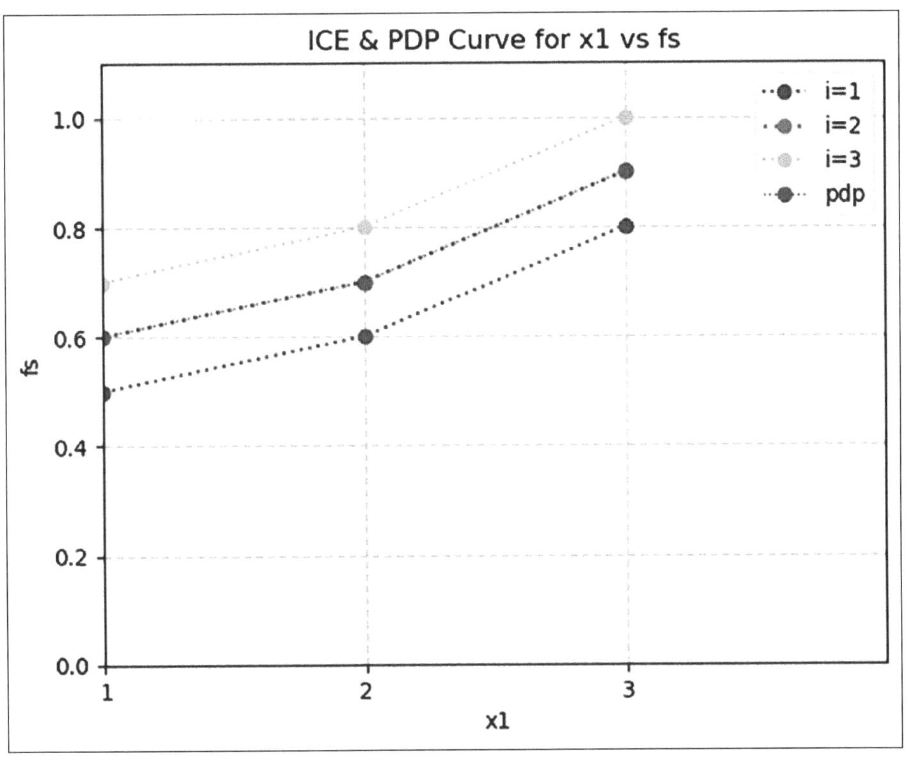

Figure 4.14: *Plot of ICE across the Three Instance Points and the PDP Plot*

A graph of the target value for a function f(x) and the input variables provides a view of the dependence. For instance, values can be represented as a scatter graph or categorical values can be represented as a bar graph. This works best for low dimensional arguments. Partial Dependence Plots provide a good approximation of Fx on selected small subsets of the input variables.

When the input features have higher dimensions, it is tough to imagine and visualize the functions. A partial dependence plot provides a useful mechanism to visualize the approximation function on multiple small subsets of the input features. Although a collection of such plots seldom provides a comprehensive insight into the approximation, it can often produce helpful hints.

Definition: Partial Dependence function is the expectation of (x_S, x_{-S}) with respect to marginal distribution of features x_{-S}:

$$f_{S,PD}(\mathbf{x}_S) = \mathbb{E}_{\mathbf{x}_{-S}}\left(\hat{f}(\mathbf{x}_S, \mathbf{x}_{-S})\right) = \int_{-\infty}^{\infty} \hat{f}(\mathbf{x}_S, \mathbf{x}_{-S})\, d\mathbb{P}(\mathbf{x}_{-S})$$

***Figure 4.15**: Partial Dependency Function*

Partial Dependence Plot (PDP) highlights the average partial relationship between a set of predictors and the predicted response. The partial dependence plot shows the marginal effect one or two features have on the predicted outcome of a machine learning model. A partial dependence plot can show whether the relationship between the target and a feature is linear, monotonic, or more complex. For example, when applied to a linear regression model, partial dependence plots always show a linear relationship.

ICE and PDP Plots

We have used the diabetes dataset from scikit-learn and trained a Linear Regression model and a Gradient Boost Regressor model. The model is then used for plotting the PDP and ICE plots for the features.

```
import matplotlib.pyplot as plt
from sklearn.datasets import load_diabetes
from sklearn.linear_model import LinearRegression
from sklearn.ensemble import GradientBoostingRegressor
from sklearn.inspection import PartialDependenceDisplay
from sklearn.model_selection import train_test_split
diabetes = load_diabetes()

X, y = diabetes.data, diabetes.target
```

```
X_train, X_test, y_train, y_test = train_test_split(X, y, test_size=0.2,
random_state=42)


clf = GradientBoostingRegressor(n_estimators=10).fit(X_train, y_train)
lm = LinearRegression().fit(X_train, y_train)
featurenames = diabetes.feature_names
```

We build a PDP plot for a feature of interest using both the Linear Regression model and the Gradient Boosting Regressor. The Linear model tends to have a linear effect on the PDP model. The features here are s5 (Triglycerides Level) and s6 (Blood sugar).

```
PartialDependenceDisplay.from_estimator(lm, X_test, [8,9], feature_
names=featurenames, kind='both')
plt.show()
```

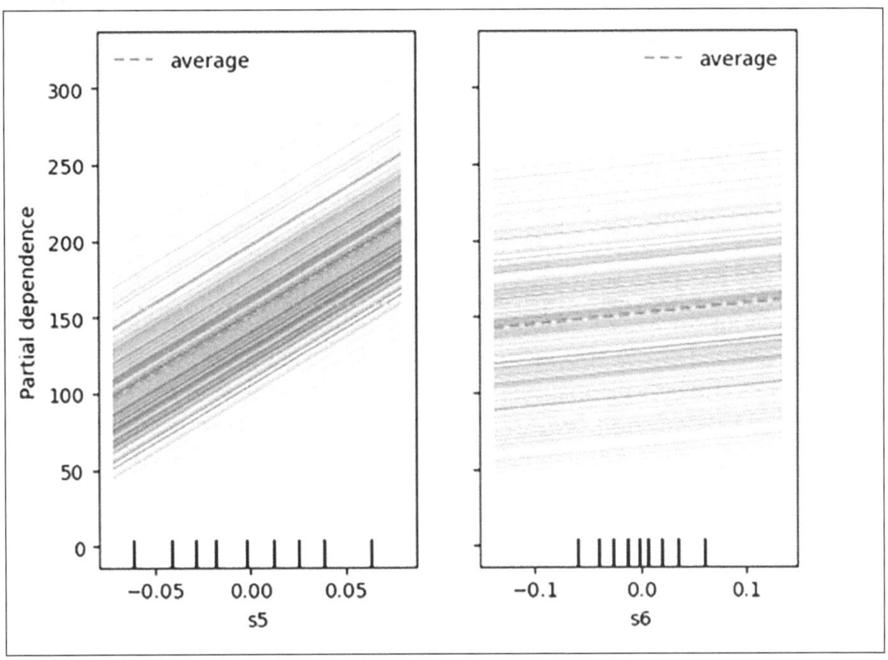

Figure 4.16: *ICE and PDP Plots for Linear Regression*

Plotting a PDP graph with a Gradient Booster Regressor gives a non-linear jagged prediction impact. The increasing pattern is similar for both models in s5 (Triglycerides) while s6 (Blood sugar) has a more uniform prediction impact until 0.05 and then it increases.

```
PartialDependenceDisplay.from_estimator(clf, X_test, [8,9], feature_
names=featurenames, kind='both')
plt.show()
```

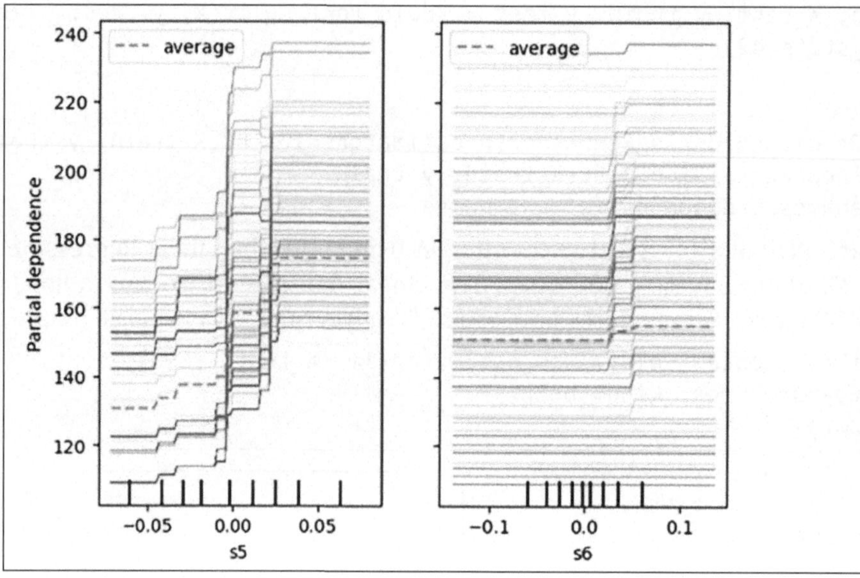

***Figure 4.17**: ICE and PDP Plots for Gradient Booster Regressor*

When features are highly correlated, PDP might include improbable combinations of feature values in its average prediction calculation because it manipulates feature values independently across the marginal distribution. This reduces the reliability of the PDP explanation in the presence of strong feature correlations. In contrast, ALE addresses feature correlations by averaging and accumulating the differences in predictions across the conditional distribution, thereby isolating the specific feature's effects. However, this method requires a larger number of observations and a nearly uniform distribution of those observations to accurately determine the conditional distribution.

PDP operates under a strict assumption that features must be uncorrelated. In real-world scenarios, features are often correlated. Some features are directly derived from others or because an observed event results in correlated distributions. For instance, in our diabetes dataset, we have features s1 and s2 where s1 is the total serum cholesterol and s2 is Low Density Lipoproteins or LDL which are highly correlated as evident in the following graph:

```
# Create a new figure for plotting
plt.figure(figsize=(10, 8))

plt.scatter(df['s1'], df['s2'], c=df['target'], cmap='viridis')
plt.colorbar()
plt.xlabel('tc')
plt.ylabel('ldl')
plt.title('Target Values')
plt.show()
```

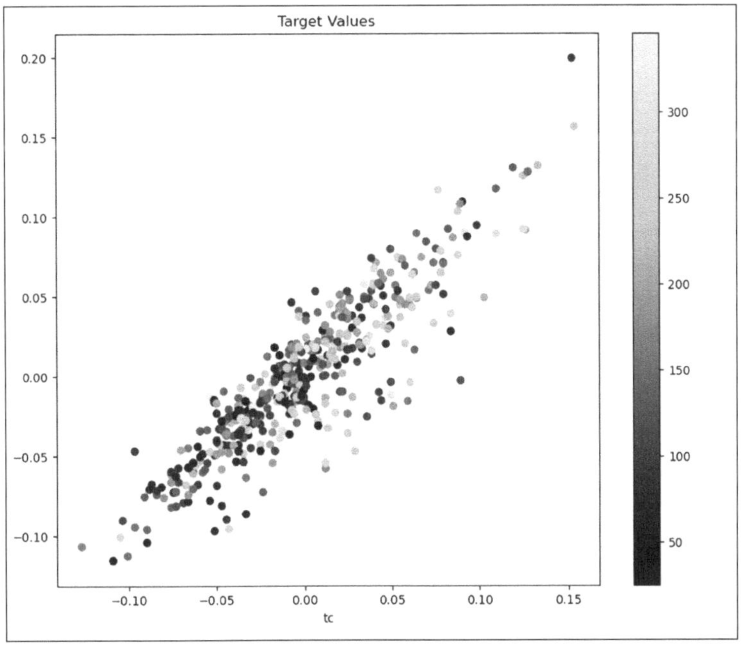

Figure 4.18: *Scatter Plot for Feature s1 (Total Serum Cholesterol) and s2 (LDL)*

The PDP graph for these features can have distribution areas that are highly unlikely like a low s1 (or total serum cholesterol) with high s2 (LDL).

```
PartialDependenceDisplay.from_estimator(lm, X , [(4, 5)],feature_names=-
featurenames)
```

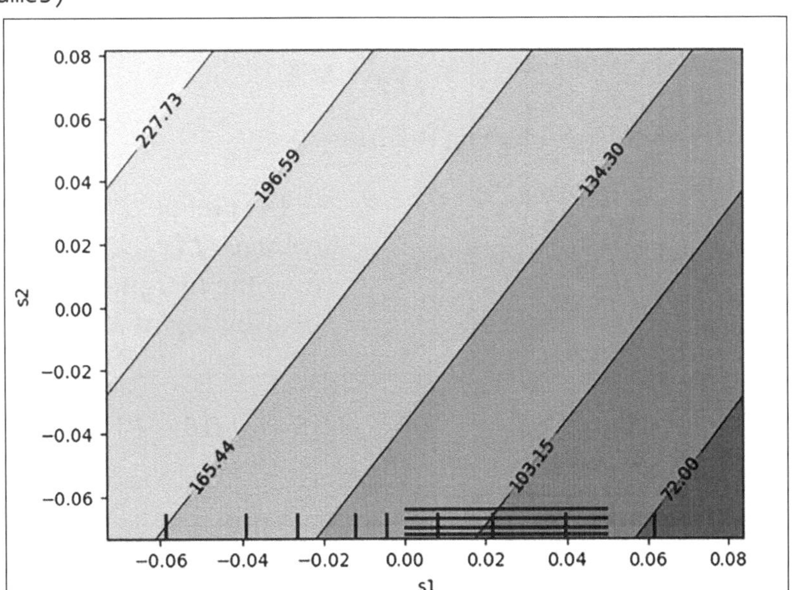

Figure 4.19: *PDP Plot for s1 (or Total Serum Cholesterol) and s2 (LDL)*

Accumulated Local Effects (ALE)

Accumulated Local Effects (ALE) is a model-agnostic global explanation method. In ALE, the relationship between feature values and target variables is evaluated similarly to Partial Dependence Plots (PDP).

The main limitation of PDP arises when there is a significant correlation between the features in a machine learning model. In those cases, PDP outputs are highly unreliable. This is mostly due to the fact that PDP outputs are based on the averages of the predictions which obscure dependencies between the features. ALE also uses a conditional feature distribution as input but focuses on differences in predictions within distribution intervals instead of the average.

Following our previous examples of a model that predicts diabetes based on blood sugar levels, BP, BMI, and other diagnostics, ALE will take the differences of the predictions of diabetes with the lowest BMI to the highest. The result provides a clear perspective of the impact of the levels without the effect of the correlated features.

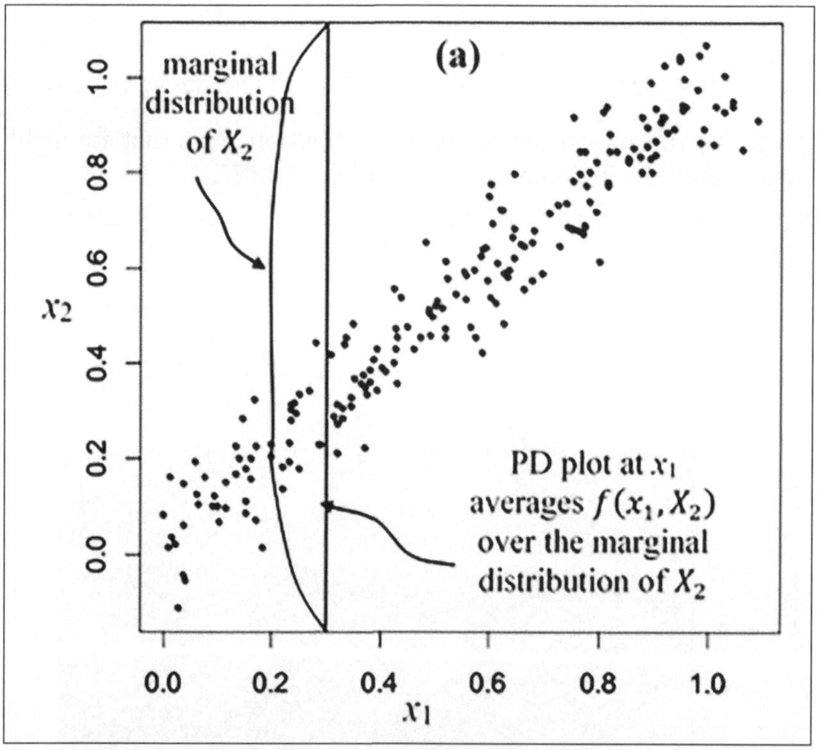

Figure 4.20: *PDP Plot with Unlikely Values for x1 (Source: Visualizing the Effects of Predictor Variables in Black Box Supervised Learning Models (2019) Apley et al)*

PDP plot where the feature distribution of x1 is across a larger distribution including some unlikely spaces.

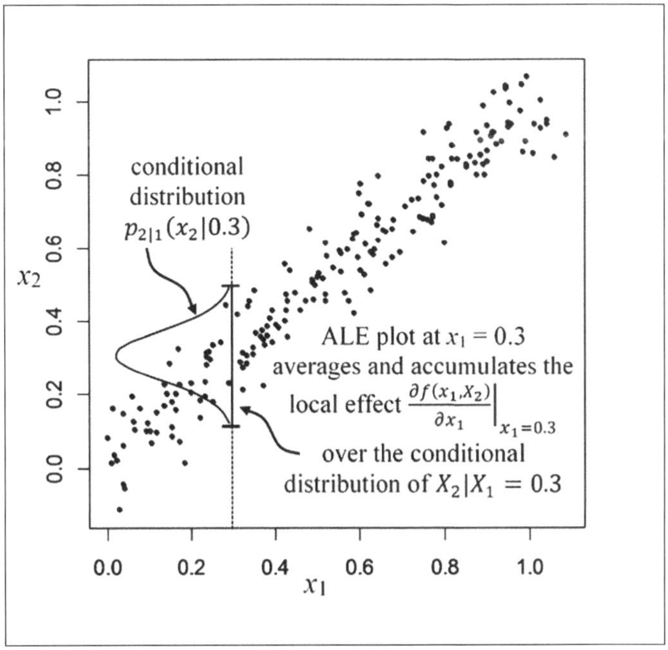

Figure 4.21: *ALE Plot with Feature Values in Distribution (Source: Visualizing the Effects of Predictor Variables in Black Box Supervised Learning Models (2019) Apley et al)*

ALE plot with a conditional distribution reduces the surface to be within the expected distribution.

The main limitation of PDP arises when there is a significant correlation between the features in an ML model. In those cases, PDP outputs are highly unreliable. This is mostly due to the fact that PDP outputs are based on the averages of the predictions which obscure dependencies between the features. ALE also uses a conditional feature distribution as input but focuses on differences in predictions instead of the average.

Here, we used the PyALE framework to chart the ALE plots.

Import the python library for ALE and display the ALE plots:

```
!pip install PyALE


from PyALE import ale

ale_eff = ale(X=df.drop('target',axis=1), model=lm, feature=["s2",
"s1"],grid_size=100,plot=True, contour=True)
```

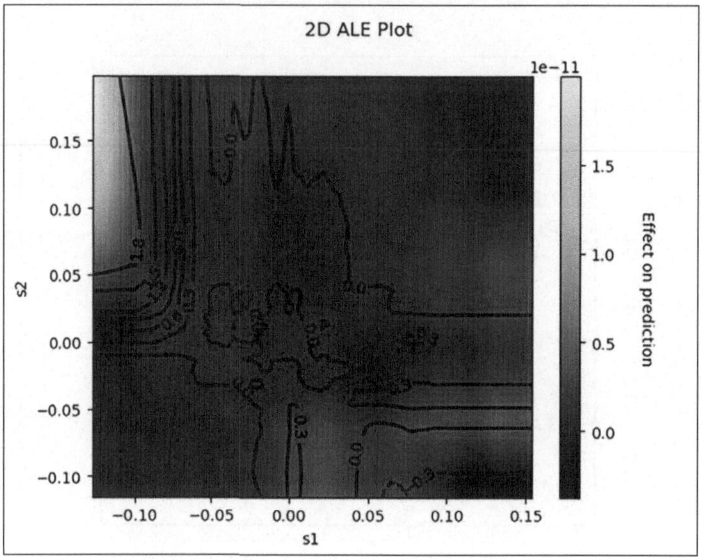

Figure 4.22: *Combined Interaction ALE Plot*

The ALE plot shows the combined interaction impact of s1 and s2. The ICE and PDP plots are good to see the individual feature effects on the prediction.

Similarly, we look at the impact of BMI on s2 (LDL).

```
## 2D - continuous
ale_eff = ale(X=df.drop('target',axis=1), model=lm, feature=["bmi",
"s2"])
```

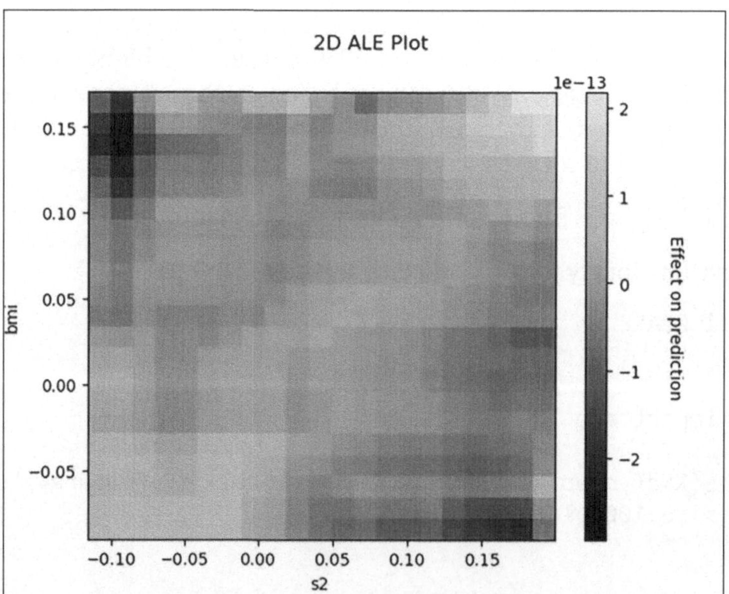

Figure 4.23: *ALE Plot for Features BMI and s2 (LDL)*

A high s2 (LDL) combined with a larger BMI has a positive impact on the prediction. While there is some effect also visible with a high BMI and low s2.

This is another example of an ALE plot of bp and s5 (Triglycerides). When bp and s5 (Triglycerides) are both low, there is a higher value on the predictions. On the other hand, low bp and a high s5 or Triglycerides have a lower than average impact on the prediction. This plot was created with intervals of 10; we notice that as the **grid_size** or intervals is increased, the plot layout changes drastically. These observations are specific to the diabetes dataset used.

```
ale_eff = ale(X=diabetes.drop('target',axis=1), model=lm, feature=["bp",
"s5"],grid_size=60,plot=True)
```

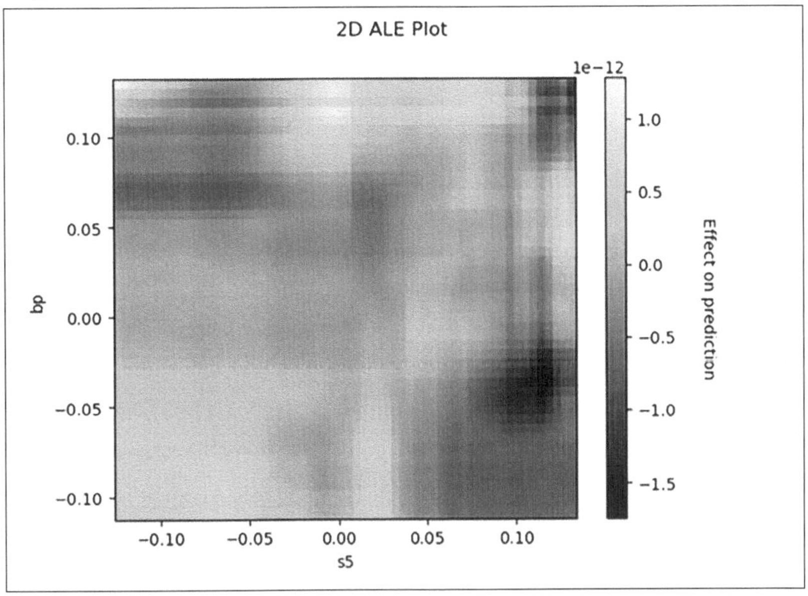

Figure 4.24: *ALE Plot for Features BP and s5 (Triglycerides)*

ALE plots are a good substitute for PDP and ICE Plots for two reasons:

The feature of interest is modified only based on distribution. This means that the possibility of ICE plots taking up unexpected combinations cannot occur.

ALE plots are computed for each interval which makes predictions applicable per interval.

These are good reasons to use an ALE plot. Although ALE does have its own set of negatives, the number of intervals chosen can impact the plots. A large interval size makes the curves very shaky while a smaller size hides the complexities. Besides, the PDP plots combined with ICE gives a sense of the heterogeneity or variance of the feature effect, which gives an understanding of the feature effect on the subsets of data. In the ALE plot, we can see the feature effect across intervals. A good guideline is to use ALE plots when the features are correlated since ALE plots stick to the feature of interest's distribution, avoiding unlikely combinations in the process. ALE plots are also faster to compute as the computations are only done for the number of intervals, while PDP plots are much wider.

Conclusion

PDP plots are focused on the marginal effects of the features on the target. While ICE plots provide granularity for individual data points. ALE is preferred when we want to ensure that the feature changes are constrained within its expected distribution. Collectively, all these plots are a good mechanism to understand feature effects.

In the next chapter, we get deeper into the Model Agnostic techniques and understand the popular methods LIME and SHAP.

References

1. Greedy function approximation: A gradient boosting machine (2001) Friedman et al https://doi.org/10.1214/aos/1013203451
2. Bringing a Ruler Into the Black Box: Uncovering Feature Impact from Individual Conditional Expectation Plots (2021) Yeh et al https://arxiv.org/pdf/2109.02724
3. Peeking Inside the Black Box: Visualizing Statistical Learning with Plots of Individual Conditional Expectation (2014) Goldstein et al https://arxiv.org/pdf/1309.6392
4. Partial Dependency PLot (PDP) https://www.studocu.com/en-gb/document/university-of-essex/machine-learning/partial-dependence-plot-pdp/17999562
5. Interpretable Machine Learning (2019) Christoph Molnar https://christophm.github.io/interpretable-ml-book/
6. Visualizing the Effects of Predictor Variables in Black Box Supervised Learning Models (2019) Apley et al https://arxiv.org/pdf/1612.08468

CHAPTER 5
Post-Hoc Methods

Introduction

This chapter progresses into Local Model Agnostic methods of LIME and SHAP to understand feature attributions. LIME perturbs the feature of interest and then builds local linear models to explain instances. SHAP identifies the marginal contributions of features and also has explainers that leverage LIME techniques. We will also have a hands-on activity to get a better sense of the techniques.

In the previous chapter, we looked at using PDP, ICE plots, and also ALE for Interpretability. The techniques also use some form of permutation variations ranging between a specific input feature being constrained within the feature's distribution or being more widespread.

These plots only show the relationship between a single feature and the model's predictions, which does not capture the complex interactions between features. Besides, they also require manual measures to identify interesting plots, which can be time-consuming and subjective.

We will now look at Post Hoc Methods like LIME and SHAP which are better equipped to handle the complexities of feature interactions.

Structure

In this chapter, we will cover the following topics:

- Model Agnostic Techniques
- Local Interpretable Model-Agnostic Explanations (LIME)
- SHapley Additive explanations (SHAP)

Model Agnostic Techniques

Model Agnostic Techniques as the name implies are applicable across Model types. We will now look at two techniques, LIME and SHAP which are Model Agnostic. Each of these techniques does have Model specific variants but the primary techniques in each were primarily designed to be model agnostic.

Local Interpretable Model-Agnostic Explanations (LIME)

Local Interpretable Model-Agnostic Explanations (LIME) is a technique for explaining the predictions of any machine learning model, and hence it is termed as Model Agnostic.

Consider a model trained to make predictions as shown in the following figure. The model uses the various symptoms to provide the "Flu" prediction. The prediction is then explained by highlighting the symptoms that were most important to the model. This information provides the rationale behind the model thus empowering the doctor to trust the model or not.

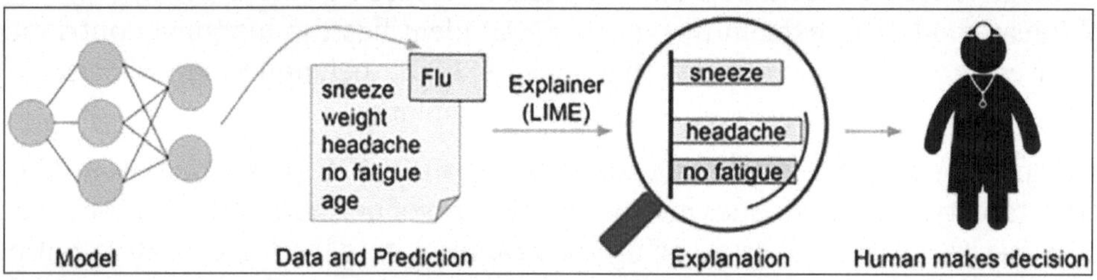

Figure 5.1: *Model Explanations (Source: "Why Should I Trust You?" Explaining the Predictions of Any Classifier (2016) Ribeiro et al)*

When deploying a machine learning model to production, it is expected to make reasonable predictions. Typically, the model's performance is evaluated using accuracy on the test set or another aggregate measure. However, anyone with practical experience in machine learning knows that these metrics can be deceptive.

Sometimes, data that should not be included inadvertently slips into the training and test sets. Additionally, the model may occasionally produce errors that are too embarrassing to overlook. These and other complex issues suggest that understanding the model's predictions can be a valuable tool in determining its reliability. Humans possess intuition and business insights that are difficult to quantify using evaluation metrics. Incorporating a "pick step," where certain representative predictions are selected for human explanation, can enhance the process, shown as follows:

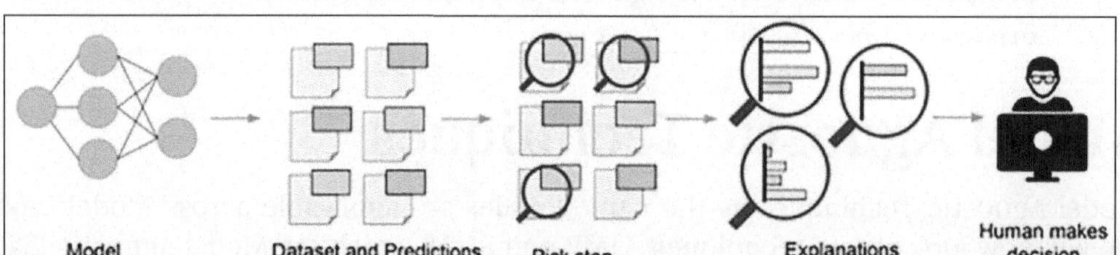

Figure 5.2: *Picked Predictions Explanations (Source: "Why Should I Trust You?" Explaining the Predictions of Any Classifier (2016) Ribeiro et al)*

A Model-Agnostic Interpreter

Local Interpretable Model-Agnostic Explanations (LIME), is a tool that excels in elucidating the predictions of any classifier or regressor whether it is a simple decision tree or a complex neural network, in a way that is understandable to humans. It accomplishes this by creating a local approximation of a model's behavior around a specific prediction, thereby providing a comprehensible explanation, also known as a 'LIME model interpretation,' for that specific instance.

LIME assumes that even a complex model can be described with the local prediction through a simpler model. In LIME the individual predictions of any model are explained by finding an approximation to the model locally on an interpretable model; the local model is called local surrogate models. For the local surrogate models often existing inherently interpretable models such as linear models or classification/regression trees are preferred. LIME can handle tabular, image, and text data. It is essentially answering the question, "why the model predicted y for input x?"

Intuition Behind LIME

The idea was first described in a 2016 paper, where the original data points are perturbed and then provided as input to the black box model. The predictions from the model for these data points which were perturbed are observed through the lens of their distance to the original points. These new data points are weighted as a measure of their nearness to the original points. Finally, a surrogate model such as linear regression is fitted onto the dataset where some of the variations use the calculated sample weights. In this way, every one of the original data points can be explained using the newly trained explanation model.

This is beneficial for interpretability because we can perturb the input by changing components that make sense to humans (for example, words or parts of an image) even if the model is using much more complicated components as features (for example, word embeddings).

An explanation is created by approximating the base model to a comprehensible model like a linear model (with only a handful of non-zero coefficients), which is learned based on perturbations of the original instance (removing words or obscuring parts of an image). The fundamental concept behind LIME is that it is significantly simpler to approximate a black-box model locally (in the vicinity of the prediction we aim to explain) rather than attempting a global approximation.

This is accomplished by assigning weights to the perturbed images based on the similarity to the instance that we are trying to explain. To illustrate with our flu prediction example, the three emphasized symptoms might provide a faithful approximation of the black-box model for patients who resemble the one under examination, but they likely do not reflect the model's behavior for all patients

In the following image, we are attempting to explain a classifier that predicts how likely it is for the image to contain a tree frog. We take the left image below and divide it into interpretable components (contiguous superpixels).

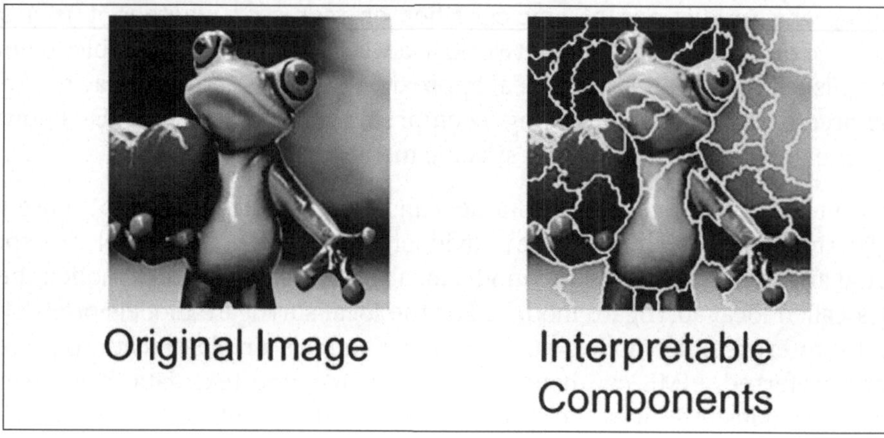

Figure 5.3: *Interpretable Components Divided from Original Image (Source: Local Interpretable Model-Agnostic Explanations (LIME): An Introduction (2016) Ribeiro et al)*

As illustrated in the following figure, we perform a set of perturbations on the original image and extract a new data set. In the new data set, some parts of interpretable areas are grayed out while the non-perturbed portions are left intact. In each of the perturbed data, the prediction from the model displays the probability of it being a tree frog. We then get a simple linear model on this data set. The model is locally weighted by being more sensitive to instances more similar to the original image such that the similar instances are correctly identified. Finally, the superpixels which have the highest positive weight are provided as the explanation while graying out the rest of the pixels.

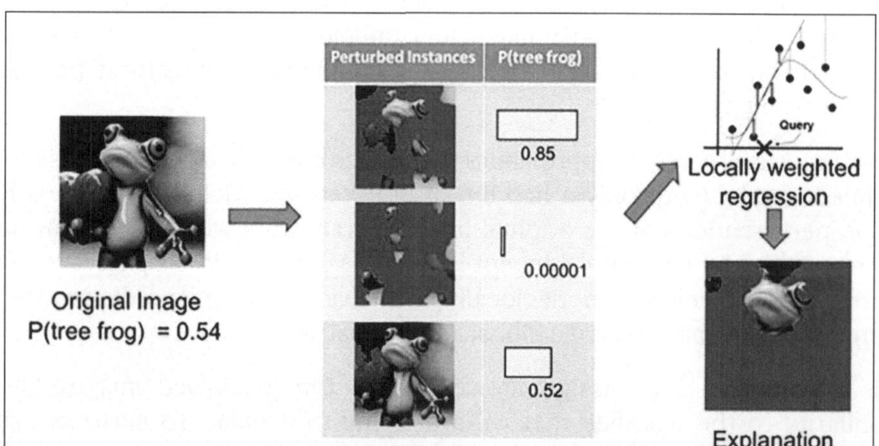

Figure 5.4: *Perturbed Image with Explanation (Source: Local Interpretable Model-Agnostic Explanations (LIME): An Introduction (2016) Ribeiro et al)*

We have a second example described in this section. In this case, illustrated in the following figure - the model has predicted the first image with the most visible portion of the head correctly as a tree frog. This is in sync with our understanding as we can clearly see most of the tree frog's head. The second image has a low predicted probability as a pool table, understandably given that the hands and eyes of the tree frog can be mistaken for billiard balls. The last image is classified as a heart with a lower probability, primarily as the balloon held by the tree frog indeed looks like a heart.

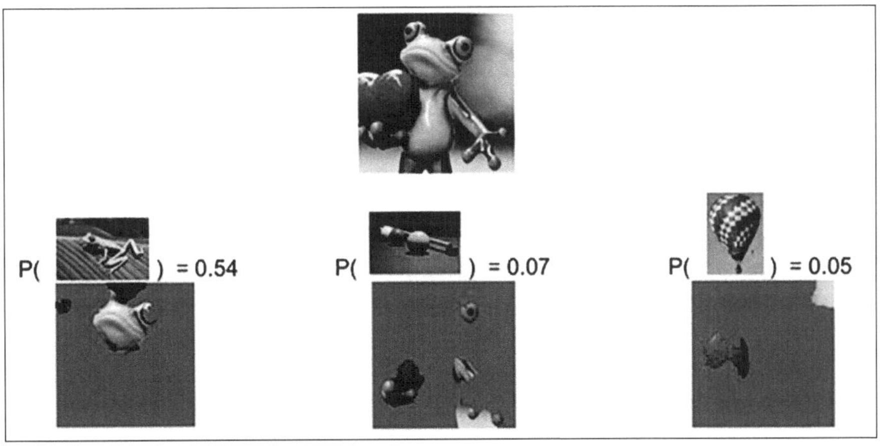

Figure 5.5: *Classifier Prediction with Explanations (Source: Local Interpretable Model-Agnostic Explanations (LIME): An Introduction (2016) Ribeiro et al)*

We demonstrate that both machine learning experts and lay users greatly benefit from explanations and are able to choose which models generalize better, improve models by changing them, and get crucial insights into the models' behavior.

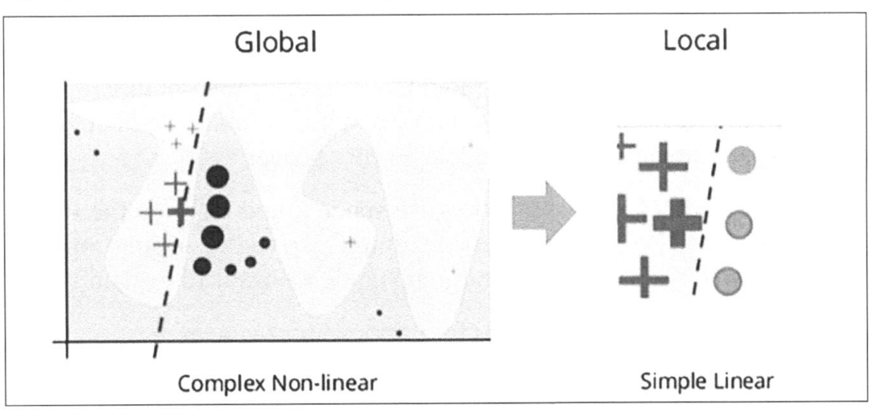

Figure 5.6: *Surrogate Models for Local Explanations (Source: "Why Should I Trust You?" Explaining the Predictions of Any Classifier (2016) Ribeiro et al)*

LIME provides a local explanation for a black-box model in the form of a model ∈ G with G as the class of potential (interpretable) models.

Model g should have two characteristics:

- Interpretable such that there is a relation between the input and the response, additionally this relation is understandable by some mechanism.
- **Locally Faithful / Fidelity:** Similar behavior as in the vicinity of the observation being predicted.

Essentially, we want to receive a model with minimal complexity and maximal local fidelity.

The optimization objective of LIME can be formulated as follows:

$$argmin_g \mathcal{L}(f, g, \pi_x) + \Omega(g)$$

***Figure** 5.7*: LIME *Optimization Objective*

In practice: LIME only optimizes L(f,g ,π_x) on model-fidelity. Users will decide the threshold on model complexity (g) beforehand.

To accomplish our goal of building a model-agnostic explainer, we should optimize L(f,g ,π_x) to learn an approximation for g. No assumptions are made about the function f.

The explanation generated by LIME for a specific prediction is an interpretable model which could be the coefficients of a linear regression. This interpretable model is trained with data points closer to our initial point of interest from the black box model hence, there is an underlying similarity maintained with the black box model.

Surrogate Models for Interpretability

The surrogate model is the interpretable representation in LIME which is essentially from the original feature space of the model. Since this interpretable representation or the surrogate model has to be easily understood by a human, the dimensions of this surrogate model are lower than the original feature space.

Let *p* be the dimension of the original feature space X and let *p'* be the dimension of the interpretable space X.' The interpretable inputs map to the original inputs through a mapping function h^y: X'→X, specific to the instance we want to explain *y*∈ X.

Different types of mappings are utilized for various input spaces:

- For text data, an interpretable representation could be a binary vector indicating the presence or absence of a word. However, the classifier might use more complex features like word embeddings. We can represent X' as the following; (X' = $\{0,1\}^{p'}$) where (p') is the number of words in the instance being explained. The mapping function converts a vector of 1's and 0's (indicating the presence or absence of a word) into the model's representations: if the model uses word counts, the mapping will convert 1 to the original word count and 0 to 0; if it uses word embeddings, the mapping should transform any sentence expressed as a vector of 1's and 0's into its embedded version.

- For images, an interpretable representation might be a binary vector indicating the presence or absence of a set of contiguous similar pixels (also known as superpixels). Formally, ($X' = \{0,1\}^{p'}$), where (p') is the number of superpixels considered, usually obtained through an image segmentation algorithm like quick shift. In this case, the mapping function maps 1 to leaving the superpixel as in the original image and 0 to graying out the superpixel (representing its absence).
- This gets more complex in tabular data as the interpretable representation is dependent on the type of data whether it is categorical, numerical, or mixed data. In categorical data, ($X'=\{0,1\}^p$), where (p) is the number of features used in the model (($p' = p$). The mapping function assigns 1 to the original class of the instance and 0 to a different class sampled according to the training data distribution. In numerical data, ($X' = X$) and the mapping function is the identity. However, numerical features can be discretized to be treated as categorical features. For mixed data, the interpretable representation is a (p)-dimensional space consisting of binary features for categorical data and numerical features for numerical data (if not discretized). Every component of the mapping function is defined according to the type of explanatory variable, as previously described.

Locality

Although a simple model may not be able to approximate the black box model globally, approximating it in the neighborhood of the individual instance we want to explain may be feasible. In other words, LIME relies on the assumption that every complex model is linear on a local scale.

Formally, we need a weight function w^y: $X \to \mathbb{R}^+$ that assigns the highest weight to instances $z \in X$ that are closest to the target instance $y \in X$, and the lowest weight to the instances that are furthest away.

LIME in GradientBoosting Model

In this example, we use the LIME method for the Gradient Boosting model on a tabular dataset. The lime package is used here.

1. Install the lime package.

```
!pip install lime
```

2. Load the diabetes dataset and train the data on a Gradient Boosting model.

```
# 1. Import necessary libraries
from sklearn.ensemble import GradientBoostingRegressor
from sklearn.datasets import load_diabetes
from sklearn.model_selection import train_test_split
from sklearn.metrics import mean_squared_error
from lime.lime_tabular import LimeTabularExplainer

# 2. Load the diabetes dataset
X, y = load_diabetes(return_X_y=True)

# 3. Split the dataset into training and testing sets
X_train, X_test, y_train, y_test = train_test_split(X, y, test_
size=0.2, random_state=42)

# 4. Train the XGBoostRegressor model
model = GradientBoostingRegressor(n_estimators=100, learning_
rate=1.0,
    max_depth=1, random_state=0).fit(X, y)
model.fit(X_train, y_train)

# 5. Predict on the test set and calculate MSE
y_pred = model.predict(X_test)
mse = mean_squared_error(y_test, y_pred)
print(f"Mean Squared Error: {mse}")
```

Output:

Mean Squared Error: 3699.612636872364

3. Instantiate the LIME explainer and plot the feature attribution.

```
# 6. Use LIME interpretation on a test datapoint
explainer = LimeTabularExplainer(X_train, mode="regression",
feature_names=load_diabetes().feature_names, class_names=
["target"], discretize_continuous=True)

i = 25
exp = explainer.explain_instance(X_test[i], model.predict, num_
features=5)

exp.show_in_notebook(show_table=True)
print("Actual Value is ", y_test[i])
```

The following figure illustrates the LIME output for the Gradient Boosting Model:

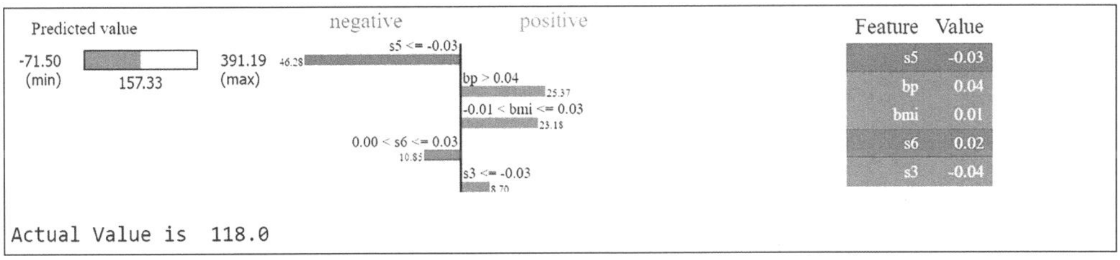

***Figure 5.8**: LIME Output for Gradient Boosting Model*

We find that the predicted value is positively influenced by the feature BP and also negatively influenced by s5 but given the actual value is lower than the predicted, the local feature influence was not sufficient.

LIME Explanations for Deep Learning

In this example, we use LIME to explain computer vision models.

1. Install the required packages.

```
!pip show tensorflow
!pip show keras
```

2. Load a hugging face dataset for classifying the leaf diseases and process the images.

```
# Step 1: Load the Dataset
from datasets import load_dataset
from tensorflow.keras.preprocessing.image import ImageDataGenerator
from tensorflow.keras.models import Sequential
from tensorflow.keras.layers import Conv2D, MaxPooling2D, Flatten,
Dense
from tensorflow.keras.optimizers import Adam
from skimage import img_as_float
from skimage.transform import resize
import numpy as np
from lime import lime_image
from lime.wrappers.scikit_image import SegmentationAlgorithm
import matplotlib.pyplot as plt


dataset = load_dataset("AI-Lab-Makerere/beans")

# Step 2: Preprocess the Data
def process_images(images):
    return np.array([resize(image, (128, 128)) for image in images])


def preprocess_images(images):
```

```
    # Convert images to numpy arrays and resize
    return np.array([resize(img_as_float(image), (128, 128)) for
image in images])

train_images = preprocess_images(dataset['train']['image'])
test_images = preprocess_images(dataset['test']['image'])
train_labels = np.array(dataset['train']['labels'])
test_labels = np.array(dataset['test']['labels'])
```

3. Train a CNN model on the training data.

```
# Step 3: Build the CNN Model
model = Sequential([
    Conv2D(32, (3, 3), activation='relu', input_shape=(128, 128,
3)),
    MaxPooling2D(2, 2),
    Conv2D(64, (3, 3), activation='relu'),
    MaxPooling2D(2, 2),
    Flatten(),
    Dense(128, activation='relu'),
    Dense(3, activation='softmax')
])

model.compile(optimizer=Adam(), loss='sparse_categorical_
crossentropy', metrics=['accuracy'])

# Step 4: Train the Model
model.fit(train_images, train_labels, epochs=10, validation_
split=0.2)
```

4. Evaluate the model and then run the LIME explainer on a sample image of a leaf. Class 0 indicates that it is diseased leaf and classified as class 0: angular leaf spot.

```
# Step 5: Test the Model
model.evaluate(test_images, test_labels)

# Load a new image, preprocess it, and make a prediction
new_image = preprocess_images([plt.imread('testleaf.jpeg')])
prediction = model.predict(new_image)
print("Prediction:", prediction)

classfound  = np.argmax(prediction, axis=-1)

print("Class:", classfound)
```

Output:

4/4 ———————————————— **0s** 37ms/step - accuracy: 0.7469 - loss: 0.8427

1/1 ———————————————— **0s** 37ms/step

Prediction: [[5.9212554e-01 4.0786180e-01 1.2739323e-05]]

Class: [0]

5. Display the highlighted portions of the image for the features impacting the classification.

```
from skimage.segmentation import mark_boundaries

# Step 6: Interpretability with LIME
explainer = lime_image.LimeImageExplainer()
segmenter = SegmentationAlgorithm('quickshift', kernel_size=1,
max_dist=200, ratio=0.2)
explanation = explainer.explain_instance(new_image[0], model.
predict, top_labels=5, hide_color=0, num_samples=1000, segmenta-
tion_fn=segmenter)

temp, mask = explanation.get_image_and_mask(explanation.top_la-
bels[0], positive_only=True, num_features=5, hide_rest=False)
plt.imshow(mark_boundaries(temp / 2 + 0.5, mask))
plt.show()
```

The following figure illustrates the image focus areas with LIME:

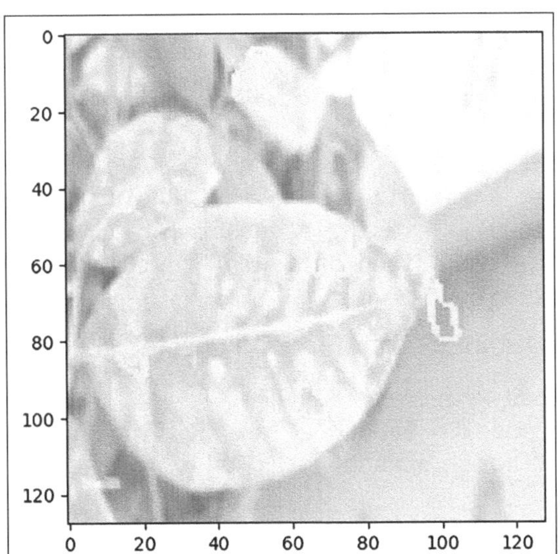

***Figure 5.9**: Image focus areas with LIME*

The preceding image explanation shows that it focuses on certain diseased portions of the image. But there are also some features from the background that could be incorrectly influencing the classification model.

Next, we will run LIME explanations for NLP. The following model is resource intensive hence, should be run on a machine with ample memory:

1. Install the required libraries.

```
pip install transformers torch datasets lime
pip install transformers[torch]
```

2. Download a hugging face dataset to run a sentiment analysis on the text instances.

```
from transformers import AutoTokenizer, AutoModelForSequence
Classification, Trainer, TrainingArguments
from datasets import load_dataset
from lime.lime_text import LimeTextExplainer
import torch

# Step 2: Load Dataset
dataset = load_dataset("emotion")

# Step 3: Preprocess Data
tokenizer = AutoTokenizer.from_pretrained("distilbert-base-
uncased")

def tokenize_function(examples):
    return tokenizer(examples["text"], padding="max_length",
truncation=True)

tokenized_datasets = dataset.map(tokenize_function, batched=True)

# Prepare dataset for training
train_dataset = tokenized_datasets["train"].shuffle(seed=42).se-
lect(range(1000))  # Using a subset for quick training
test_dataset = tokenized_datasets["test"].shuffle(seed=42).se-
lect(range(200))
```

3. Finetune the DistilBERT transformer model for NLP on the dataset.

```
# Step 4: Load Pre-trained Model
model = AutoModelForSequenceClassification.from_pretrained
("distilbert-base-uncased", num_labels=6)

# Step 5: Fine-tune Model
training_args = TrainingArguments(output_dir="test_trainer",
evaluation_strategy="epoch", num_train_epochs=1)
```

```
trainer = Trainer(model=model, args=training_args, train_data-
set=train_dataset, eval_dataset=test_dataset)
trainer.train()
```

The following figure illustrates the training run of the transformer model:

```
{'eval_loss': 0.9988493323326111, 'eval_runtime': 222.5652, 'eval_samples_per_second': 0.899, 'eval_steps_per_second': 0.112, 'epoch': 1.0}
{'train_runtime': 4209.8713, 'train_samples_per_second': 0.238, 'train_steps_per_second': 0.03, 'train_loss': 1.44066455078125, 'epoch': 1.0}
```

Figure 5.10: *Training Run of Transformer Model*

4. Instantiate the LIME explainer on the trained model.

```
# Step 6: Generate LIME Explanations
explainer = LimeTextExplainer(class_names=["sadness", "joy",
"love", "anger", "fear", "surprise"])

def predictor(texts):
inputs = tokenizer(texts, return_tensors="pt", padding=True,
truncation=True, max_length=512)
outputs = model(**inputs)
predictions = torch.softmax(outputs.logits, dim=1).detach().
numpy()
return predictions

# Example text for explanation
text = dataset["test"]["text"][0]

exp = explainer.explain_instance(text, predictor, num_features=6)
exp.show_in_notebook(text=True)
```

The following figure illustrates the explanations for the NLP model with LIME:

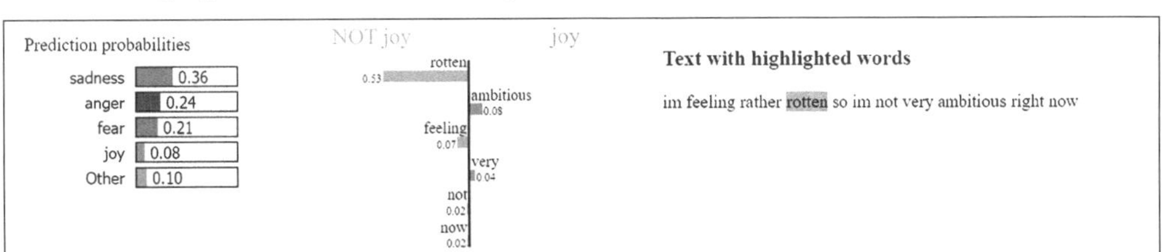

Figure 5.11: *Explanations for the NLP Model with LIME*

Challenges of the LIME Algorithm

One limitation of LIME is its instability. A new explanatory model is generated for each prediction. If there is a small change in the data, this can result in different interpretations leading to inconsistencies in the model explanations which seemingly make it seem unstable.

High dimensionality is another challenge in LIME. In low dimensional spaces, local linear models are effective in LIME or for instances near the decision boundary. But this assumption starts to unravel as dimensionality increases. The model explanation could be overtly simplified or misrepresented when trying to represent the complexity of the higher dimensionality of the original model. This can cause lesser accuracy or meaningful interpretations.

LIME, or Local Interpretable Model-Agnostic Explanations, is adept at providing explanations for individual predictions due to its local perspective. However, this focus on individual instances can also be a drawback, as it may miss broader patterns or structures within the model. While LIME is excellent at explaining specific predictions, it may struggle to offer a comprehensive understanding of the model as a whole. In its pursuit to provide localized interpretability, LIME tends to lose out on the global view.

This creates a tradeoff between model fidelity and its complexity for LIME. The field of explainable AI is constantly evolving, and so are the methods and techniques it uses. Although the current version of LIME has its limitations, its potential and value in enhancing interpretability in machine learning are undeniable.

Despite its constraints, LIME remains a powerful tool for model interpretation. Its ability to extract explanations from complex models is unmatched. However, practitioners must be aware of its limitations and use it wisely.

SHapley Additive exPlanations (SHAP)

SHAP in Interpretability is a concept from cooperative game theory. Shapley values were introduced in the year 1951 by Lloyd Shapley, who won the Nobel Memorial Prize in Economic Sciences in 2012. The underlying concept of SHAP is primarily the computation of Shapley values in coalitional game theory.

Shapley Values in Game Theory

Game theory is a study of strategic games between players where a game is a series of interactions between the agents with gains and losses of quantifiable utility value.

1. In a Cooperative game, consider all possible players $P = \{1, \ldots, p\}$ where each subset of the players $S \subseteq P$ forms a coalition, and each coalition S wins a specific payout.
2. A value function $v : 2^{|P|} \rightarrow R$ maps all $2^{|P|}$ possible coalitions to their payout (or gain).

3. Consider v(S) as the payout of coalition S ⊆ P (a payout of an empty coalition must be zero: v(∅) = 0 where ∅ is an empty coalition).

Some players contribute more than others hence, we want to fairly divide the total achievable payout v(P) among the players depending on a specific player's individual contribution.

We call the individual payouts per player as φj , j ∈ P (the Shapley value).

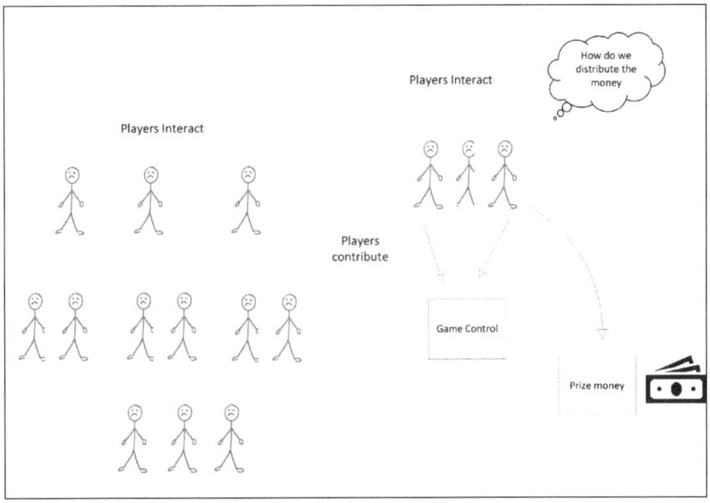

Figure 5.12: *Cooperative Game Illustration*

Let us look at what can be considered the fair payouts for the players.

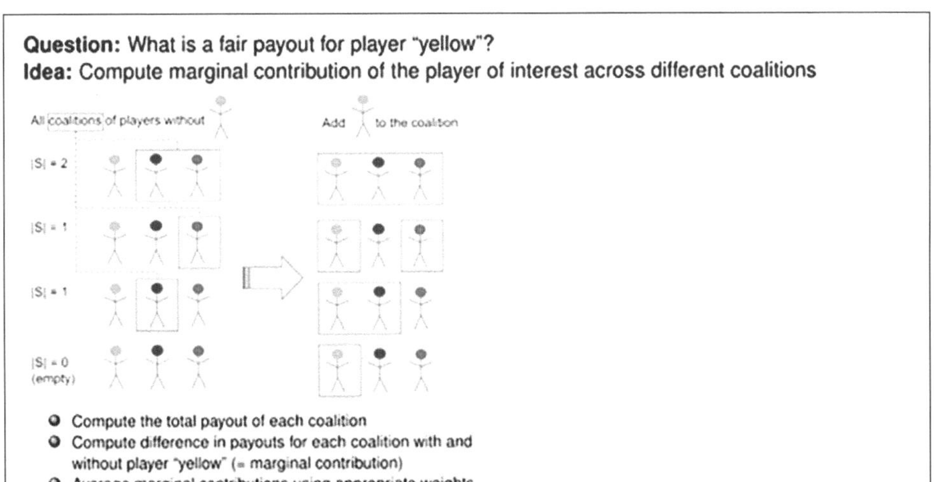

Figure 5.13: *Cooperative Game Illustration for Payouts*

This refers to the Shapley value which assigns a payout value to each player. The payout value is based on their marginal contributions done across all coalitions.

1. Let v(S ∪ {j}) – v(S) be the marginal contribution of player j to coalition S which measures how much player j increases the value of a coalition S.
2. Average marginal contributions for all possible coalitions S ⊆ P \ {j} where the order of how players join the coalition matters and also has different weights depending on the size of S.

Shapley value formulation is as follows:

$$\phi_j = \sum_{S \subseteq P \setminus \{j\}} \frac{|S|!(|P| - |S| - 1)!}{|P|!}(v(S \cup \{j\}) - v(S))$$

From Game Theory to Machine Learning

Shapley values are used to capture the relative impact of each feature on the prediction to compare it with the average effect of the input for the machine learning model.

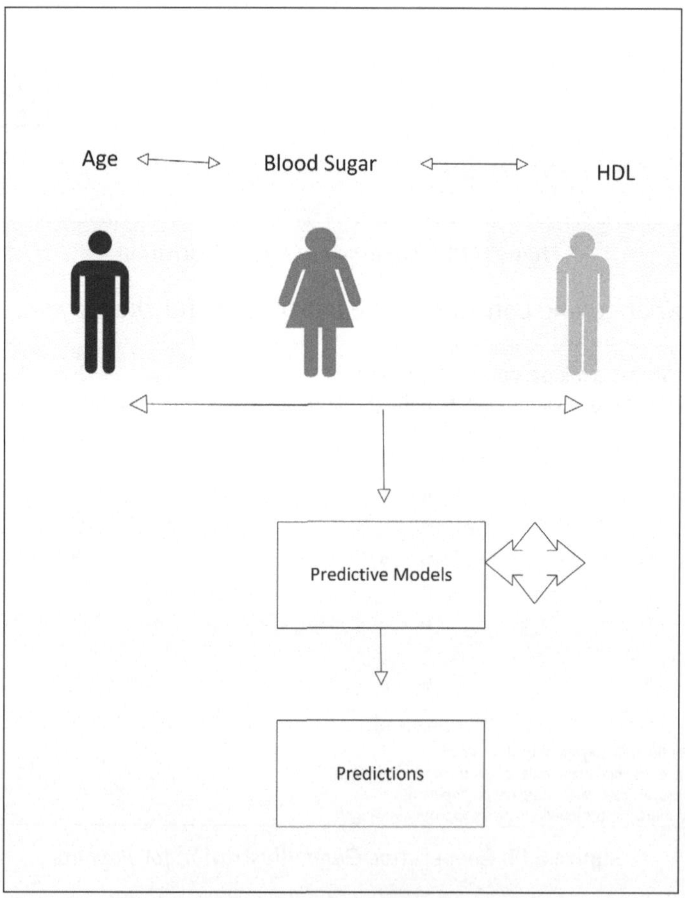

Figure 5.14: *Prediction Model with Features*

Shapley Values

How much does a feature j contribute to the prediction of a single observation? Shapley values from cooperative game theory are used to determine the feature contribution.

1. This is done by comparing the "reduced prediction function" of feature coalition S with S ∪ {j}
2. Next, we iterate over all possible coalitions to calculate the marginal contribution of feature j to the sample.

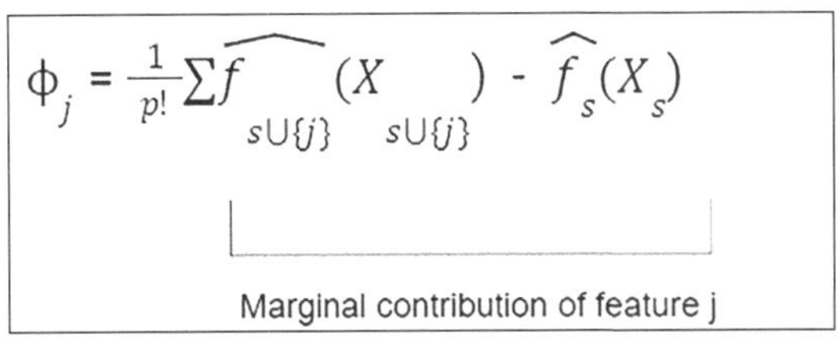

Figure 5.15: *Shapley Values*

f ̂is the prediction function, and p denotes the number of features. Non-existent features in a coalition are replaced by values of random feature values. And S_j defines the coalition as the set of players before player j.

Shapley to SHAP

Our aim is to find an additive combination that explains the prediction of an observation x. An estimation procedure is used to find the explanation which computes the contribution of each feature to the prediction.

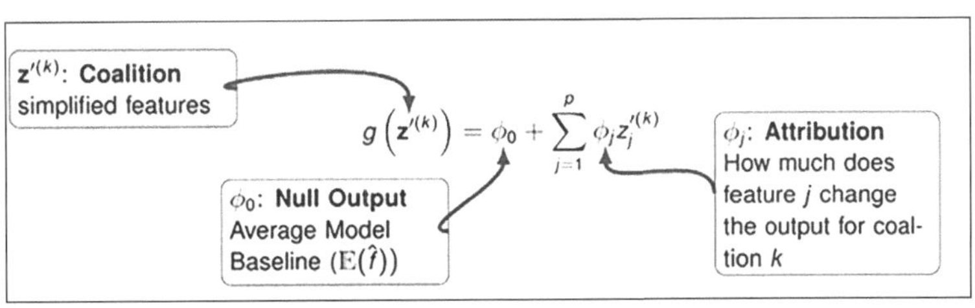

Figure 5.16: *SHAP Equation*

The feature change attribution is the shapley value in our calculation shown as follows:

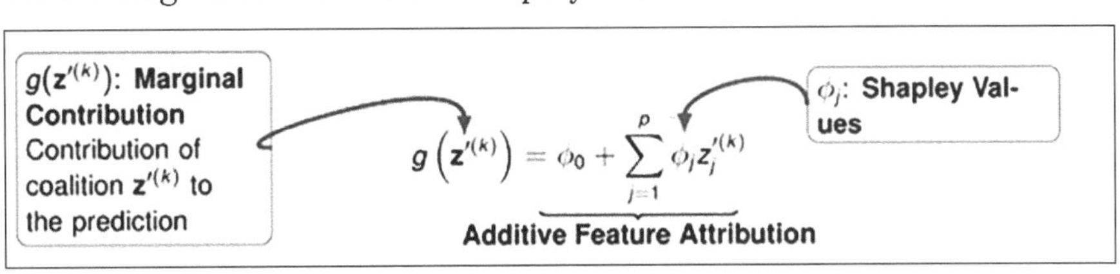

Figure 5.17: *Shapley Value Calculation*

SHAP Analysis Explained

Consider a model to identify loan default scores. The model has an expected base rate of 18%. While the predicted rate for a specific instance is 22%. The shapley values for each feature can explain the gap between the expected rate and the prediction.

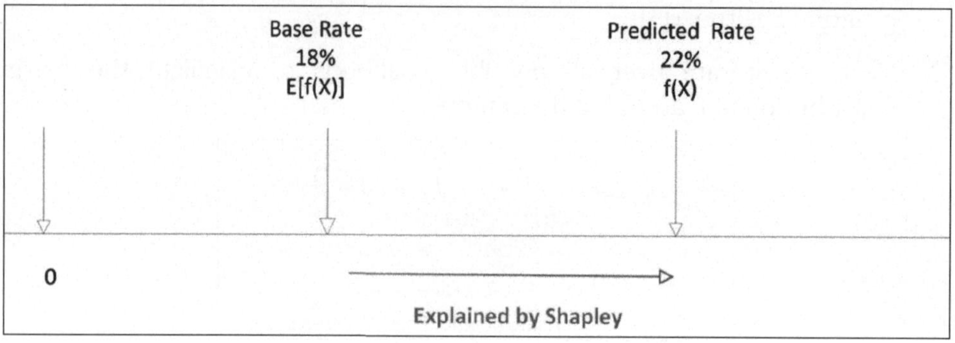

Figure 5.18: *Shapley Explanations for Model*

The shapley values are determined from the marginal contribution of each feature across the multiple coalitions possible. This gives the feature marginal contribution to the model's prediction.

SHAP in Linear Models

In this section we will use SHAP to add interpretability in a Linear Model.

1. Install the **shap** package.

   ```
   !pip install shap
   ```

2. Build a Linear model and create a SHAP explainer.

   ```
   # 1. Import necessary libraries
   import pandas as pd
   import numpy as np
   from sklearn import linear_model
   from sklearn.datasets import load_diabetes
   from sklearn.model_selection import train_test_split
   from sklearn.metrics import mean_squared_error
   import shap

   # 2. Load the diabetes dataset
   diabetes = load_diabetes()

   df = pd.DataFrame(data = np.c_[diabetes['data'],diabetes
   ['target']],columns = diabetes.feature_names+['target'])
   X, y = df.drop('target',axis=1),df['target']
   ```

```
feature_names = diabetes.feature_names

# 3. Split the dataset into training and testing sets
X_train, X_test, y_train, y_test = train_test_split(X, y, test_
size=0.2, random_state=42)

X100 = shap.utils.sample(X, 100)  # 100 instances for use as the
background distribution

# a simple linear model
model = linear_model.LinearRegression()
model.fit(X, y)
```

3. Instantiate the SHAP explainer and display the summary plot. The summary plot gives an understanding of the feature impact on shap values. The color coding adds further granularity in understanding the impact of a high feature value versus a low value on shap.

```
# Create a SHAP explainer and calculate SHAP values
explainer = shap.Explainer(model, X)
shap_values = explainer(X)

# Summary plot
shap.summary_plot(shap_values, X)
```

Here is the plot of SHAP values for Linear Model prediction:

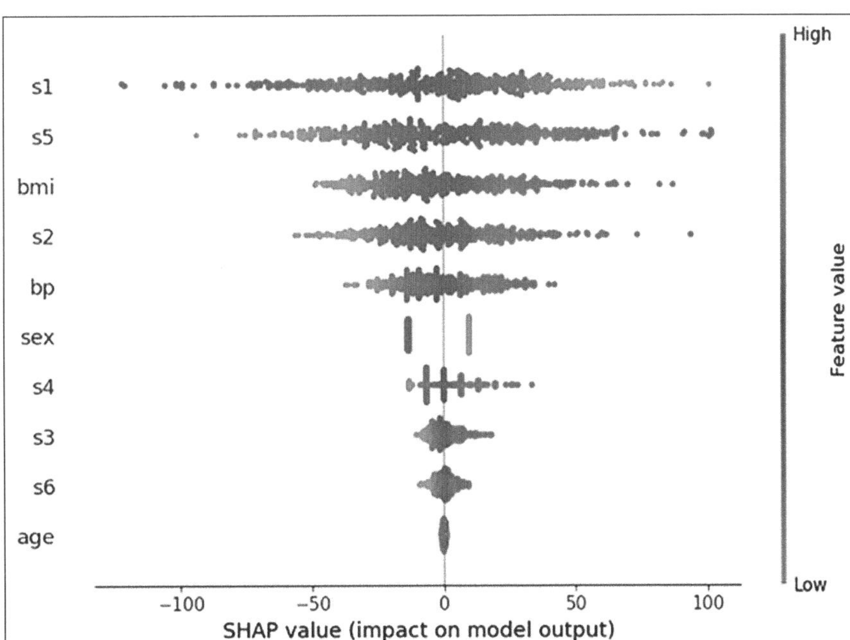

***Figure 5.19**: Plot of SHAP Values for Linear Model Prediction*

5. The bar plot provides a global summary of the average effect of each feature on the shap values.

```
# Bar plot
shap.plots.bar(shap_values)
```

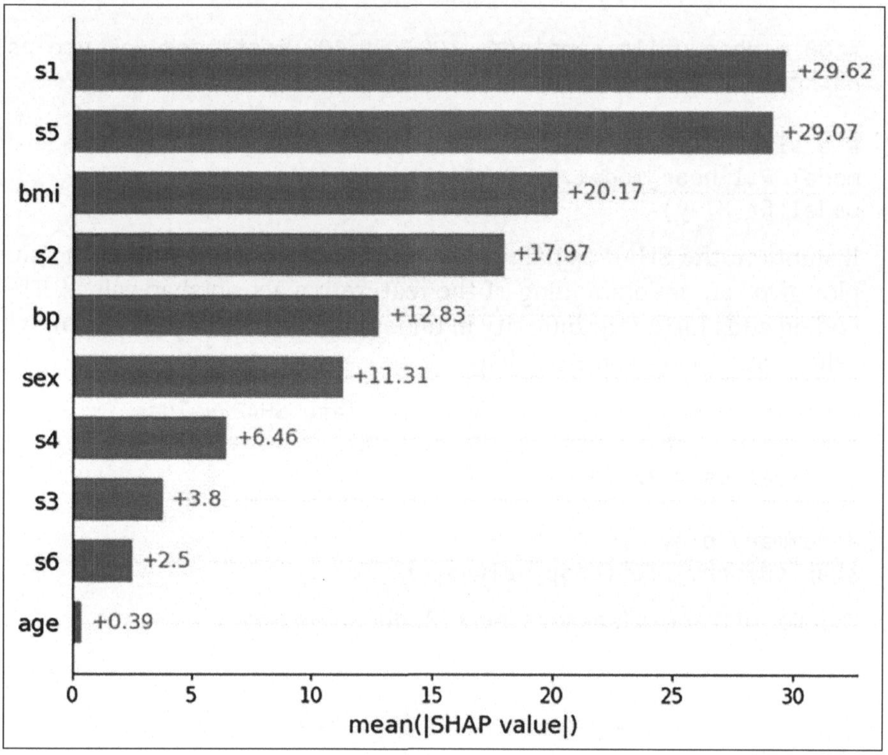

Figure 5.20: SHAP Global Summary

6. The waterfall plot provides the marginal feature effect from the average prediction on the shap values.

```
# Waterfall plot for the first prediction
shap.plots.waterfall(shap_values[0])
```

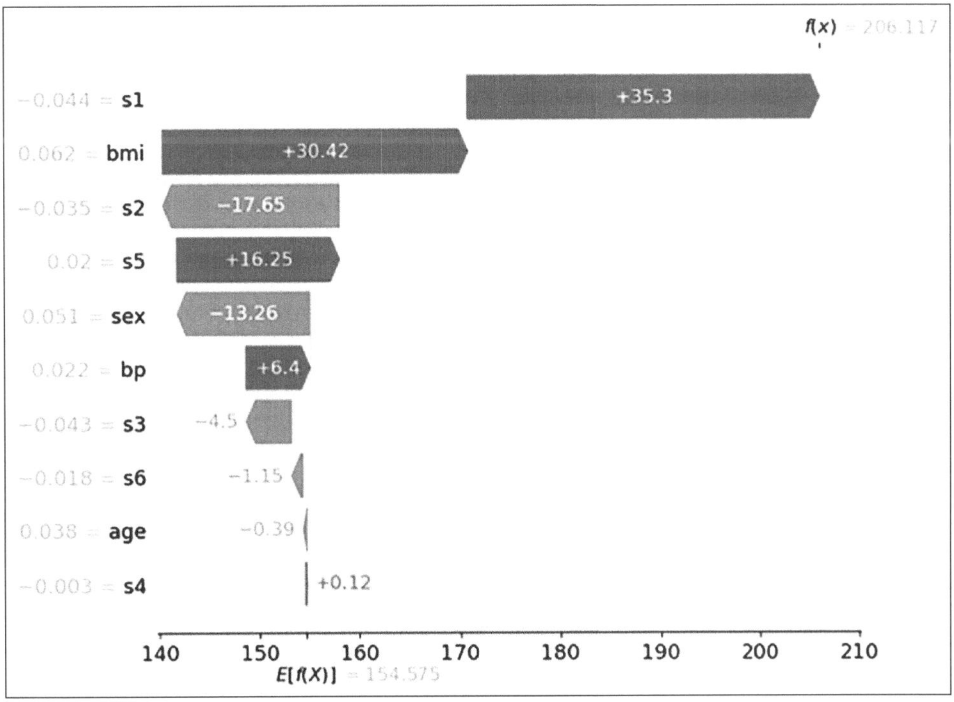

Figure 5.21: *SHAP Marginal Feature Effects*

7. The force plot provides the local explanation for a specific instance and it shows the marginal effect of each feature on the shap values.

```
# Force plot for the first prediction
shap.force_plot(explainer.expected_value, shap_values.val-
ues[0,:], X.iloc[0,:])
```

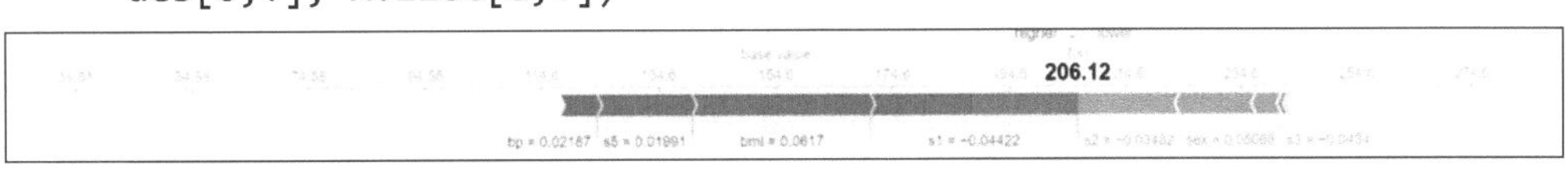

Figure 5.22: *Force Plot for a Prediction*

8. The violin plot is a new addition that provides a similar view as the summary plot but is clearer to understand the impact of high-valued features on the shap values.

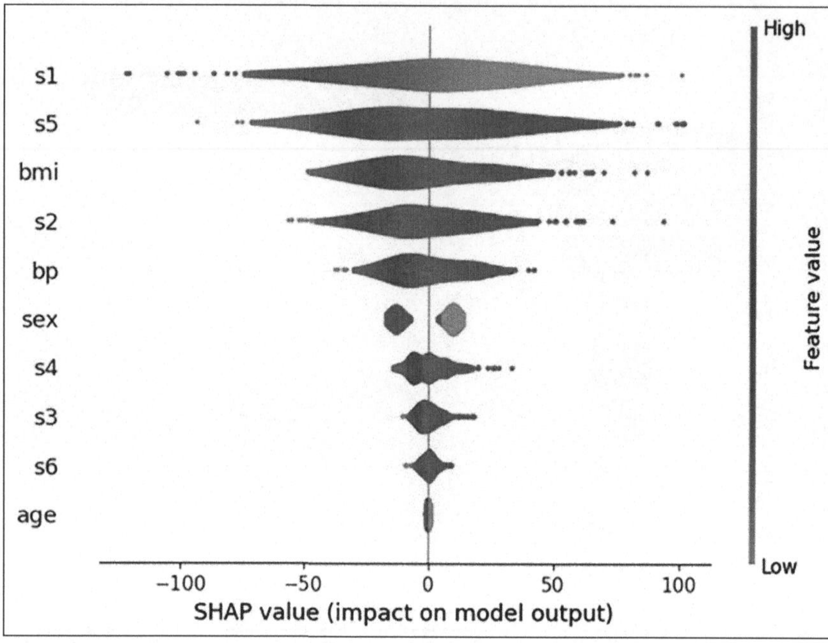

Figure 5.23: *Violin Plot on SHAP Values*

9. Similar to the violin plot, the heatmap is a new addition and summarizes a lot of detail in one visual.

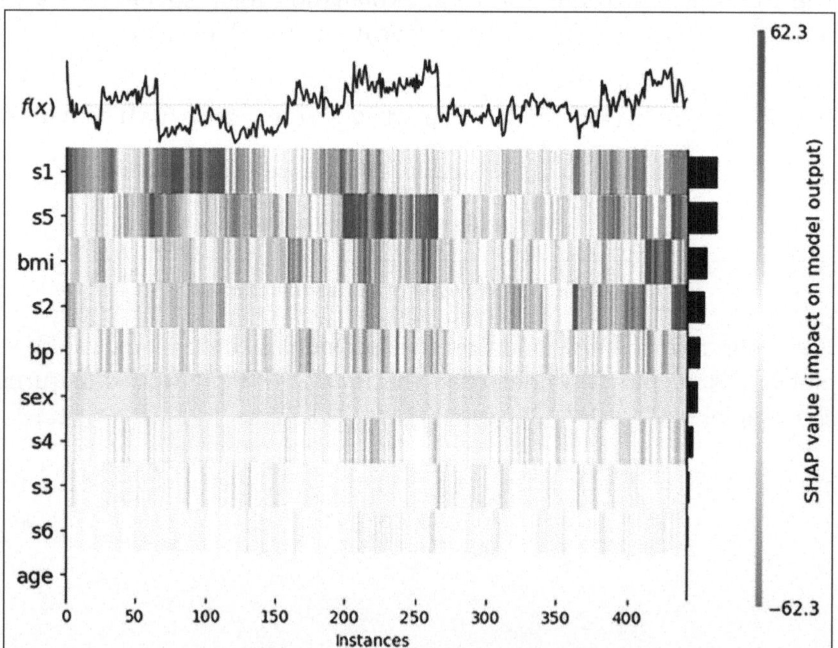

Figure 5.24: *Heatmap Summary*

SHAP Explainer for XGBoost

In this example, we use SHAP to explain an XG boost on a tabular dataset.

1. Install all the required packages.

```
!pip install xgboost
```

2. Load a dataset and train the data on a XGBoostRegressor model.

```
import xgboost
import shap

# train an XGBoost model
X, y = shap.datasets.california()
model = xgboost.XGBRegressor().fit(X, y)
```

3. Instantiate the shap explainer and plot various views.

```
# explain the model's predictions using SHAP
# (same syntax works for LightGBM, CatBoost, scikit-learn, trans-
formers, Spark, etc.)
explainer = shap.Explainer(model)
shap_values = explainer(X)
# visualize the first prediction's explanation
shap.plots.waterfall(shap_values[0])
```

The following figure illustrates the waterfall plot summary:

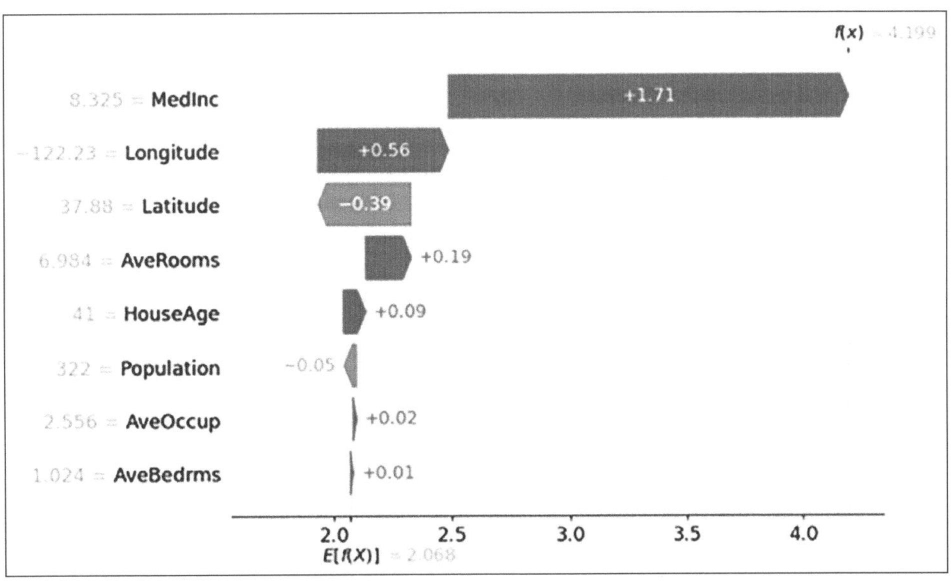

***Figure 5.25**: Waterfall Plot Summary*

4. The **initjs** is required for the interactive view in the force plot which shows the impact of a specific data point.

```
shap.initjs()
# visualize the first prediction's explanation with a force plot
shap.plots.force(shap_values[0])
```

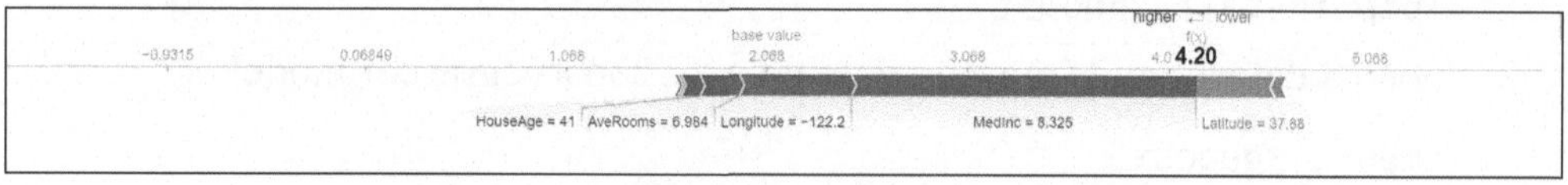

Figure 5.26: *Force Plot*

Limitations of SHAP

SHAP does not scale well in the higher dimensions due to the exponential complexity in calculating the Shapley values. The higher dimensionality deficiency is handled in the specialized SHAP methods, KernelSHAP and TreeSHAP.

KernelSHAP

KernelShap, is related to LIME and extends on it. When the LIME equation parameters are modified, this can be used to retrieve Shapley values. The LIME framework is essentially utilized by Kernel SHAP to compute Shapley Values. Setting the loss function, weighting kernel, and regularization terms appropriately in the LIME framework allows theoretically obtaining Shapley Values more efficiently than directly computing Shapley Values.

It is a perturbation-based Shapley approach that is model agnostic. Kernel SHAP works by calculating the contributions of each feature value to the prediction for an instance "x." Kernel SHAP has five main steps: evaluate the coalitions, run predictions for each coalition, calculate the weight for each using kernel SHAP and then use the shap values to create a weighted linear model, and finally return the Shapley values "k," the linear model's coefficients.

Additionally, setting a loss function, weighting the kernel, and using regularization terms appropriately in the LIME framework is more efficient in obtaining the Shapley Values as against directly computing the Shapley Values.

The KernelShap method involves a number of steps:

1. In the first step, a set of binary masked instances is generated from a randomly selected combination of features.
2. In each instance, the output of the black box model is computed.
3. In the next stage, a weighted linear regression model is fitted on the generated

dataset from step 1. The weights for the linear model are computed based on the similarity between the generated instances and the instance of interest.

4. Finally, the coefficients of the linear regression model are an indication of the approximate Shapley values.

$$\pi_x(z') = \frac{(M-1)}{\binom{M}{|z'|}|z'|(M-|z'|)}$$

***Figure* 5.27**: *KernalShap Calculation*

In the aforementioned KernelShap calculation, M represents the maximum coalition size while |z'| is the number of features also present in the instance z.'

Advantages and Limitations

Advantages of KernelShap include:

- It can be applied to any black-box model, regardless of its model design or the underlying training algorithm.
- A combined measure of feature importance is produced from KernelShap which is consistent across different models.
- Finally, the interactions between the features are considered.

Limitations of KernelShap include:

- The Computational cost can be higher especially for higher dimensional data or complex models.
- A large number of samples are required to get better accuracy in the estimates of the Shapley values.

TreeSHAP

TreeSHAP is a fast explainer used for analyzing decision tree models in the Shap python library. TreeSHAP is designed for tree-based machine learning models such as decision trees, random forests, and gradient boosted trees. TreeSHAP is offered as a rapid, model-specific alternative to KernelSHAP although it can sometimes produce feature attributions that are not intuitive.

The popularity of XGBoost as the de facto model in a lot of scenarios means that TreeSHAP as an explainer approach is also heavily used. The tree explainer makes use of the structure of the tree algorithm to extract and generate SHAP values much faster than the Kernel explainer.

TreeExplainer forgoes the model-agnosticism of LIME and KernelExplainer in lieu of improving the computation speed. TreeExplainer is a good substitute for algorithms like SP-LIME. SP-LIME is a method for selecting predictions that represent a global view to users while being distinct for explaining the best subsets in a dataset. TreeExplainer is in fact, faster in computing Shapley values for entire datasets thus allowing global feature importance calculation. The magnitude of each Shapley value can be averaged for any feature over the entire dataset. Alternatively, the relationship between the feature's Shapley value and the original value can be plotted. The one caveat in TreeExplainer is that it often requires transforming a model's output non-linearly; such as converting a log-odds output to probability while assuming that features are independent.

TreeShap is a specialized explanation method for tree-based models like decision trees, random forests, and gradient boosting machines. Similarly to KernelShap, it relies on Shapley values but leverages the structure of tree-based models for efficient computation.

In TreeShap, the exact Shapley value for each feature is calculated using recursion. This is done through recursive traversal of the decision tree while assigning the contributions of each feature during the traversal. Additionally, dynamic programming is used to handle redundancy in the calculations and reduce the computational complexity.

The following steps are followed in TreeShap:

1. In the first step, the tree is traversed. The decision path is noted for the instance of interest while traversing from the root to the leaf nodes.
2. Each feature's contributions are assigned during the traversal, considering the number of possible feature combinations and their probabilities.
3. Repeat for all trees in the ensemble where applicable.
4. Finally, average the contributions across all trees to obtain the Shapley values.

TreeSHAP Explainer for LightGBM

The following code is a model for Census income classification using LightGBM. The notebook uses LightGBM to predict the probability of an individual making over $50K a year in annual income. It uses the standard UCI Adult income dataset.

1. Install required packages.

   ```
   pip install lightgbm
   ```

2. Train a LightGBM model on a `shap` dataset.

   ```
   from sklearn.model_selection import train_test_split
   import lightgbm as lgb
   import shap
   ```

```
# print the JS visualization code to the notebook
shap.initjs()
```

3. Instantiate a TreeExplainer and run on the model to explain values.

```
X,y = shap.datasets.adult()
X_display,y_display = shap.datasets.adult(display=True)

# create a train/test split
X_train, X_test, y_train, y_test = train_test_split(X, y, test_
size=0.2, random_state=7)
d_train = lgb.Dataset(X_train, label=y_train)
d_test = lgb.Dataset(X_test, label=y_test)

params = {
    "max_bin": 512,
    "learning_rate": 0.05,
    "boosting_type": "gbdt",
    "objective": "binary",
    "metric": "binary_logloss",
    "num_leaves": 10,
    "verbose": -1,
    "min_data": 100,
    "boost_from_average": True
}

model = lgb.train(params, d_train, 10000, valid_sets=[d_test],
callbacks=[lgb.callback.early_stopping(50),lgb.log_evalua-
tion(1000)])

explainer = shap.TreeExplainer(model)
shap_values = explainer.shap_values(X)

shap.force_plot(explainer.expected_value, shap_values[0,:], X_
display.iloc[0,:],  matplotlib=True)
```

The following figure illustrates the force plot explainer for an instance:

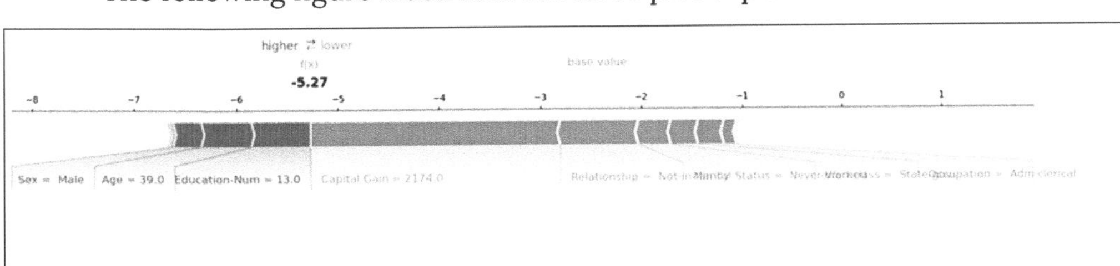

Figure 5.28: *Force Plot Explainer for an Instance*

4. This is a force plot, similar to the one aforementioned but instead of a single instance, the plot captures the feature effect across multiple instances. It is also interactive and can be applied to multiple features or factors.

```
shap.force_plot(explainer.expected_value, shap_values[:1000,:],
X_display.iloc[:1000,:])
```

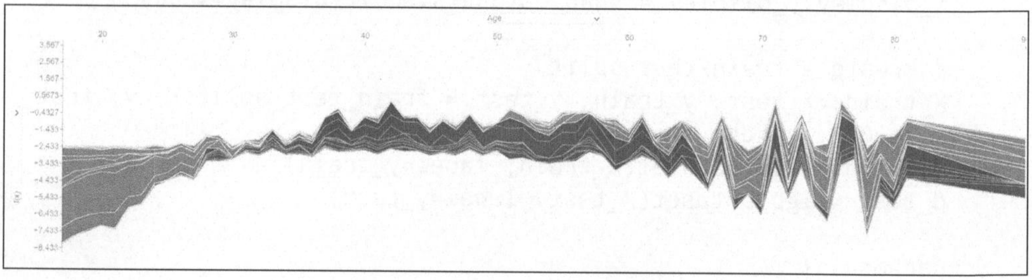

Figure 5.29: *Force Plot Summary*

5. Similarly, we can see the summary plot to see the effect of each feature. As can be seen in the figure, a high capital gain has mostly a positive impact on the shapley value.

```
shap.summary_plot(shap_values, X)
```

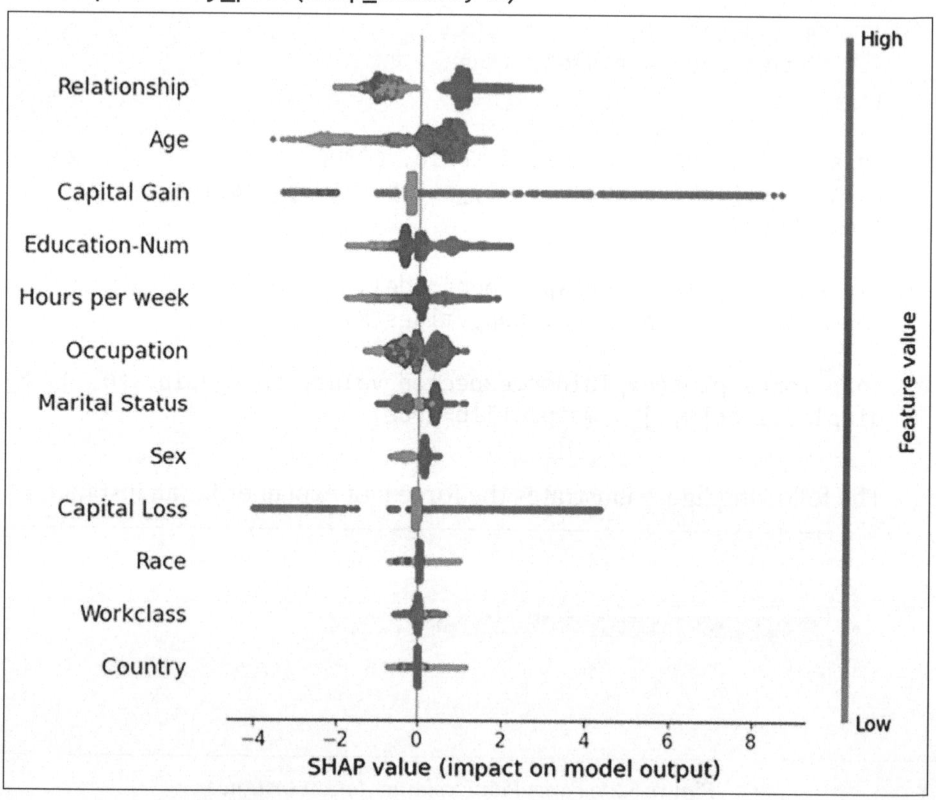

Figure 5.30: *Summary Plot for Feature Effect*

6. Lastly, we look at SHAP dependence plots. Here we can see the impact of a feature over the entire dataset. The preceding plot shows the feature's actual value as against the SHAP value of that feature. The biggest difference between the SHAP dependence plots and the partial dependence plots is that they account for the interaction effects in the features of the input space. In a feature, the vertical dispersion of the SHAP value is a result of the interaction effects. Multiple colors are chosen to highlight the different interactions.

```
for name in X_train.columns:
    shap.dependence_plot(name, shap_values, X, display_
features=X_display)
```

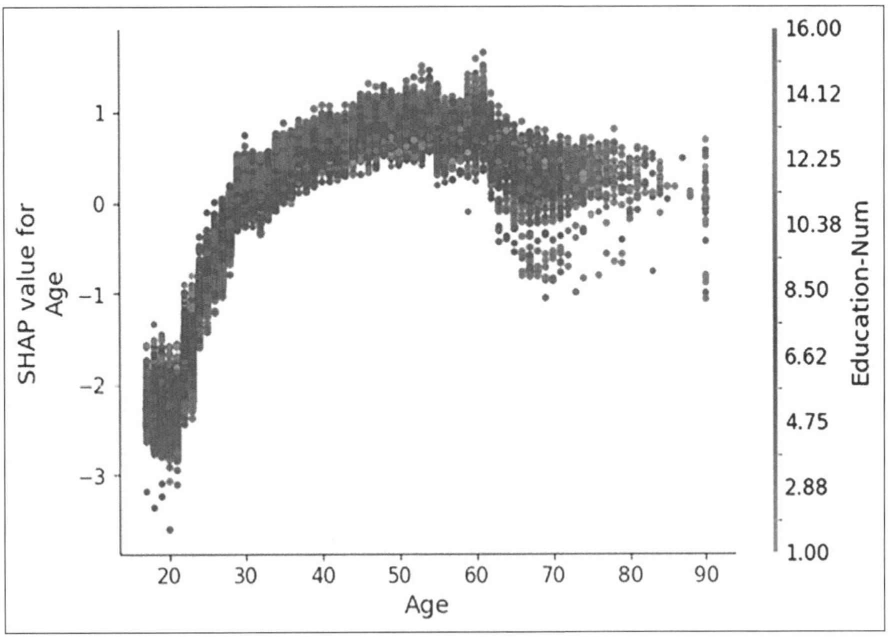

***Figure* 5.31**: *SHAP Dependence Plot for Feature Age*

The preceding code plots the dependence plot for each feature. The following plot is for the Workclass feature:

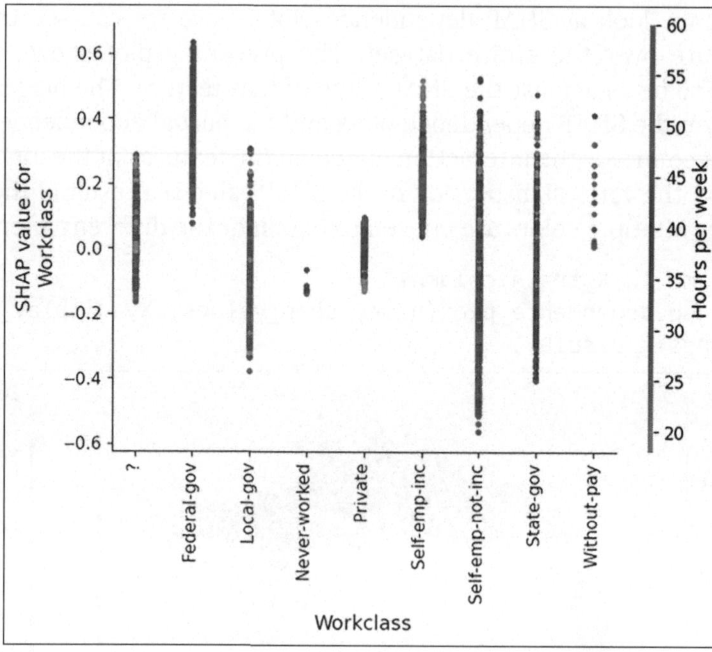

Figure 5.32: *Dependence Plot for Feature Workclass*

The following plot is for the Education-Num feature which is the numeric equivalent for the level of education:

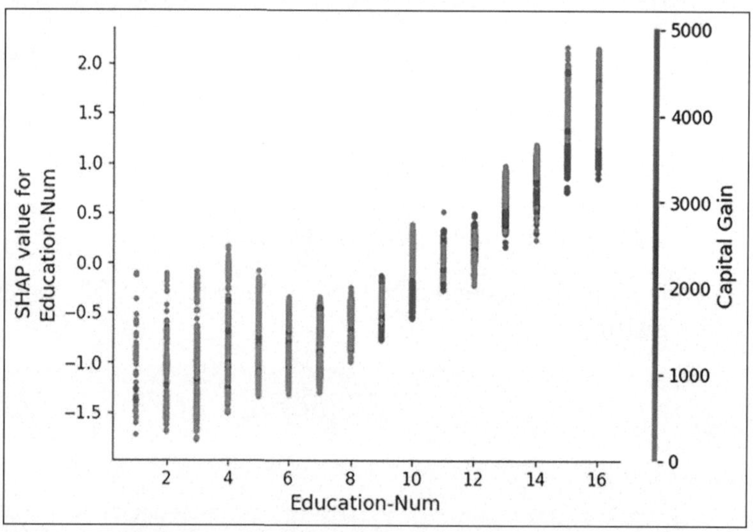

Figure 5.33: *Dependence Plot for Feature Education*

There are similar dependence plots across the feature combinations each providing the interaction effects of the features.

We can also Train a model with only two leaves per tree hence, no interaction terms between features. This can be achieved by setting the num_leaves to 2 in the parameters.

Advantages and Limitations

Advantages:

- In TreeShap, we can compute the exact Shapley values without any sampling or approximations.
- The dynamic programming approach makes it computationally efficient.
- Particularly designed for tree-based models which are popular and commonly used.

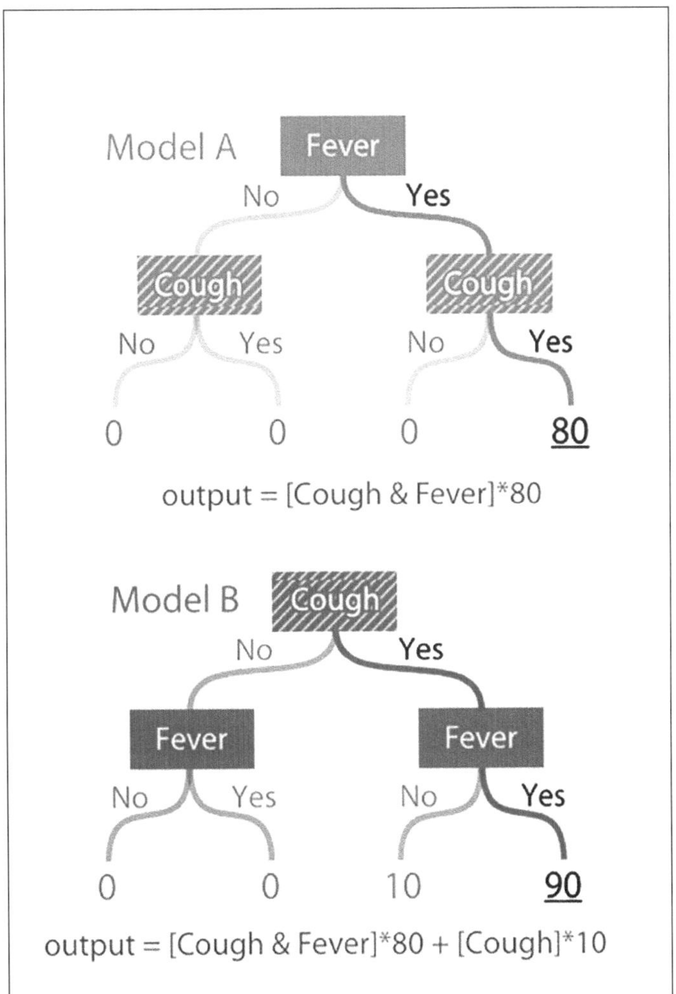

Figure 5.34: *TreeShap Illustration*

Limitations:

TreeSHAP calculates in polynomial time, not exponential time. The basic idea is to move all possible subsets down the tree at the same time. To calculate the single-tree forecast, you need to track the number of subsets in each decision node. This depends on the subset of parent nodes and the split function.

As implied in its name, TreeShap is restricted to tree-based models. It cannot be used in other types of models like support vector machines, linear regression, or neural networks. To address this gap, there are model specific techniques like LinearSHAP and DeepSHAP which add efficiency to the techniques.

Conclusion

LIME and SHAP are powerful as model agnostic explainer methods. Although the model specific methods like the TreeShap tend to be more efficient hence, more popular. Also, a feature dependency causes an incorrect representation of the feature impact.

LIME is a perturbation-based technique with local surrogate models for local explainability. While SHAP is an additive feature attribution approach, it does not allow "what if" analysis. So, if we change a feature value to a different value, how does it impact the outcome? We will look at these techniques for anchors and "what if" analysis through counterfactuals in the next chapter.

References

1. "Why Should I Trust You?" Explaining the Predictions of Any Classifier (2016) Ribeiro et al https://arxiv.org/pdf/1602.04938
2. Local Interpretable Model-Agnostic Explanations (LIME): An Introduction (2016) Ribeiro et al https://www.oreilly.com/content/introduction-to-local-interpretable-model-agnostic-explanations-lime/
3. A Unified Approach to Interpreting Model Predictions (2017) Lundberg et al https://arxiv.org/abs/1705.07874
4. Consistent Individualized Feature Attribution for Tree Ensembles (2019) Lundberg et al https://arxiv.org/pdf/1802.03888
5. Are There Any Limitations to Using LIME https://deepchecks.com/question/are-there-any-limitations-to-using-lime/

Chapter 6
Anchors and Counterfactuals

Introduction

This chapter continues the Model Agnostic explainability methods. Anchors and Counterfactual Explanations are an extension of the LIME and SHAP techniques discussed in the previous chapter. While Anchors provide rules to quantify a local explanation, Counterfactual explanations add additional detail on the changes required in a local instance to get to an alternate outcome.

Structure

In this chapter, we will cover the following topics:

- Anchors
- Counterfactuals

Anchors

Anchors is another interpretation technique for classification models. It was developed by Marco Tulio Ribeiro who is also the creator of LIME. Similar to LIME, Anchor uses a perturbation-based approach to generate local explanations. It can elucidate the individual predictions of any "black box" model, making it "Local," "Post hoc," and "Model agnostic." Compared to other interpretability methods such as LIME or SHAP, Anchor's explanations are more intuitive for humans, providing prediction rules that clarify how the model arrived at its results.

An anchor explanation is a rule that firmly grounds the prediction locally, meaning that changes to other feature values do not affect the prediction. Essentially, for instances where the anchor holds, the prediction remains largely consistent.

The anchor method can explain any black-box classifier with two or more classes, as long as the classifier has a function that accepts raw text or a numpy array and outputs an integer prediction.

Anchors vs LIME

We compare the two methods and their interpretability variances as follows:

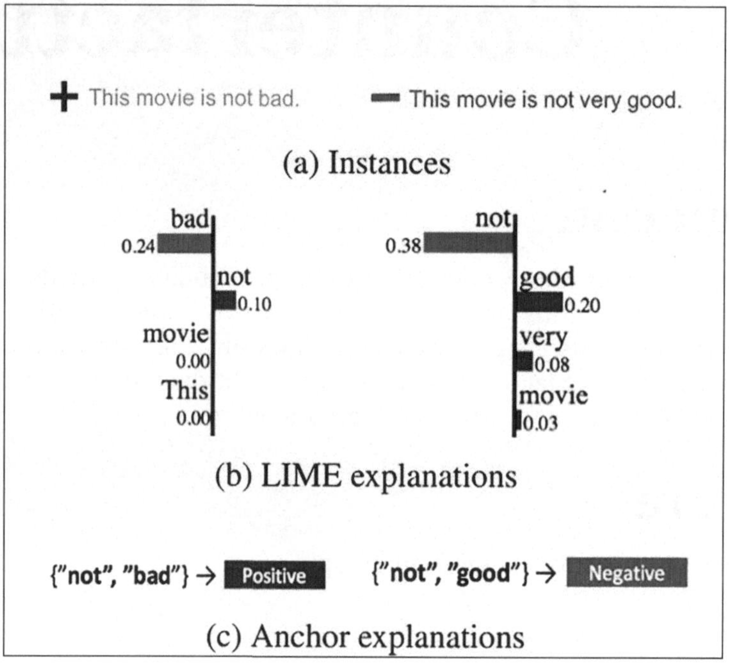

Figure 6.1: *Anchors in Comparison to LIME*
(Source: Anchors: High-Precision Model-Agnostic Explanations (2018) Ribeiro et al)

LIME provides explanations for two sentiment predictions made by an LSTM in *Figure* 6.1. Although both explanations are locally accurate, applying the explanation from the left to the sentence on the right might misleadingly suggest that the word "not" has a positive influence, which it does not. While these explanations offer insights into the model, their coverage is unclear, such as when "not" positively influences sentiment. This leads us to the novel model-agnostic explanations based on if-then rules, called anchors. An anchor explanation is a rule that basically "anchors" the prediction locally, meaning changes to other feature values do not affect the prediction. For instances where the anchor holds, the prediction remains almost always the same. For example, the anchors in *Figure 6.1(c)* indicate that the presence of "not bad" guarantees a positive sentiment prediction (and "not good" a negative sentiment). Anchors are intuitive, easy to understand, and have clear coverage–they apply only when all conditions in the rule are met, ensuring high precision.

Image Classification

The explanations for the label prediction of an image use the method of segmenting the image into superpixels and then uses the presence or absence of those superpixels as the interpretable representation. The visual question answer (VQA) has anchors in bold.

(a) Original image (b) Anchor for "beagle"

What animal is featured in this picture ?	**dog**
What floor is featured in this picture?	dog
What toenail is paired in this flowchart ?	dog
What animal is shown on this depiction ?	dog

Figure 6.2*: Image Classification Explanation*
(Source: Anchors: High-Precision Model-Agnostic Explanations (2018) Ribeiro et al)

High Precision Rules

Anchors are primarily concerned with explaining the individual predictions of any ML classifier. This is accomplished by identifying high-precision rules called anchors. These rules predict locally, disregarding changes in the other feature values of an instance. Anchors also overcome a limitation of the local explanation method LIME, which approximates the model's local behavior linearly. However, the anchor method has some limitations, such as potentially conflicting anchors and overly specific anchors. In the case of conflicting anchors, multiple anchors with different predictions might apply to the same test instance, making it unclear which anchor to choose. For overly specific anchors, predictions near the boundary of the model's decision function or for rare classes may require very specific conditions, resulting in complex anchors with low coverage.

The rule generation process involves successive iterations on potential rule candidates. Each iteration selects the best candidates and perturbs them by adding new features. This loop continues until the rule meets the accuracy conditions.

Anchor Intuition

Given a black-box model f : X → Y and an instance x ∈ X, the goal of Local Model-Agnostic Interpretability (LIME) is to explain the behavior of f(x) to a user, where f(x) is the individual prediction, for instance x. The assumption is that while the model is globally too complex to be explained succinctly, "zooming in" on individual predictions makes the explanation task feasible. Most model-agnostic methods work by perturbing the instance x according to some "perturbation distribution" D_x (for simplicity, D from now on). The paper emphasizes that perturbations D (and explanations) must use an interpretable representation (that is, one that makes sense to humans), even if the model uses an alternative representation of the input.

Let A be a rule (set of predicates) acting on such an interpretable representation, such that A(x) returns 1 if all its feature predicates are true for instance x.

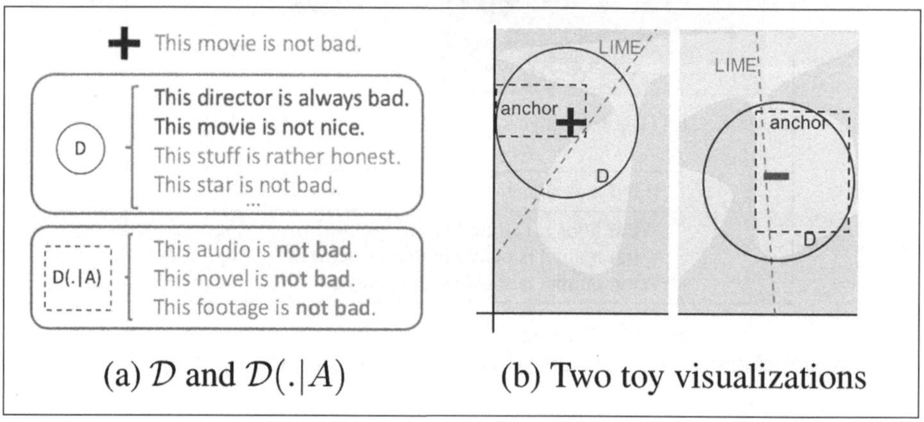

Figure 6.3: *Anchors and LIME Working*
(Source: Anchors: High-Precision Model-Agnostic Explanations (2018) Ribeiro et al)

For example, in *Figure 6.3(a)* (top),

x = "This movie is not bad.",

f(x) = Positive, A(x) = 1 where A = {"not", "bad"}.

Let D(·|A) denote the conditional distribution when rule A applies (for example, similar texts where "not" and "bad" are present, *Figure 6.3(a)* bottom). 'A' is an anchor if A(x) = 1 and 'A' is a sufficient condition for f(x) with high probability – in our running example, if a sample z from D(z|A) is likely predicted as Positive (that is, f(x) = f(z)).

Formally, A is an anchor if,

$$\mathbb{E}_{\mathcal{D}(z|A)}[\mathbb{1}_{f(x)=f(z)}] \geq \tau, A(x) = 1.$$

Figure 6.4: *Anchor Equation*

Figure 6.2(b) shows two "zoomed in" regions of a complex model, with particular instances (+ and -) being explained. LIME explanations work by learning the lines that best approximate the model under D, with some local weighting. The resulting explanations give no indication of how faithful they are (the explanation on the right is a much better local approximation of the black-box model than the one on the left), or what is in their "local region." In contrast, even though they use the same D, anchors are by construction faithful, adapting their coverage to the model's behavior (the anchor on the right of *Figure 6.2(b)* is broader) and making their boundaries clear.

Anchor Explanations on Tabular Data

1. We use the alibi package for Anchor explanations. Install the alibi package.

```
!pip install alibi
```

2. Import required packages, load the iris dataset from **sklearn,** and train a **RandomForestClassifier**.

```
import numpy as np
from sklearn.datasets import load_iris
from sklearn.ensemble import RandomForestClassifier
from alibi.explainers import AnchorTabular

dataset = load_iris()
feature_names = dataset.feature_names
class_names = list(dataset.target_names)

idx = 145
X_train,Y_train = dataset.data[:idx,:], dataset.target[:idx]
X_test, Y_test = dataset.data[idx+1:,:], dataset.target[idx+1:]

np.random.seed(0)
clf = RandomForestClassifier(n_estimators=50)
clf.fit(X_train, Y_train)
```

The following figure illustrates random forest training:

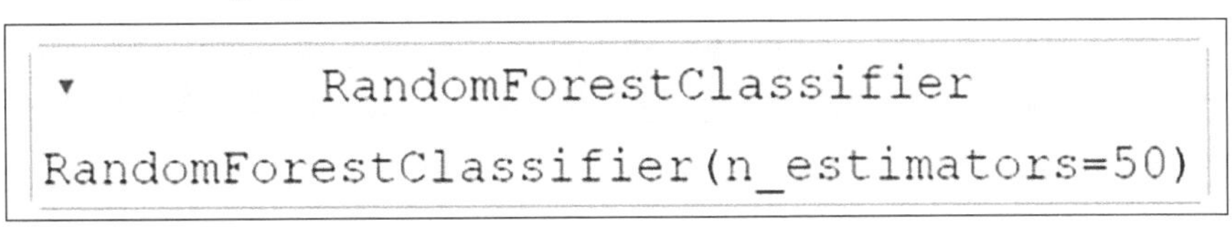

Figure 6.5: *Random Forest Training*

3. Initialize the Anchor explainers and visualize the anchor rules.

```
predict_fn = lambda x: clf.predict_proba(x)
explainer = AnchorTabular(predict_fn, feature_names)
explainer.fit(X_train, disc_perc=(25, 50, 75))
```

Output:

```
AnchorTabular(meta={
  'name': 'AnchorTabular',
  'type': ['blackbox'],
  'explanations': ['local'],
  'params': {'seed': None, 'disc_perc': (25, 50, 75)},
  'version': '0.9.6'}
)
```

Figure 6.6: *Anchor Implementation*

4. Print prediction for the first item in the holdout test data.

```
idx = 0
print('Prediction: ', class_names[explainer.predictor(X_
test[idx].reshape(1, -1))[0]])
```

Output:

```
Prediction:  virginica
```

Figure 6.7: *Model Prediction*

5. Getting anchor rules for the first item in the dataset.

```
explanation = explainer.explain(X_test[idx], threshold=0.95)
print('Anchor: %s' % (' AND '.join(explanation.anchor)))
print('Precision: %.2f' % explanation.precision)
print('Coverage: %.2f' % explanation.coverage)
```

Output:

```
Anchor: petal width (cm) > 1.80 AND sepal width (cm) <= 2.80
Precision: 0.98
Coverage: 0.08
```

Figure 6.8: *Anchor for Model*

Counterfactuals

In the previous chapter, we covered SHAP as an explanation method. Shap is an additive feature attribution method but it does not allow for "what if" analysis.

The feature importance in SHAP is primarily concerned with finding the most prominent features which are impacting the model's global accuracy or in a particular prediction. The role of Counterfactual explanations is to augment the algorithm predictions through instances leading to alternative but desirable outcomes.

History of Counterfactual Explanations

Counterfactual explanations have been used in multiple fields such as philosophy, psychology, and the social sciences for many years. There are many published articles on Counterfactuals by philosophers. As quoted in his book, James Woodward notes that a satisfactory explanation must follow patterns of counterfactual dependence. Philosophers and psychologists alike believe that counterfactuals elicit causal reasoning in humans. Multiple studies have rated counterfactual explanations as being preferred over case-based reasoning or feature importance methods. We will look at counterfactual explanations through an example, the methods, and challenges.

An Example

Consider a bank that is disbursing home mortgage loans. The loan decision is influenced largely by a machine learning classifier model which considers feature vectors of {Income, CreditScore, LoanAmount, Education, Age}. Unfortunately, the loan is denied to one of the applicants Olga and she is left wondering:

1. Why was the loan denied?

   This can be answered with explanations of the following: "CreditScore was too low." This is similar to the majority of traditional explainability methods.

2. Is there anything different she can do to get the loan approved in the future?

This question is synonymous with a counterfactual explanation. What are the smallest changes in Olga's feature vectors that will lead to an outcome that is on the other side of the classifier's decision boundary? If there was a counterfactual, we can assume that Olga got guidance on what can be changed so that the loan gets approved the next time.

A possible counterfactual recommendation might be to increase her Income by $5K, to reduce the loan amount, to get a new master's degree, or a combination of the three. The first answer stated that the credit score was low but did not give a clear indication to Olga on what action to take while the counterfactual explanation explicitly helps her to identify the actions.

Features x: Customer information

Prediction y: Loan granted or denied

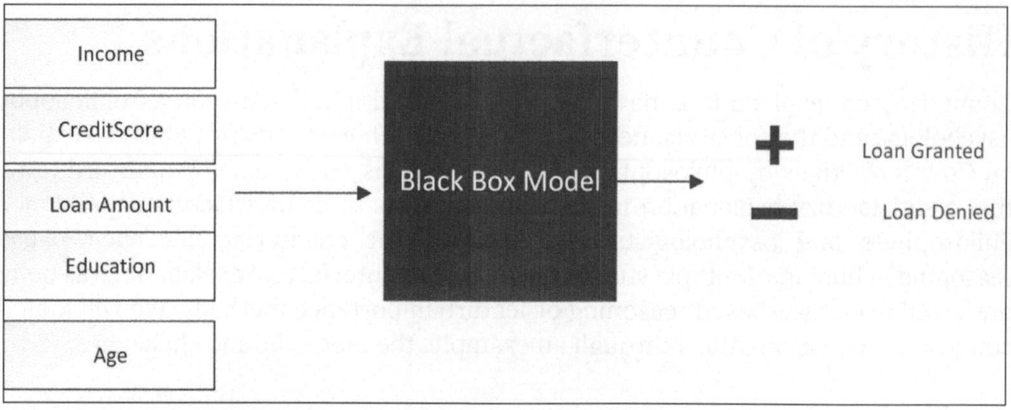

***Figure 6.9**: Typical Explanations from a Black-Box Model*

Why was the loan denied?

Is it a fair outcome?

How can x be changed so that the loan is accepted?

Counterfactual explanations provide answers in the form of "What-if" scenarios:

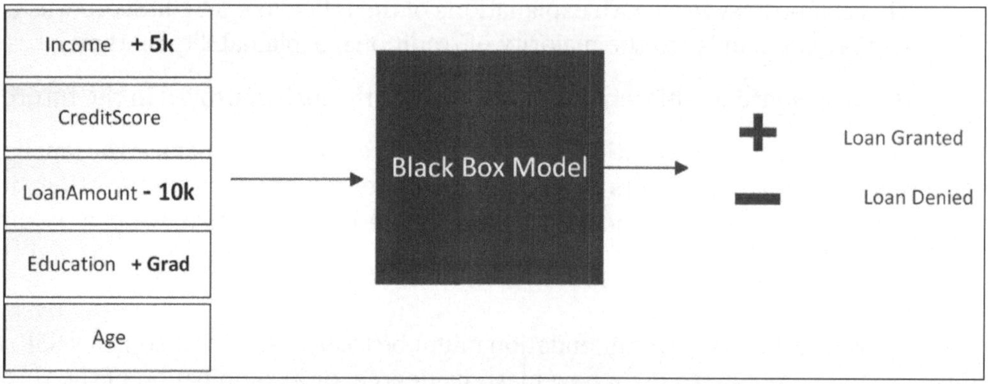

***Figure 6.10:** Counterfactual Explanations*

"If the income was increased by $5k, loan amount reduced by 10, or was more skilled, the loan would have been accepted."

The counterfactual is illustrated in *Figure* 6.11. A datapoint representing an individual who is initially classified in the negative class can follow three paths to cross the decision boundary into the positive class region. Counterfactual explanations presume that the underlying classifier model will remain unchanged in the future when the applicant reapplies. On the basis that this assumption holds true, the counterfactual ensures that the model will provide the desired outcome at a future time.

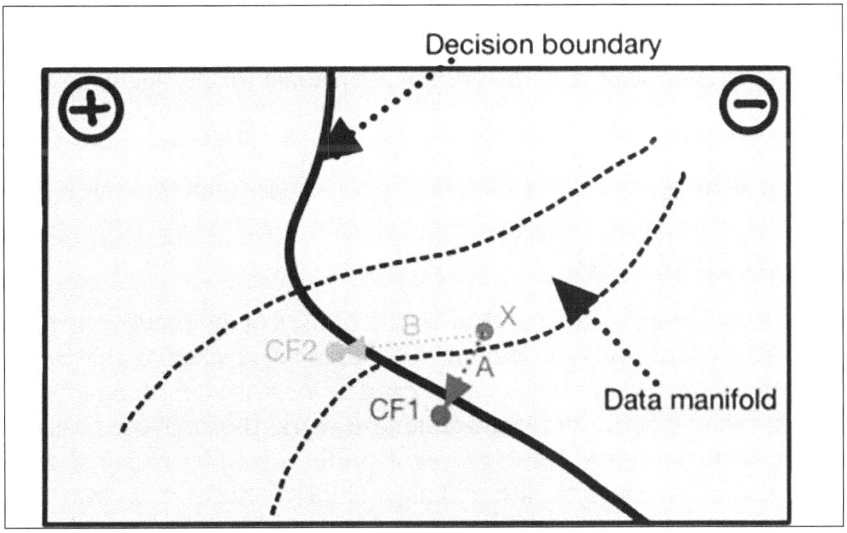

Figure 6.11: *Counterfactual for Input Value X (Source: Counterfactual Explanations and Algorithmic Recourses for Machine Learning: A Review (2022) Verma et al)*

Intuition

In Counterfactuals, we explain particular predictions of an ML model by presenting an alternative input whose prediction equals a desired outcome.

- Represent close neighbors of a data point we are interested in which leads to the desired outcome.
- Identify which minimal changes to the input are sufficient to receive a different outcome. The input feature change makes sense only if there is a possibility to change it. (for example, by changing behavior).
- The targeted audience of Counterfactual Explanations is often end-users.

Counterfactual Explanations serve various purposes, the user can decide what to learn from them.

For Example

"If the person had been one year older and the credit amount had been increased to $12.000, the credit would have been granted."

Guidance for Future Actions:

Ok, I will apply again next year for the higher amount.

Provide Reasons:

Interesting, I did not know that age plays a role in loan applications.

Provide Grounds to Contest the Decision:

How dare you, I do not want to be discriminated against for my age in an application.

Detect Model Biases:

There is a bug, an increase in amount should not increase approval rates.

Factors of Interest

The previous example highlights several key attributes of an effective counterfactual explanation. The counterfactual should indicate a small change that leads to the desired outcome. For instance, Olga might need to increase her income by $5K to get loan approval. While a $30K increase would also work, the smallest possible change is more practical for her. Besides Olga might prefer a simpler explanation, focusing on changing just a few aspects rather than multiple features. It is also crucial that the counterfactual provides realistic and actionable advice. A suggestion to decrease her age by ten years would be impractical. These considerations have driven recent advancements in counterfactual explainability.

Working of Counterfactuals

Creating such scenarios is both an art and a science. It requires understanding the decision boundaries of an AI model and adjusting the input variables just enough to influence the decision. Consequently, research in counterfactual explanations has concentrated on finding Counterfactual Explanations that ensure qualities such as credibility, minimality, similarity, plausibility, discriminative power, actionability, causality, and diversity. These can be grouped into three main categories:

- **Quantum of Change**: The aim is to identify the smallest change that makes the most significant impact. This involves precision–altering the inputs just enough to change the outcome without suggesting unrealistic or impractical modifications.
- **Grounding in Reality**: It is not just about finding any change; it is about finding a plausible one. The suggestions must be realistic. For instance, advising someone to become ten years younger is not a practical counterfactual.
- **Tools**: Various algorithms and tools are used to create such explanations. From optimization techniques to causal inference models, these tools strive to balance simplicity with thoroughness.

Methods of Counterfactual Explanations

The simplest method involves trial and error, randomly changing the feature values for the instance of interest until the desired output gets predicted.

Optimization Method:

The initial counterfactual explanations framed CFE as an optimization problem. The goal, as stated in Equation (1), is to minimize the distance between the counterfactual (x ') and the original datapoint (x), while ensuring that the classifier's output for the counterfactual matches the desired label (y ' ∈ Y). Transforming this objective into a differentiable and unconstrained form results in two components as shown in Equation (2). The first component aims to make the classifier's output for the counterfactual close to the desired class, while the second component ensures the counterfactual remains similar to the original datapoint. The distance between the two datapoints x and x ' ∈ X is measured using a metric d. This distance can be the L1/L2 distance, quadratic distance, or distance functions that consider the CDF of the features or pairwise feature costs as perceived by users. This original definition highlighted that an effective counterfactual should involve only a small change from the starting point.

$$\arg\min_{x'} d(x, x') \text{ subject to } f(x') = y' \quad (1)$$

$$\arg\min_{x'} \max_{\lambda} \lambda (f(x') - y')^2 + d(x, x') \quad (2)$$

Figure 6.12: *Counterfactual Equation*

Where f is the model, x is the original instance, y is the original target response, x' is the counterfactual instance, y' is the desired target class, d is the distance function, and λ is the balancing/regularizer parameter.

Of particular importance is the choice of distance function used to decide which synthetic data point x' is closest to the original data point x_i. As a sensible first choice, which should be refined based on subject- and task-specific requirements, we suggest the use of the L1 norm, or Manhattan distance, weighted by the inverse median absolute deviation. This is written as MAD_j for the median absolute deviation of feature j, over the set of points P. This can be formulated as follows:

$$\arg\min_{\mathbf{x}'} \max_{\lambda} \lambda \underbrace{(\hat{f}(\mathbf{x}') - y')^2}_{o_p(\hat{f}(\mathbf{x}'), y')} + \underbrace{\sum_{j=1}^{p} |x'_j - x_j| / MAD_j}_{o_f(\mathbf{x}', \mathbf{x})}$$

Figure 6.13: *Counterfactual Equation in MAD*

MAD_j is the median absolute deviation of feature j.

The equation for x' is solved by looping through the iterations using optimizers. λ is then increased to get to a close enough solution. The optimization problem has its problems. For one we do not have a good enough method for deducing the λ. Besides, the focus is firstly on the minimization operation. Other factors such as sparsity and plausibility of counterfactuals are not accounted for.

Multi-Objective Counterfactual (MOC):

In the prior method, we captured all objectives into a single objective. Alternatively, we could optimize all the objectives simultaneously. This is MOC or Multi-Objective Counterfactual.

$$\arg\min_{\mathbf{x}'} \left(o_p(\hat{f}(\mathbf{x}'), y'), o_f(\mathbf{x}', \mathbf{x}), o_s(\mathbf{x}', \mathbf{x}), o_4(\mathbf{x}', \mathbf{X}) \right).$$

Figure 6.14: *Multi-Objective Counterfactual*

An adjusted multi-objective genetic algorithm is used to get diversity in the counterfactual output handling a combination of mixed discrete and continuous feature spaces. Weighing parameters such as the λ we used previously are no longer needed. This means there is not just one counterfactual. The output in multi-objective counterfactuals is multiple counterfactuals with varying tradeoffs which are devised with a diversity in the feature space.

Methods with Sparsity

The underlying assumption is that a counterfactual should only change the smallest number of features to be effective. Also, the number of features and amount of change required to get to an output needs to be weighed as they can have contrasting impacts. Besides, there can be a positive in shorter counterfactuals as humans tend to be biased towards simpler explanations. This leads to the inclusion of sparsity in building explanations. The loss function is updated to add a penalty function, this penalty function promotes sparsity in the difference between the changed data point and its original.

$$g(x' - x) - \text{L0/L1 norm}$$

$$\arg\min_{x' \in \mathcal{A}} \max_{\lambda} \lambda(f(x') - y')^2 + d(x, x') + g(x' - x)$$

Figure 6.15: *Sparse Counterfactual*

Data Manifold Proximity

The counterfactual also needs to be grounded in reality and possible to accomplish. For instance, if we get a mix of features that are not plausible and not like any observation seen earlier, building trust in such a counterfactual is also tough. To accomplish this requirement of the counterfactual being realistic, we can use the training data as a guideline to ensure that the changed data is close enough. This leads to the concept of data manifold which indicates the space with all the training data points can be quantified in multiple different ways. One mechanism is to add a penalty to our loss function to ensure that it is abiding by the data manifold from our training set as denoted by $l(x'; X)$.

$$\arg\min_{x' \in \mathcal{A}} \max_{\lambda} \lambda(f(x') - y')^2 + d(x, x') + g(x' - x) + l(x'; \mathcal{X})$$

***Figure 6.16**: Adding Plausibility to Counterfactuals*

The area between the dashed lines is the data manifold in *Figure* 6.5. In the figure, we see that there are two routes to go across the decision boundary from the blue datapoint. There is a green path which is longer but sticks to the data manifold region. The red path to the counterfactual across the decision is much shorter but it is important to note that it is outside of the data manifold region. Hence adding a loss term for the data manifold promotes proximity to the data manifold such that the algorithm selects the green path instead of the red path although it is longer.

Methods with Diversity

There can be multiple counterfactuals for a single input data point. The positive of having multiple counterfactuals is that applicants are able to attain at least one counterfactual state. Counterfactuals provided should be diverse so the applicants have multiple options to select. When sparsity is enforced by an algorithm, multiple sparse subsets of the features can be altered. Diversity in counterfactuals is hence useful. Maximizing the distance counterfactuals also increases the diversity. This is done either by adding it as a term in the optimization objective or by minimizing the mutual information between all the pairs of the modified feature. Diverse Counterfactual Explanations (DiCE) primarily work to provide a balance between diversity and feasibility.

Other factors considered in counterfactual explanations are the following:

Causality:

Features within a dataset are seldom independent, meaning that altering one feature in the real world often impacts others. For instance, obtaining a new educational degree requires the individual to age by at least a certain amount. To be realistic and actionable, a counterfactual must preserve any known causal relationships between features. Consequently, our loss function now considers

- Validity of the counterfactual
- Sparsity in the feature vector and the actionability of features

- Similarity to the training data, data manifold
- Causal relationships

Adversarial Learning:

Adversarial learning is closely related but not synonymous with counterfactual generation. The goal of adversarial learning is to make minimal changes to input to classify it differently, often aiming to significantly exceed the decision boundary and result in a highly confident misclassification. Although the optimization problem is similar to that of counterfactual generation, the objectives differ. For instance, in adversarial learning, particularly with images, the aim is to make indistinguishable changes to the input image. This contrasts with the Counterfactual Explanation (CFE) goal of sparsity and parsimony, though single-pixel attacks are an exception. Additionally, concepts such as data manifold and actionability/causality are seldom considered in adversarial learning. Some studies highlight the similarities and potential synergies between the two fields, such as the connection between the optimization objectives and outcomes of adversarial and CFE techniques. Another study notes that the differences in the desired class label and the distance from the original data point distinguish CFEs from adversarial examples. Additionally, there are suggestions for generating semantically meaningful adversarial perturbations to create CFEs for images. The emphasis is that the requirement to produce plausible data points sets CFEs apart from adversarial examples.

CFE in Python Using DiCE:

1. Install the DiCE library.

```
!pip install dice-ml
```

2. We will be using the iris dataset from sklearn to train the classification model.

```
import dice_ml
from dice_ml import Dice

from sklearn.datasets import load_iris, fetch_california_housing
from sklearn.pipeline import Pipeline
from sklearn.preprocessing import StandardScaler, OneHotEncoder
from sklearn.model_selection import train_test_split
from sklearn.compose import ColumnTransformer
from sklearn.ensemble import RandomForestClassifier, RandomFore-
stRegressor

import pandas as pd

df_iris = load_iris(as_frame=True).frame
df_iris.head()
```

The following figure illustrates the iris dataset:

	sepal length (cm)	sepal width (cm)	petal length (cm)	petal width (cm)	target
0	5.1	3.5	1.4	0.2	0
1	4.9	3.0	1.4	0.2	0
2	4.7	3.2	1.3	0.2	0
3	4.6	3.1	1.5	0.2	0
4	5.0	3.6	1.4	0.2	0

Figure 6.17: *Iris Dataset*

```
outcome_name = "target"
continuous_features_iris = df_iris.drop(outcome_name, axis=1).
columns.tolist()
target = df_iris[outcome_name]
# Split data into train and test
datasetX = df_iris.drop(outcome_name, axis=1)
x_train, x_test, y_train, y_test = train_test_split(datasetX,tar-
get,
test_size=0.2, random_state=0, stratify=target)

categorical_features = x_train.columns.difference(continuous_fea-
tures_iris)

# We create the preprocessing pipelines for both numeric and cat-
egorical data.
numeric_transformer = Pipeline(steps=[
    ('scaler', StandardScaler())])

categorical_transformer = Pipeline(steps=[
    ('onehot', OneHotEncoder(handle_unknown='ignore'))])

transformations = ColumnTransformer(
    transformers=[
        ('num', numeric_transformer, continuous_features_iris),
        ('cat', categorical_transformer, categorical_features)])
```

3. Train the model.

```
# Append classifier to preprocessing pipeline.
# Now we have a full prediction pipeline.
clf_iris = Pipeline(steps=[('preprocessor', transformations),
                           ('classifier', RandomForestClassifier
())])
model_iris = clf_iris.fit(x_train, y_train)
```

4. Find the Counterfactual Explanations.

```
d_iris = dice_ml.Data(dataframe=df_iris,
                      continuous_features=continuous_features_iris,
                      outcome_name=outcome_name)

# We provide the type of model as a parameter (model_type)
m_iris = dice_ml.Model(model=model_iris, backend="sklearn",
model_type='classifier')
exp_genetic_iris = Dice(d_iris, m_iris, method="genetic")
# Single input
query_instances_iris = x_test[2:3]
genetic_iris = exp_genetic_iris.generate_counterfactuals(query_
instances_iris, total_CFs=7, desired_class=2)
genetic_iris.visualize_as_dataframe()
```

The following figure illustrates the diverse counterfactuals for provided input:

```
100%|██████████| 1/1 [00:01<00:00,  1.60s/it]
Query instance (original outcome : 0)
```

	sepal length (cm)	sepal width (cm)	petal length (cm)	petal width (cm)	target
0	5.1	3.8	1.9	0.4	0

```
Diverse Counterfactual set (new outcome: 2)
```

	sepal length (cm)	sepal width (cm)	petal length (cm)	petal width (cm)	target
0	7.9	3.8	6.4	2.0	2
0	7.7	3.8	6.7	2.2	2
0	4.7	3.8	5.1	2.1	2
0	4.7	3.8	5.6	2.1	2
0	5.2	3.9	6.0	2.1	2
0	4.3	3.8	5.1	2.1	2
0	4.3	3.8	5.6	2.1	2

***Figure 6.18**: Diverse Counterfactuals for Provided Input*

```
# Multiple queries can be given as input at once
query_instances_iris = x_test[17:19]
genetic_iris = exp_genetic_iris.generate_counterfactuals(query_
instances_iris, total_CFs=7, desired_class=2)
genetic_iris.visualize_as_dataframe(show_only_changes=True)
```

The following figure illustrates the counterfactuals for multiple inputs:

	sepal length (cm)	sepal width (cm)	petal length (cm)	petal width (cm)	target
0	6.7	3.1	4.4	1.4	1

```
Diverse Counterfactual set (new outcome: 2)
```

	sepal length (cm)	sepal width (cm)	petal length (cm)	petal width (cm)	target
0	-	-	5.6	2.4	2.0
0	6.4	-	5.5	1.8	2.0
0	6.9	-	5.4	2.1	2.0
0	6.9	-	5.1	2.3	2.0
0	-	3.0	5.2	2.3	2.0
0	-	3.3	5.7	2.1	2.0
0	-	3.3	5.7	2.5	2.0

```
Query instance (original outcome : 1)
```

	sepal length (cm)	sepal width (cm)	petal length (cm)	petal width (cm)	target
0	7.0	3.2	4.7	1.4	1

```
Diverse Counterfactual set (new outcome: 2)
```

	sepal length (cm)	sepal width (cm)	petal length (cm)	petal width (cm)	target
0	7.2	-	6.0	1.8	2.0
0	6.5	-	5.1	2.0	2.0
0	6.9	-	5.7	2.3	2.0
0	6.8	-	5.9	2.3	2.0
0	6.4	-	5.3	2.3	2.0
0	6.9	3.1	5.4	2.1	2.0
0	6.2	3.1	4.8	1.8	2.0

***Figure 6.19**: Counterfactuals for Multiple Inputs*

Requirements from CFE

In this section, we outline the desirable properties of Counterfactual Explanations (CFEs) which are primarily the focus at this point. Listing them here allows us to discuss some challenges identified in the subsequent section.

- **Actionability:** Mutability and actionability of features should be accounted for when suggesting changes. A CFE should not attempt to alter immutable features such as an individual's birthplace or race.
- **Sparsity:** A CFE is more actionable if it suggests changes to a few features as against proposing small changes to many features. This is the case even if the magnitude of those individual changes is larger.

- **Adherence to Data Manifold:** A more actionable CFE is closer to the manifold of the data that was used to train the underlying ML model. The training dataset projects the distribution of its features. Hence, a CFE that far from the dataset is likely unactionable. In *Figure* 6.5, the green CFE is closer to the data manifold than the red CFE.
- **Respect for Causal Relations:** A CFE should stick to causal relations between features so as to reflect real-world relations. For instance, suggesting a decrease in one's age or degree is not plausible.
- These are the desirable properties of the CFE generating algorithm:
- **Black-Box and Model-Agnostic CFEs:** Algorithms that generate CFEs for black-box models and are model-agnostic can be applied to various scenarios. This is true for proprietary ML models too.
- **Speed in CFEs:** Algorithms that can generate CFEs for multiple data points from the same distribution from a single optimization are faster and easier to deploy.

Properties of Counterfactual Algorithms

This section expounds on the key properties of a counterfactual explanation generation algorithm.

The properties of the models are the following:

- **Model Access**: The access to the underlying model may be needed based on the algorithm in use for Counterfactual generation. Three distinct access level types come into play including, access to all of the model internals, access to only gradients, and access to the prediction function in case of black-box models. Complete model internals are needed for solver-based methods such as mixed integer programming or decision trees, which require access to all internal nodes. Most methods use gradient-based algorithms to solve the optimization objective, modifying the loss function proposed in the original paper of Counterfactual Explanations from 2017, but this is limited to differentiable models. Blackbox approaches use gradient-free optimization algorithms, growing spheres, or genetic algorithms. Some methods do not frame the goal as an optimization problem and instead use heuristics. For example, the use of Dijkstra's algorithm to find the shortest path between existing training datapoints to find counterfactuals for a given input, thus not generating new datapoints. Other techniques involve dividing the entire feature space into class-based delineations such that all datapoints belonging to a class are marked and then graph traversal methods are used to find the nearest counterfactual explanations. Alternatively, some methods suggest changes in the training phase, for instance, the addition of adversarial loss while training to improve the likelihood of occurrence for training datapoints.

Other techniques proposed are CounterNet which is a unique architecture to predict the class and generate the CFE for a datapoint through training. There are also methods that train a sum-product network to function as a classifier and density estimator for generating CFEs.

- **Model Agnostic**: This property describes the range of models an algorithm can operate on. For instance, gradient-based algorithms can only handle differentiable models, while solver-based algorithms require linear or piece-wise linear models. Some algorithms are model-specific, such as those for tree ensembles. Blackbox methods, however, have no restrictions on the underlying model and are thus model-agnostic.
- **Optimization Amortization**: In the reviewed papers, most algorithms generate a single counterfactual for each input datapoint, requiring the optimization problem to be solved for each counterfactual individually. However, some methods can produce multiple counterfactuals (often diverse by some diversity metric) for a single input, needing only one run per input to generate several counterfactuals. Some approaches use a Variational Auto-Encoder (VAE) to map datapoints to counterfactuals, allowing the generation of multiple counterfactuals for all inputs without separate optimization, making it very fast. In other methods, we train a reinforcement learning model to learn the actions needed to generate CFEs for data distribution, thus amortizing the process. We examine two aspects of optimization amortization:
    - **Amortized Inference**: The algorithm generates counterfactuals for many data points without the need for separate optimizations or it is marked No.
    - **Multiple Counterfactuals (CF)**: The algorithm generates multiple counterfactuals for one input datapoint or it is marked No.
- **Counterfactual (CF) Attributes**: These columns assess algorithms based on sparsity, adherence to the data manifold, and causality. The tendency is to use solver-based methods explicitly to enforce sparsity, and black-box methods to constrain the L0 norm of the counterfactual and the input data point while gradient-based methods typically use the L1 norm. Some methods modify only a fixed number of features, change features iteratively, or flip the minimum possible split nodes in decision trees to introduce sparsity. Other methods achieve sparsity post-hoc by sorting the features in increasing order of the relative change and then using a greedy mechanism to restore their values to match the input data point. This is continued until the prediction for the Counterfactual Explanation (CFE) is different from the input.

  Adherence to the data manifold is addressed through various approaches, such as training VAEs on the data distribution, constraining the distance of a counterfactual from the k-nearest training datapoints, directly sampling points from the latent space of a VAE and passing them through the decoder. This can also be achieved using an ensemble of models to capture predictive entropy, using a Kernel Density Estimator (KDE) to estimate the PDF of the underlying data manifold. The other ways to ensure adherence to the data manifold includes using cycle consistency loss in GANs, mapping back to the data domain, using a combination of existing datapoints, using Gaussian Mixture Models to approximate the probability of being in-distribution (training data is an independent identical distribution which is also called in-distribution data), using feature correlations, or simply not generating any new datapoint.

A causal graph shows the relationship between different features and this is represented as a directed graph. Access to the complete causal graph is required in this case which seldom is possible in the real world. However, there are methods available that can work with partial causal graphs.

These three properties are reported in the table:

- **Sparsity**: This applies if the algorithm does not consider sparsity; otherwise, it specifies the sparsity constraint.
- **Data Manifold**: This indicates that the algorithm makes sure that the generated counterfactual is close to the data manifold using some mechanisms or it is marked as No.
- **Causal Relation**: This applies if the algorithm considers the causal relations between features when generating counterfactuals; otherwise, it is marked No.

- **Counterfactual (CF) Optimization Problem Attributes**: These attributes relate to the optimization problem. Most studies that examine feature actionability classify features as either immutable or mutable. Some methods further divide features into immutable, mutable, and actionable categories, with actionable features being a subset of mutable ones. They point out that some features, such as CreditScore, are mutable but not directly actionable by the individual, as they are influenced by other factors such as income or credit amount. Other studies use an oracle to learn user preferences for changing features amongst the mutable ones and can also uncover hidden preferences.

  Most tabular datasets contain both continuous and categorical features. While arithmetic operations on continuous features are straightforward, handling categorical variables in gradient-based algorithms can be complex. Some algorithms exclude categorical variables, while others combine all categorical features to each of their values, leading to scalability issues. Some methods convert categorical features to one-hot encoding and treat them as numerical features, though maintaining one-hotness can be challenging. Other approaches use different distance functions for categorical features, such as an indicator function, or methods such as Markov chain transitions are used to encode categorical distances. Other works suggest using Gaussian mixture models to normalize the continuous features and techniques such as Gumbel-Softmax to convert categorical features into continuous ones. Similarly, techniques such as genetic algorithms, evolutionary algorithms, and SMT solvers can also handle categorical features.

These properties are reported in the table:

- **Feature Preference**: The feature being actionable is validated in the algorithm or it is marked No.
- **Categorical Distance Function**: When a separate distance function is not used for categorical data by the algorithm, this property applies else the specific distance function is provided.

Metrics for Evaluation:

Evaluation of counterfactual generation algorithms is based on the desirable properties of counterfactuals. Counterfactuals serve as actionable feedback for individuals when there are undesirable outcomes from automated decision-makers. The ability to act on a recommended counterfactual is measured using quantifiable proxies:

- **Validity:** Measures the ratio of counterfactuals having the desired class label as against the total number of counterfactuals generated. Higher validity is preferable and is commonly reported in most papers.
- **Proximity:** Measures the distance between the input data point and the counterfactual. Counterfactuals closer to the input data point are easier to act upon. Common distance metrics include the L1 norm, L2 norm, and Mahalanobis distance.
- **Sparsity**: Short explanations are more understandable to humans, so counterfactuals should generally recommend only a small number of feature changes. A general sense is to minimize the sparse counterfactuals to at most two feature changes.
- **Counterfactual Generation Time:** This measures the time required to generate counterfactuals. It can be averaged over the generation of counterfactuals for a batch of input data points or for multiple counterfactuals for a single input data point.
- **Diversity:** Some algorithms generate multiple counterfactuals for a single input data point to increase the ease of reaching at least one counterfactual state. Diverse counterfactuals allow applicants to choose the easiest one. Diversity is encouraged by maximizing the distance between counterfactuals, minimizing mutual information between modified features, or using other methods. Higher diversity values are preferable.
- **Closeness to Training Data:** This measures the actionability and realism of modified features by grounding them in the training data distribution. Methods include measuring the average distance to the k-nearest data

points, local outlier factor, reconstruction error from a VAE, PDF using KDE, or Maximum Mean Discrepancy (MMD). Lower values are preferable.

- **Causal Constraint Satisfaction:** Metric captures the feasibility of the modifications in the counterfactual by measuring if they satisfy the causal relations between features.
- **IM1 and IM2:** These metrics are specific to algorithms using autoencoders. Lower IM1 values imply better reconstruction by the autoencoder trained on the counterfactual class, indicating closeness to the data manifold of the counterfactual class. Lower IM2 values imply similar reconstruction from autoencoders trained on the counterfactual class and all classes, indicating more interpretable counterfactuals.
- **Label Variation Score and Oracle Score:** When there are multiple labels for each datapoint then Label Variation Score applies. This ensures that a counterfactual for one label has no effect on the predictions for other labels except if they are highly correlated. The Oracle Score also uses predictions from another classifier for the ground truth validity.

Rashomon Effect

In counterfactual explanations, we face the Rashomon effect; there exist many plausible counterfactuals that explain the same data point. This raises the question of which one we should show to the user.

The solution to the optimization problem might not be unique, and many equally close counterfactual explanations might exist that obtain the desired prediction. Essentially, there can be many different equally good explanations for the same decision.

Some of the more recent papers mention methods such as returning only the Pareto-optimal set of counterfactuals, which at least guarantees that no strictly dominated option is shown. In future works, integrating user preferences or considering additional objectives are being considered to improve the final selection.

Conclusion

We looked at multiple post hoc explanation methods in these previous few chapters. Anchors and Counterfactual Explanations are additional techniques in the same bucket serving a different purpose. Anchors are simple to understand and aim to give precise explanations, unlike techniques such as LIME which can be misinterpreted depending on the visual presented. While Counterfactuals serve the purpose of providing the minimal feature changes required to achieve an alternate outcome.

In the next chapter, we discuss explainability challenges in neural networks and understand the various gradient-based techniques in vision models.

References

1. Anchors: High-Precision Model-Agnostic Explanations (2018) Ribeiro et al https://dl.acm.org/doi/abs/10.5555/3504035.3504222
2. Counterfactual Explanations for Machine Learning: Challenges Revisited (2021) Verma et al https://arxiv.org/pdf/2106.07756
3. Counterfactual Explanations and Algorithmic Recourses for Machine Learning: A Review (2022) Verma et al https://arxiv.org/pdf/2010.10596
4. Explaining Machine Learning Classifiers through Diverse Counterfactual Explanations (2019) Mothilal et al https://arxiv.org/pdf/1905.07697
5. Counterfactual Explanations for Machine Learning: A Review (2020) Verma et al https://ml-retrospectives.github.io/neurips2020/camera_ready/5.pdf

CHAPTER 7

Interpretability in Neural Networks

Introduction

In this chapter, we will take a deep dive into explanations in neural networks, specifically computer vision. We have seen a few examples of using LIME and SHAP in deep neural networks, but there are more specific gradient-based and non-gradient based techniques for integrating explainability and interpretability in Deep Learning.

Structure

In this chapter, we will cover the following topics:

- Explainable AI
- Interpretability in Neural Networks
- Interpretability Techniques in Vision Model
- DeconvNet
- Guided Backpropagation
- Axiomatic Approaches
- DeepLIFT
- Integradient Gradients
- Improvements on Integrated Gradients
- TCAV

Explainable AI (XAI)

In the past few chapters, we have explored many explanation methods. Essentially, we looked at generalizable frameworks for explaining a machine learning model and provide a good justification.

The explainable machine learning methods fit into one of the following:

- Interpretable models
    - Linear regression, logistic regression, decision trees, and so on.
    - These models are often simple to use.
- Model-specific interpretation methods
    - It is model-dependent and, hence, cannot be generalized.
- Model-agnostic methods

In model-agnostic methods, we looked at techniques such as LIME and SHAP in *Chapter 5, Post-Hoc Methods*, and Anchors and Counterfactuals in *Chapter 6, Anchors and Counterfactuals*. These techniques focus on various aspects of explainability, from local explainability and feature attribution to what-if scenario decomposition.

The interpreted models using LIME and SHAP were applied across tabular, image, and language data. This brings us to an interesting aspect of interpretability and the fact that some techniques are applicable across data types such as image, language, and model architectures, including neural networks.

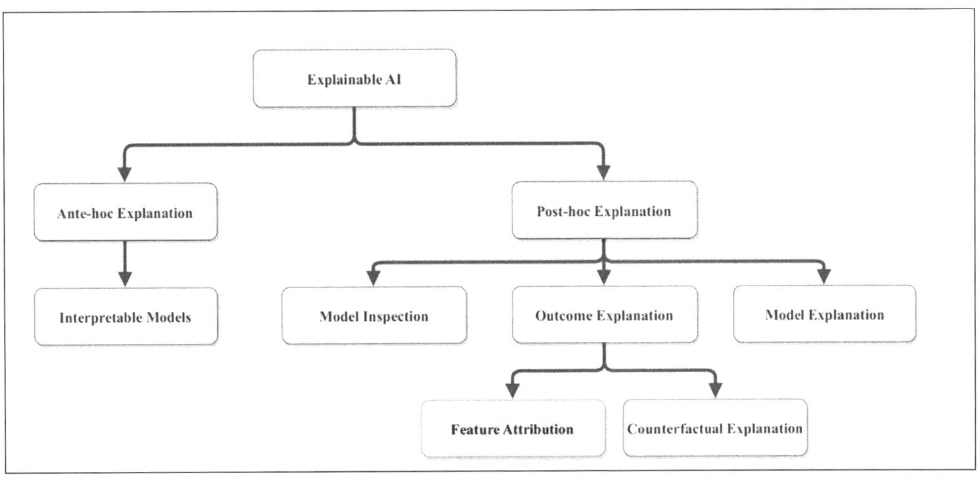

***Figure 7.1**: Methodology in Explainable AI*
(Source: Gradient based Feature Attribution in Explainable AI: A Technical Review (2024) wang et al)

Explainable AI (XAI) encompasses a range of techniques aimed at understanding and reasoning about model behaviors, providing insights to correct model errors or biases, and ultimately fostering user trust in the model's predictions. XAI can be divided into two main categories: ante-hoc explanations (or inherently interpretable models) and post-hoc explanations.

Ante-hoc explanations focus on creating transparent models that users can easily understand without additional tools, such as decision trees. Post-hoc explanations, on the other hand, seek to clarify the workings of a trained black-box model by examining the relationship between input features and model predictions. These post-hoc explanations can be further broken down into model explanation, outcome explanation, and model inspection.

Model explanation involves approximating the overall logic of a black-box model with an interpretable and transparent model on a global scale. Outcome explanation delves into the reasons behind a specific prediction at a local level. Model inspection provides visual and textual representations to help users grasp the model's mechanisms.

In outcome explanation, two common approaches are feature attribution (also known as feature importance) and counterfactual explanation. Feature attribution identifies the significance of input features to the model's output, while counterfactual explanation explores minimal and meaningful changes in input values to determine how they might affect the model's prediction.

Interpretability in Neural Networks

The past decade has witnessed the rise of Deep Neural Networks (DNN) as they have become crucial in many industries, empowering complex systems and solutions. While machine learning was primarily dealing with tabular data, deep learning performs well in many modalities, including natural language processing, computer vision, and speech, amongst others. In most instances, deep learning models tend to outperform many previous machine learning models, such as decision trees and gradient boosting methods. In fact, neural networks have achieved human parity in some of these areas. Voice assistants and character recognition have become common place, leading to products used by many people. Healthcare and manufacturing are industries that have benefited from these state-of-the-art models, and they are getting even more ingrained in science.

A neural network is built with many layers where each layer is composed of numerous neurons. Training a neural network involves learning the weights that are essentially the parameters to be learned. The complexity and size of neural networks increase with the achieved efficiency. For instance, AlexNet, one of the earliest popular neural networks, has 62 million parameters. Deep Learning with all its benefits, does pose a critical drawback, given its sheer size and complexity. The internals of the neural network are not easy to decipher, and determining the backdrop for a specific prediction is not possible for this reason.

Interpretability Techniques in Vision Models

Convolutional neural networks (CNNs) were introduced in the 1980s and, just like other early neural networks, were largely unused until the rise of modern machine learning. They quickly became essential for solving contemporary computer vision problems.

Since then, CNN-based deep learning models have driven remarkable advancements in various computer vision tasks, including image classification, semantic segmentation, image captioning, and visual question answering, sometimes reaching near-human performance levels. Today, advanced computer vision models are employed in face recognition, monitoring factory floors, designing smart cities, developing self-driving cars, medical imaging, and diagnosing diseases.

The significant rise in the number of intelligent systems that are reliant on image models points to the importance of explainability in analyzing and understanding these systems. Unfortunately, these highly complex systems can fail without warning or explanation, sometimes leading to serious consequences.

Similarly, Explainable AI (XAI) encompasses a variety of techniques aimed at making the decision-making processes of deep learning models more transparent and understandable.

In this chapter, we will focus on the explainability methods for transparent computer vision models. The main difference between traditional machine learning and computer vision tasks is the most basic feature, which is a pixel in vision. Pixels are seldom significant separately and have meaning in collectives. These combinations of pixels form features to create high level features such as edges, textures, or patterns that we humans understand. The nature of features in computer vision, being a combination of pixels, requires differential treatment in its usage with explanation methods. Various techniques and methods have been devised to handle these variations in vision models. The explainability methods we discuss in this chapter will explore multiple aspects of features in images, using that detail to arrive at explanations.

The explainability methods for image models can be classified into the following types: backpropagation methods, perturbation methods, methods that depend on the internal state, or a combination of these approaches. The techniques that we will discuss in this chapter belong to these groups. The algorithm in LIME is reliant on perturbing input examples to obtain an equivalent interpretable model. As the name implies, the methods Integrated Gradients and XRAI depend on backpropagation, while Guided Backpropagation, Grad-CAM, and a few others depend on the model's internal state.

Based on different methodological approaches, feature attribution contains the following branches of research: perturbation-based methods, surrogate-based methods, decomposition-based methods, and gradient-based methods.

In deep learning for computer vision tasks, a Convolutional Neural Network (ConvNet or CNN) is trained for tasks such as image classification and visual question answering. CNN models are typically seen as black boxes that process a dataset and produce an output, such as predictions in image classification or captions in image captioning, depending on the task. For example, the model's prediction is optimized for accuracy in image classification.

The challenge lies in determining which parts of the image are in focus for the network when making a prediction, thus transforming these black box models into interpretable ones.

Explainability is critical in industries such as healthcare, where outcomes are extremely impactful. In fields such as medical imaging, adding an explainability layer to ConvNets is highly beneficial for disease prognosis. In a classification model trained on medical images such as MRI scans, fMRI, and X-rays, the model predicts the presence or absence of a medical condition. Utilizing the crucial details of the images for its predictions makes the model more trustworthy compared to a black box model with high prediction accuracy.

We have seen feature attribution in the previous chapters. Similarly, pixel attribution is a type of feature attribution specifically concerned with images. As noted earlier, feature attribution is a method for explaining individual predictions. This is accomplished by attributing each input feature depending on how much it caused a change in the prediction, either negatively or positively. These features can be either input pixels, tabular data, or language. Techniques such as SHAP, Shapley values, and LIME are examples that use these general feature attribution methods.

Let us consider a neural network that outputs a prediction as a vector of length c. This could be a regression network when c=1. The neural network has an output for image I, $S(I) = [S_1(I),\ldots,S_C(I)]$. Input to all these methods is considered to $x \in R_p$ where the input can be image pixels, tabular data, language with p features. The output as an explanation is a relevance score for each of the p input features: $R^c=[R_1^c,\ldots,R_p^c]$. The c indicates the relevancy for the c-th output $S_C(I)$.

As mentioned earlier, there are two types of attribution methods:

Occlusion- or Perturbation-Based

SHAP and LIME are explainability methods where we manipulate parts of the image to generate explanations. These are model-agnostic methods, and we have delved into the details of SHAP and LIME in the previous chapters.

Gradient-Based Methods

Gradient-based methods utilize the gradients that are obtained through backpropagation to create heatmaps. These heatmaps emphasize the distinguishing features in an image for each of the specific categories identified by Convolutional Neural Networks (CNNs).

Many of these methods calculate the gradient of the prediction (or classification score) with respect to the input features. The primary difference among the various gradient-based methods lies in how the gradient is computed. Both approaches share the characteristic that the explanation matches the size of the input image (or can be meaningfully projected onto it), assigning each pixel a value that indicates its relevance to the prediction or classification of the image.

Another useful way to categorize pixel attribution methods is by considering the baseline question:

- **Gradient-only methods** indicate whether a change in a pixel would alter the prediction. The examples include Vanilla Gradient and Grad-CAM. The gradient-only attribution method indicates that when the color values of a pixel increases, the predicted class probability would rise for a positive gradient or fall for a negative gradient. The larger the absolute value of the gradient, the stronger the effect of changing that pixel.
- **Path-attribution methods** compare the current image to a reference image, which can be a completely grey image or noise. The difference between the actual and baseline predictions is distributed among the pixels.

The baseline image can also be represented as a distribution of images. Model-specific gradient-based techniques, such as Deep Taylor and Integrated Gradients, are included in this category, as well as model-agnostic methods such as LIME and SHAP. In some path-attribution methods, completeness is a factor, meaning that the total relevance scores for all input features equal the difference between the image's prediction and that of a reference image, as seen in methods such as SHAP and Integrated Gradients. In path-attribution methods, the interpretations are always relative to a baseline. The pixels are considered in the difference of the classification scores between the actual image and the baseline image. The choice of the reference image or distribution has a considerable impact on the explanation, with the common assumption being to use a "neutral" image or distribution.

"Image Specific Class Saliency" or Vanilla Gradient are synonymous and involve calculating the gradient of the loss function for the class of interest with respect to the input pixels. This results in a map of the input features' size with values ranging from negative to positive. The concept of Vanilla Gradient was one of the first pixel attribution approaches introduced in 2013 and is straightforward if you are familiar with backpropagation.

Saliency Maps or Vanilla Gradient

In this section, we describe how a classification ConvNet can be queried about the spatial support of a particular class in a given image. Given an image I_0, a class c, and a classification ConvNet with the class score function $S_c(I)$, we would like to rank the pixels of I_0 based on their influence on the score $S_c(I_0)$.

We start with a motivational example. Consider the linear score model for the class c:

$$S_c(I) = w_c^T I + b_c,$$

Figure 7.2: *Linear Score for Class c*

Here, the image I is represented in the vectorized (one-dimensional) form, and w_c and b_c are, respectively, the weight vector and the bias of the model. In this case, it is easy to see that the magnitude of elements of w defines the importance of the corresponding pixels of I for the class c.

In the case of deep ConvNets, the class score $S_c(I)$ is a highly non-linear function of I, so the reasoning of the previous paragraph cannot be immediately applied. However, given an image I_0, we can approximate $S_c(I)$ with a linear function in the neighborhood of I_0 by computing the first-order Taylor expansion:

$$S_c(I) \approx w^T I + b,$$

Figure 7.3: *Approximate Linear Function for Class c*

Here, w is the derivative of S_c with respect to the image I at the point (image) I_0:

$$w = \left. \frac{\partial S_c}{\partial I} \right|_{I_0} .$$

Figure 7.4: *Derivate for Class c with the Pixel in Image*

A saliency map can be defined as the pixel effect representing saliency. A bright pixel indicates the salient aspects of the pixel and hence it can be implied that the brightness of a pixel is directly proportional to its saliency. Salient maps are most useful in finding the prominent or striking areas at every location of the visual field, guiding the selection of attended locations based on the spatial distribution of saliency.

dumbbell **cup** **dalmatian**

Figure 7.5: *Saliency Maps of Images (Source: Deep Inside Convolutional Networks: Visualising Image Classification Models and Saliency Maps (2014) Simonyan at al)*

Problems with Vanilla Gradient

There is a saturation issue in Vanilla Gradient. This happens when using ReLU, and if the activation falls below zero, it is capped at zero and then no longer changes, leading to saturation.

For instance, consider an input to the layer with two neurons having weights of -1 and -1, and a bias of 1. When this input passes through the ReLU layer, the activation will be the sum of neuron1 and neuron2 if their combined value is less than 1. If their sum exceeds 1, the activation will remain saturated at 1. Additionally, the gradient at this point will be zero, leading Vanilla Gradient to indicate that this neuron is not significant.

DeconvNet

The objective of a DeconvNet is to reverse a neural network. In this, the output label map is obtained by gradual deconvolution and unpooling. The operations performed are reversals of filtering, pooling, and activation layers. Vanilla Gradient is similar to the DeconvNet except for the ReLU layer. DeconvNet makes a different choice when backpropagating the gradient through ReLU.

The reconstruction of an input image is not trivial due to the max pooling layers. Hence, DeconNet proposes the unpooling operation by storing the pooled location. By using the DeconvNet, the input image can be reconstructed from the feature representation. This technique is useful to visualize activated features in a trained CNN.

Deconvnets are similar to convolutional networks but operate in the reverse order, reversing pooling, filters, and so on. They can be trained using an unsupervised approach. In this method, the CNN model is probed for explanations rather than being trained.

In the following figure, we can see how the deconv layers are attached to the corresponding CNN layers. This is done to reconstruct the activation on that specific layer. The image is then passed through the CNN model, and the network calculates the output. For a given class c, all activations except the one responsible for predicting the class are set to zero. In the next stage, the Deconvnet layers are traversed where the feature maps are provided as inputs to the corresponding layers.

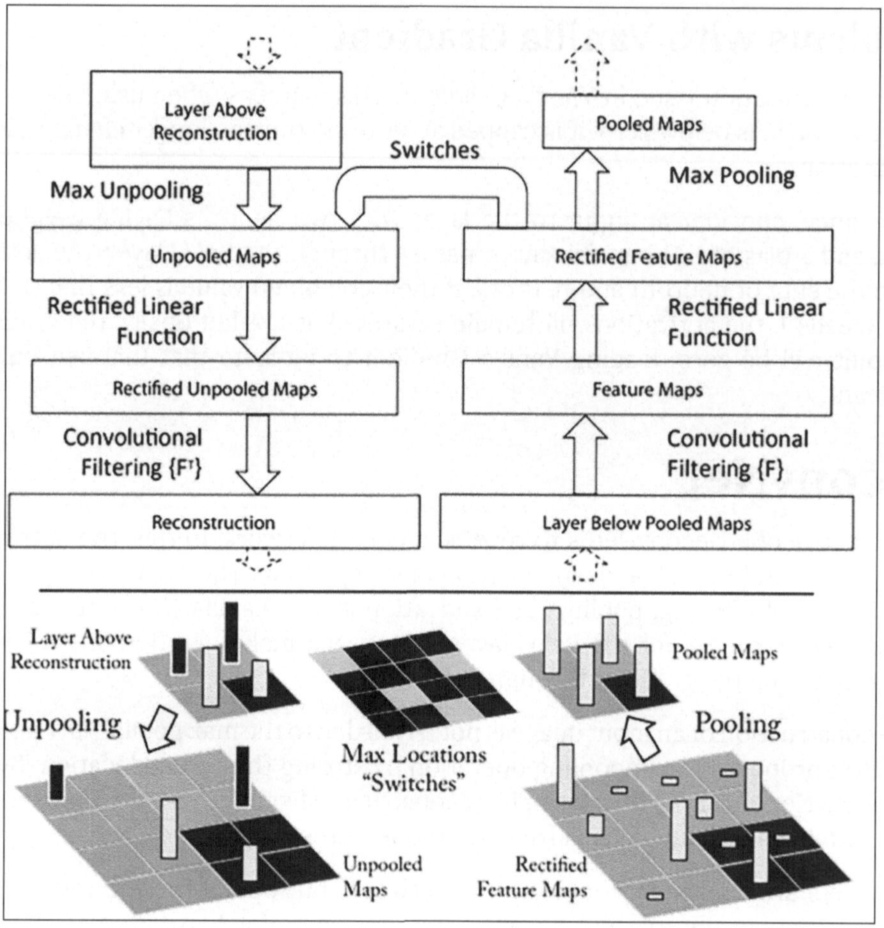

Figure 7.6: *Deconvnet Implementation (Source: Visualizing and Understanding Convolutional Networks (2013) Zeiler et al)*

Guided Backpropagation

This method computes attribution using guided backpropagation. Guided backpropagation computes the gradient of the target output with respect to the input, but the gradients of ReLU functions are overridden so that only non-negative gradients are back propagated.

When comparing the equations of Deconvnet and gradient with back propagation, we notice that all the equations are the same until they get to the ReLU layer. In Deconvnet, the regenerated signal (similar to gradient) is propagated forward only when it is positive; signals that help boost the activation are only forwarded. Alternatively, in regular gradient propagation, the gradient is forwarded through the ReLU only when the ReLU passes the inputs forward in the forward pass. This is the primary difference between the two methods.

Guided Backpropagation is a combination of vanilla backpropagation at ReLUs (leveraging which elements are positive in the preceding feature map) with DeconvNets (keeping only positive error signals). We are focused solely on the image features detected by the neuron. Therefore, when propagating the gradient, we set all negative gradients to zero. We disregard any pixel that "suppresses" (that has a negative value) a neuron along the path to our target neuron. A value greater than zero in the filter map indicates the importance of a pixel, which is then overlaid on the input image to highlight the pixels that contributed the most.

Axiomatic Approaches

So far, we have explored gradient-based methods for interpreting neural network decisions. However, this approach has a significant limitation. The presence of components such as ReLU and MaxPooling implies that the score function can sometimes be locally "flat" for certain input pixels, resulting in zero gradients. Consequently, gradient-based methods may incorrectly assign zero contribution to pixels that saturate the ReLU or MaxPool, which is counter-intuitive. To overcome this issue, we need:

- A formal definition of explainability or relevance that goes beyond simple gradients is needed. We should identify the properties we want this "relevance" to have. Ideally, relevance should behave like vanilla gradients in linear layers, as gradients effectively explain linear functions.
- Potential candidates that meet our criteria for "relevance" and are computationally efficient, preferably calculable in a single back pass.

Taylor Decomposition

A reference image X_0 is selected, which is referred to as the Baseline Image. The baseline image is utilized in explaining the pixels of the original image X. The class score of the baseline image should be as low as possible to provide robust results.

In Axiomatic relevance, the comparison of the input image to a baseline image is a common technique. This comparison is expected to highlight the important pixels in the image.

Some effective baseline images are:

- **Blurred input images**: Effective for colored images.
- **Blank or dark images**: Effective for grayscale or black-and-white images.

Layer-Wise Relevance Propagation (LRP)

Layer-Wise Relevance Propagation (LRP) redistributes the output relevance or the prediction score of a neural network back to its input features. This backward propagation of relevance helps identify the contribution of each input feature in the final prediction. The relevance scores are propagated through the neural network layers, ensuring that their sum equals the model's output relevance.

LRP is a propagation-based explanation method, meaning it requires access to the model's internals, such as topology, weights, and activations. This additional information allows LRP to simplify and more efficiently solve the explanation problem. Unlike model-agnostic methods that explain predictions in one step, LRP leverages the network structure to redistribute explanatory factors such as relevance. It goes layer by layer, starting from the model's output and moving towards the input variables, which could be pixels. Each redistribution addresses a simpler explanation problem between two adjacent layers. Thus, LRP explains by decomposition, iteratively redistributing the total evidence of the prediction f(x).

Originally developed for convolutional neural networks and bag-of-words models, LRP has been extended to various applications, making it a widely used XAI technique today. It has been applied in diverse domains such as computer vision, natural language processing, EEG analysis, and meteorology.

The main advantages of LRP include its high computational efficiency (comparable to a single backward pass), its theoretical foundation that ensures robustness and trustworthiness, and its long-standing popularity and successful application across various problems and domains. However, the method's flexibility is somewhat limited, as careful adaptation of redistribution rules may be necessary for novel model architectures.

Deep Learning Important Features (DeepLIFT)

Deep Learning Important FeaTures (DeepLIFT) is an explainability method in deep learning. It uses backpropagation to compare each neuron's activation to a "reference activation," then assigns a contribution score based on the differences between neurons.

In essence, DeepLIFT delves into the neural network's feature selection to identify neurons and weights that significantly impact the output. It separately considers positive and negative contributions and can uncover dependencies that other methods might miss. Scores are efficiently computed in a single backward pass.

DeepLIFT relies on a reference image alongside an input image for explaining the input pixels, similar to LRP. While LRP adheres to the conservation dictum, it lacks a clear method for distributing net relevance among pixels. DeepLIFT addresses this by enforcing an additional axiom for relevance propagation.

The two axioms followed by DeepLIFT are:

- **Conservation of Total Relevance:** The sum of relevance for all inputs must equal the difference between the input image's score and the baseline image's score at every neuron. This is the same as LRP's axiom.
- **Backpropagation/Chain Rule:** Relevance per input follows the chain rule, similar to gradients, allowing gradient-like relevance backpropagation. This makes DeepLIFT closer to vanilla gradient backpropagation.

Integrated Gradients

In the last section, we discussed how Taylor Decomposition assigns relevance to individual pixels by using the product of the gradient and the difference of pixel values (including those of the baseline image). Similarly, DeepLIFT assigns relevance through a product of the coarse gradient and the difference in pixel values between the input and baseline image. The RevealCancel rule is a concept used in the context of explainability methods such as DeepLIFT. It helps in understanding how the relevance of individual pixels is calculated.

RevealCancel Rule Explained:

1. **Relevance Calculation**: The rule states that the relevance of each pixel is determined by a discrete path integral of the gradient. This path integral is computed along the positive and negative parts of the difference in pixel values (Δx) between the input image and the baseline image.
2. **Positive and Negative Contributions:** The path integral is split into two parts:
    a. **Positive Part of** Δx: This part considers the positive differences in pixel values.
    b. **Negative Part of** Δx: This part considers the negative differences in pixel values.
3. **Discrete Path Integral**: By integrating the gradient along these paths, the rule effectively captures how changes in pixel values contribute to the overall prediction. This method ensures that both positive and negative contributions are accounted for, providing a more comprehensive explanation of the model's decision.

Why It Matters:

The RevealCancel rule is important because it allows for a more nuanced attribution of relevance to individual pixels. By considering both positive and negative changes, it provides a clearer picture of how each pixel influences the model's output. This approach helps in identifying the most critical features in the input image that drive the prediction.

This raises the question: How effective are path integrals over gradients of the score function in attributing features to input image pixels? The favored feature attribution methods currently break on two desirable axioms.

Gradients and Sensitivity in Attribution Methods

In linear models, the products of model coefficients and feature values are used for debugging the predictions. While in deep networks, the gradients of the output with respect to the input serve as a natural analog to model coefficients. Thus, the product of the gradient and feature values is a logical starting point for an attribution method. However, gradients fail to satisfy the sensitivity property, which is crucial for all attribution methods. Gradients have a sense of the local information about the model function behavior, but this linear interpretation is incomplete. After a model is trained and is predicting with higher confidence, minor modifications to the inputs would not make much difference. For instance, consider an image of a cockatoo. If your model is robust with a very high prediction score around 90%, changing a few pixels and even pixels portraying the cockatoo itself will likely not change the prediction score for that class. After the model is trained on how the value of a specific pixel affects the model's prediction class, the gradient of that model prediction for the specific pixel will become smaller and smaller, eventually becoming zero. We can say that the gradient for the model's prediction with respect to that pixel has saturated.

Axiom 1: Sensitivity: An attribution method satisfies Sensitivity if, for any input and baseline that differ in one feature and have different predictions, the differing feature receives a non-zero attribution.

Gradients Violate Sensitivity: Consider a simple example: a one-variable, one-ReLU network, $f(x) = 1 - ReLU(1-x)$. If the baseline is $x = 0$ and the input is $x = 2$, the function changes from 0 to 1. However, because f becomes flat at $x = 1$, the gradient method assigns an attribution of 0 to x. This occurs because the prediction function may flatten at the input, resulting in a zero gradient despite a different function value at the input compared to the baseline. Practically, this lack of sensitivity causes gradients to focus on irrelevant features.

Other Backpropagation-Based Approaches: Another group of methods involves back propagating the final prediction score through each network layer down to the individual features. These methods include DeepLIFT, Layer-wise Relevance Propagation (LRP), Deconvolutional Networks (DeConvNets), and Guided Backpropagation. They differ in their specific backpropagation logic for various activation functions. However, DeConvNets and Guided Backpropagation violate Sensitivity because they only backpropagate through a ReLU node if the ReLU is activated at the input. This makes them similar to gradients, assigning zero attribution to features with zero gradient at the input, even if there is a non-zero gradient at the baseline.

Addressing Sensitivity with DeepLIFT and LRP: Methods such as DeepLIFT and LRP address the Sensitivity issue by using a baseline and computing discrete gradients at the input. Although these methods differ in how they compute the discrete gradient, the idea is that a large, discrete step avoids flat regions, thus maintaining Sensitivity. However, these methods may violate other requirements for attribution methods.

Ensuring Sensitivity: LRP and DeepLIFT maintain Sensitivity due to the Conservation of Total Relevance. In contrast, gradient-based methods do not ensure the Sensitivity Axiom because of saturation at ReLU or MaxPool stages, where the score function becomes locally "flat" for some input features. Effectively passing relevance or attribution through saturated activations is a common challenge in feature attribution research.

Axiom 2: Implementation Invariance

Two models are considered functionally equivalent if they produce identical attributions to input features, even if their implementations differ. Attribution methods should satisfy Implementation Invariance, meaning the attributions must be the same for two functionally equivalent networks. This concept is based on the idea that attribution assigns blame (or credit) for the output to the input features, independent of implementation details.

Why DeepLIFT and LRP Break Implementation Invariance:

- **Gradients and Implementation Invariance**: Gradients are inherently invariant to implementation. The chain rule for gradients, $\partial f/\partial g = \partial f/\partial h \cdot \partial h/\partial g$, illustrates this. Here, g and f represent the input and output of a system, while h is an implementation detail. The gradient of the output f with respect to the input g, that is, $\partial f/\partial g$, can be computed directly, ignoring h, or by using the chain rule through h. It is the basis of backpropagation.
- **Discrete Gradients in LRP and DeepLIFT:** Methods such as LRP and DeepLIFT replace gradients with discrete gradients and use a modified form of backpropagation to combine these discrete gradients into attributions. However, the chain rule does not generally apply to discrete gradients.

  Formally, $\frac{f(x1)-f(x0)}{g(x1)-g(x0)} \neq \frac{f(x1)-f(x0)}{h(x1)-h(x0)} \cdot \frac{h(x1)-h(x0)}{g(x1)-g(x0)}$.

  As a result, these methods fail to satisfy Implementation Invariance.

Implications of Failing Implementation Invariance:

If an attribution method does not satisfy Implementation Invariance, the attributions may be influenced by irrelevant aspects of the models. For example, if a network has more degrees of freedom than necessary to represent a function, there could be multiple parameter sets that yield the same function. The training process might converge to different parameter sets based on initialization or other factors, but the underlying function remains unchanged. It is undesirable for attributions to vary due to such reasons.

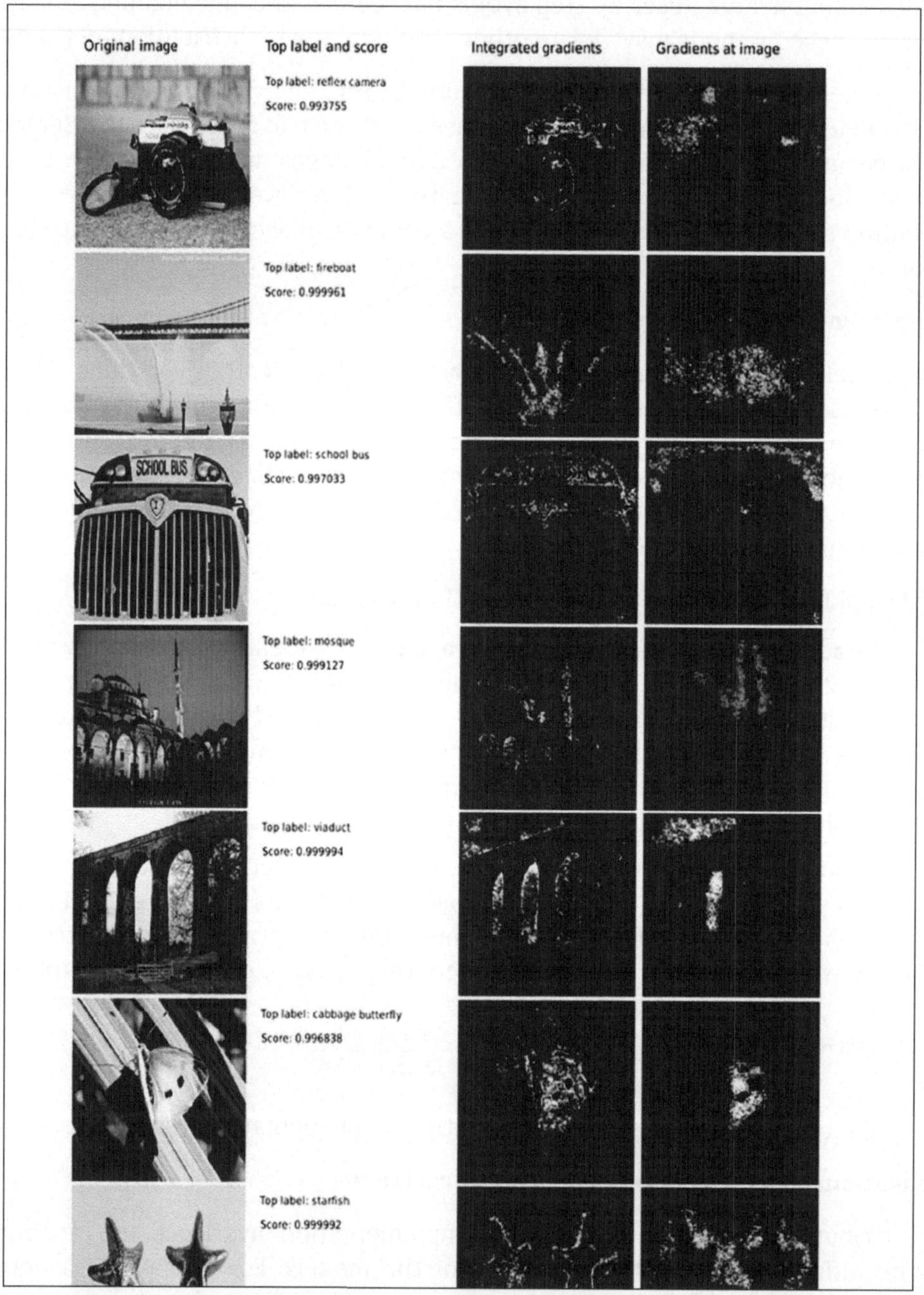

Figure 7.7: *Comparing Integrated Gradients with Gradients at the Image (Source: Axiomatic Attribution for Deep Networks (2017) Sundararajan et al)*

Integrated Gradients is a local attribution method. It provides an explanation for a model's prediction for a single example image. It also produces an easily interpretable saliency mask highlighting the pixels or areas in the image contributing primarily to the model's prediction.

Integrated Gradients for feature attribution:

$$\text{IntegratedGrads}_i(x) ::= (x_i - x_i') \times \int_{\alpha=0}^{1} \frac{\partial F(x' + \alpha \times (x - x'))}{\partial x_i} \, d\alpha$$

Figure 7.8: *Integrated Gradients (Source: https://arxiv.org/pdf/1703.01365.pdf)*

This technique is a combination of the Implementation Invariance of Gradients along with the Sensitivity of techniques such as LRP or DeepLift.

We have a function $F : R^n \rightarrow [0, 1]$ representing a deep network. Let $x \in R^n$ be the input at hand, and $x \in R^n$ be the baseline input. The baseline could be a black image in image networks, while for text models, it could be a zero embedding vector.

We take the straight line path in R^n from the baseline x' to the input x, computing the gradients at all points along the path. Integrated gradients are derived by accumulating these gradients. Integrated gradients are essentially the path integral of the gradients along the straight line path from the baseline x' to the input x.

The integrated gradient along the ith dimension for an input x and baseline x' is defined as follows. Here, (∂F (x))/∂xi is the gradient of F(x) along the ith dimension.

Axiom: Completeness: The axiom of completeness can be attributed to Integrated Gradients given that the attributions add up to the difference between the output of F at the input x and the baseline x'. This is an important check to ensure that the attribution method is understandable in its accounting, especially when the network's score is utilized in a numeric sense, and not just for picking the top label. For example, a model estimating insurance premiums from the credit features of individuals.

- **Sensitivity**: According to the Fundamental Theorem of Calculus, Integrated Gradients sum up to the difference in feature scores, similar to LRP and DeepLIFT. Therefore, they adhere to sensitivity just like LRP and DeepLIFT.
- **Implementation Invariance**: Since Integrated Gradients are entirely defined in terms of gradients, they follow implementation invariance.

By default, the integral is a straight line from the baseline to the input. The choice of path does not affect the adherence to the aforementioned axioms. The straight line path is also symmetric with respect to the baseline and the input image.

Positives of Integrated Gradients:

- Integrated Gradients were among the first successful and widely used methods for model explainability.

- They can be applied to any differentiable model across various data types, including images, text, and tabular data.
- The implementation is straightforward and intuitive, making it accessible even to novice practitioners. Additionally, many XAI libraries offer easy-to-use implementations.
- Integrated Gradients are particularly effective for low-contrast images or those taken in non-natural environments, such as X-rays.

Challenges of Integrated Gradients:

- Integrated Gradient relies on the differentiability of the model and also requires access to the gradients. It is easily applicable to tree-based models.
- There is a sensitivity on the hyperparameters or choice of baseline, so the results can be sensitive.

Improvements on Integrated Gradients

Integrated Gradients is one of the most widely used and well-known gradient-based attribution techniques in explaining deep networks. Though for some inputs, this method can produce spurious or noisy pixel attributions that are not related to the model's predicted class. This issue arises partly due to the accumulation of noise from regions with correlated, high-magnitude gradients for irrelevant pixels along the straight line path used in computing Integrated Gradients. It is also closely related to the choice of baseline used in the computation.

To address these issues, various techniques have been introduced. Blur Integrated Gradients and Guided Integrated Gradients are two improvements on the classic Integrated Gradients, which users can consider.

Testing with Concept Activation Vectors (TCAV)

Testing with Concept Activation Vectors (TCAV) is a concept-based neural network approach designed to measure how strongly a concept, such as color, influences classification. It relies on Concept Activation Vectors (CAVs), which describe how neural activations relate to the presence or absence of a user-defined concept.

Steps to Calculate CAVs:

1. **Data Collection:** Gather two datasets–one with images representing the concept and another with images where the concept is absent.

2. **Training a Model**: Train a logistic regression model on this combined dataset to classify whether the concept is present in an image. The activations from a specific layer of the neural network serve as features for this model.

3. **CAVs as Coefficients**: The coefficients of the logistic regression model are the CAVs.

Example: To determine how much the concept "stripes" contributes to classifying an image as "zebra," you would need a dataset of images with stripes and another dataset without stripes. The CAVs derived from this setup help to calculate the conceptual sensitivity, which is the product of the CAV and the derivative of the classification with respect to the specified neural network layer and class. This sensitivity indicates how strongly the concept influences the desired class.

Local versus Global Explanation:

- **Local Explanation**: CAVs provide a local explanation for a single classification.
- **Global Explanation**: TCAV aggregates CAVs across the dataset to offer a global explanation, answering how much a concept contributes overall to a given classification.

The TCAV process primarily involves the following series of steps:

1. **Calculate CAVs**: Compute CAVs for the entire dataset for the selected class, concept, and level.
2. **Ratio of Positive Sensitivity**: Determine the ratio of images with positive conceptual sensitivity, indicating how many images the concept contributed to the class prediction.
3. **Statistical Testing**: Repeat this process with different "negative" samples and apply a two-tailed Student t-test to check if the conceptual sensitivity is significantly different from zero. This statistical test indicates the "T" in TCAV.

By following these steps, TCAV provides a robust method to quantify the influence of specific concepts on neural network classifications.

Explanations using pytorch and Captum

In this example, we use the `Captum` library to extract multiple explanations using various methods discussed in the previous sections.

1. Install the libraries.

   ```
   pip install torch torchvision pillow captum
   ```

2. Import the required modules.

   ```
   import torch
   import torch.nn.functional as F
   from PIL import Image
   import os
   import json
   ```

```
import numpy as np
from matplotlib.colors import LinearSegmentedColormap
import torchvision
from torchvision import models
from torchvision import transforms

from captum.attr import IntegratedGradients
from captum.attr import GradientShap
from captum.attr import LRP
from captum.attr import Occlusion
from captum.attr import NoiseTunnel
from captum.attr import visualization as viz
from captum.attr._utils.lrp_rules import EpsilonRule, GammaRule,
Alpha1_Beta0_Rule
```

3. Load a foundational model.

```
model = models.resnet18(pretrained=True)
model = model.eval()
```

4. Transform the image and normalizing functions.

```
transform = transforms.Compose([
 transforms.Resize(256),
 transforms.CenterCrop(224),
 transforms.ToTensor()
])
transform_normalize = transforms.Normalize(
     mean=[0.485, 0.456, 0.406],
     std=[0.229, 0.224, 0.225]
 )
img = Image.open('swan-3299528_1280.jpg')
transformed_img = transform(img)
input = transform_normalize(transformed_img)
input = input.unsqueeze(0)
```

5. Predict the class for the image using the model.

```
output = model(input)
output = F.softmax(output, dim=1)
prediction_score, pred_label_idx = torch.topk(output, 1)

pred_label_idx.squeeze_()
predicted_label = idx_to_labels[str(pred_label_idx.item())][1]
print('Predicted:', predicted_label, '(', prediction_score.
squeeze().item(), ')')
```

```
Predicted: goose ( 0.4569336771965027 )
```

Figure 7.9: *Prediction Score for Model*

6. Initialize the Integrated Gradients.

```
print('Predicted:', predicted_label, '(', prediction_score.
squeeze().item(), ')')
integrated_gradients = IntegratedGradients(model)
attributions_ig = integrated_gradients.attribute(input, tar-
get=pred_label_idx, n_steps=200)
```

7. Visualize the image and the corresponding attributions.

```
default_cmap = LinearSegmentedColormap.from_list('custom blue',
                                                  [(0, '#ffffff'),
                                                   (0.25,
'#000000'),
                                                   (1,
'#000000')], N=256)

_ = viz.visualize_image_attr(np.transpose(attributions_
ig.squeeze().cpu().detach().numpy(), (1,2,0)),
             np.transpose(transformed_img.squeeze().cpu().de-
tach().numpy(), (1,2,0)),
             method='heat_map',
                           cmap=default_cmap,
                           show_colorbar=True,
                           sign='positive',
                           outlier_perc=1)
```

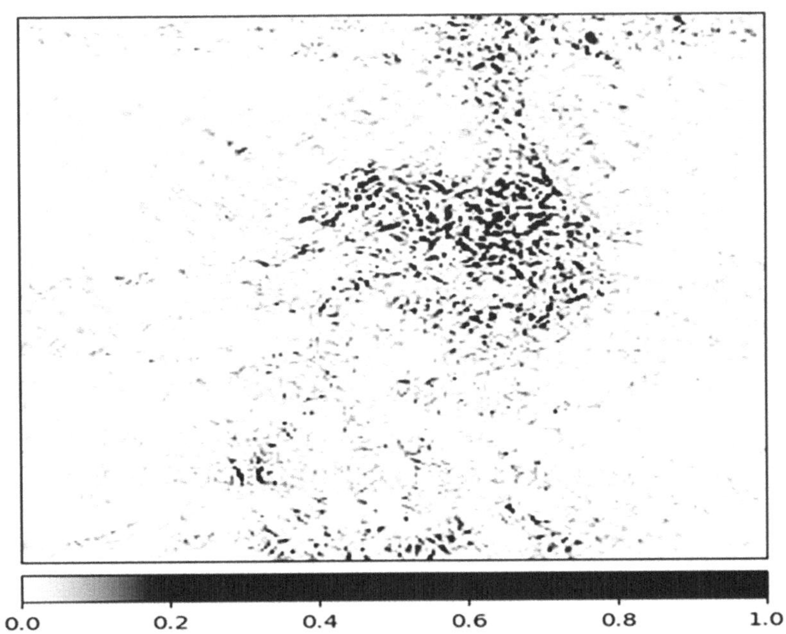

***Figure 7.10**: Integrated Gradients of Image*

8. Explanations with a **GradientShap**.

```
torch.manual_seed(0)
np.random.seed(0)
gradient_shap = GradientShap(model)
# Defining baseline distribution of images
rand_img_dist = torch.cat([input * 0, input * 1])

attributions_gs = gradient_shap.attribute(input,
                                          n_samples=50,
                                          stdevs=0.0001,
                                          baselines=rand_img_dist,
                                          target=pred_label_idx)
_ = viz.visualize_image_attr_multiple(np.transpose(attributions_
gs.squeeze().cpu().detach().numpy(), (1,2,0)),
                                      np.transpose(transformed_
img.squeeze().cpu().detach().numpy(), (1,2,0)),
                                      ["original_image", "heat_
map"],
                                      ["all", "absolute_value"],
                                      cmap=default_cmap,
                                      show_colorbar=True)
```

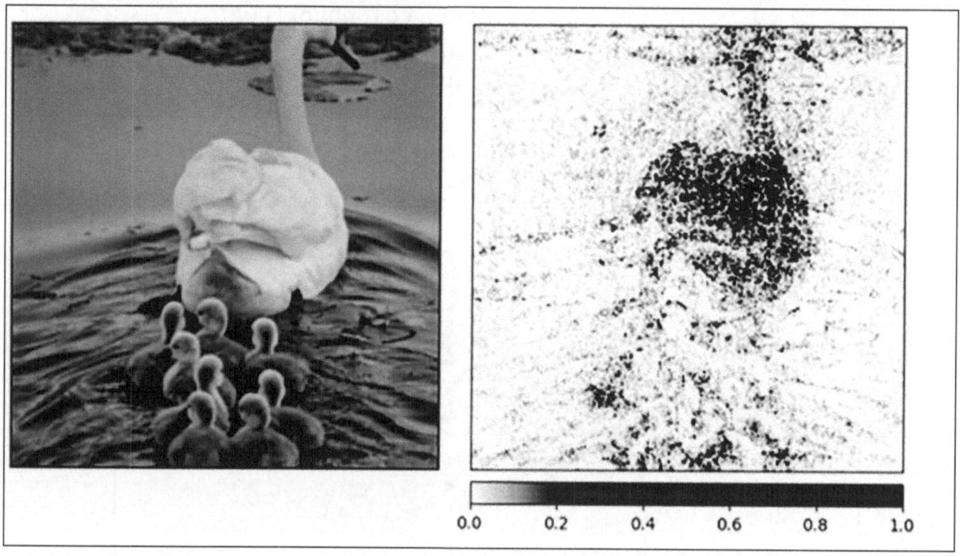

Figure 7.11: *Original Image and GradientShap Explanation*

Conclusion

In the previous chapters, we focused on the various techniques for Interpretability. The technique selection depends on the model used, and some Interpretability methods worked for tabular data and other media types. The biggest consideration factor was the complexity of neural networks. Hence, the techniques we discussed in this chapter, such as the gradient-based methods or Integrated Gradients, were suited for neural networks. In some of these techniques, access to the model internals was also required. This may not always be possible, and to address this challenge, we will look at additional techniques for neural networks.

In the next chapter, we will expand into methods such as Class Activation Maps and the multiple variations of the CAM methods.

References

1. The Building Blocks of Interpretability: https://distill.pub/2018/building-blocks/
2. Axiomatic Attribution for Deep Networks (2017) Sundararajan et al:https://arxiv.org/pdf/1703.01365
3. Explainability and Auditability in ML: Definitions, Techniques, and Tools: https://neptune.ai/blog/explainability-auditability-ml-definitions-techniques-tools
4. A Survey Of Methods For Explaining Black Box Models (2018) Guidotti et al: https://arxiv.org/pdf/1802.01933
5. Learning Deep Features for Discriminative Localization (2015) Zhou et al: https://arxiv.org/pdf/1512.04150
6. Deep Inside Convolutional Networks: Visualising Image Classification Models and Saliency Maps (2014) Simonyan at al https://arxiv.org/pdf/1312.6034
7. Interpretable Machine Learning (2019) Christoph Molnar https://christophm.github.io/interpretable-ml-book
8. A Survey of Explainable AI in Deep Visual Modeling: Methods and Metrics (2023) Naveed Akhtar: https://arxiv.org/pdf/2301.13445
9. Layer-wise Relevance Propagation for Neural Networks with Local Renormalization Layers (2016) Binder et al https://arxiv.org/pdf/1604.00825
10. Explainable AI Methods - A Brief Overview (2022) Holzinger et al https://link.springer.com/chapter/10.1007/978-3-031-04083-2_2
11. Gradient based Feature Attribution in Explainable AI: A Technical Review (2024) wang et al https://arxiv.org/pdf/2403.10415
12. Visualizing and Understanding Convolutional Networks (2013) Zeiler et al https://arxiv.org/pdf/1311.2901

CHAPTER 8
Explainable Neural Networks

Introduction

In the previous chapter, we explored multiple techniques for explainability in Neural Networks. We will look at additional techniques that aid in neural network explainability.

This chapter extends on the explainability techniques in Neural Networks. In particular, we will focus on class activation maps as a technique to enhance explainability. We will also look at the variations of class activation maps to improve explainability.

Structure

In this chapter, will cover the following topics:

- Class Activation Maps (CAM)
- CAM Explanations Using pytorch and torchcam
- Improvements in the Basic CAM
- Neural Network Explainability Approaches
- Feature Ablation

Class Activation Maps (CAM)

The idea behind Class Activation Maps is to identify the regions within an image that a Convolutional Neural Network (CNN) considers most relevant for recognizing a specific class. This approach is motivated by the unique spatial information within each activation map. The convolutional layers closer to the end, that is, near the network's point of classification, provide more effective high-level activations for visual localization to explain the final prediction.

Class activation maps, also known as CAMs, can help explain the predictions of a

ConvNet. These maps are class-discriminative saliency maps. Saliency maps highlight the most important parts of an image for a particular class, while class-discriminative saliency maps help in differentiation between classes. Generally, a ConvNet consists of a series of convolutional layers, each with a set of filters, followed by fully connected layers.

A method is developed to project the weights of the CNN's output layer back onto the feature maps generated by the convolutional layers. This projection effectively creates a heatmap, highlighting the areas within the image that significantly influence the network's decision-making process.

The original CAM method creates class-discriminative visualization maps by linear combination of activation maps from the final convolutional layer with importance coefficients, which is represented by the fully connected weights associated with the target class. Activation maps highlight the salient regions of an image for a particular prediction. CAM uses a global average pooling (GAP) layer after the last convolutional layer. Let us understand how it works.

Let us look at the process for computing the Class Activation Map.

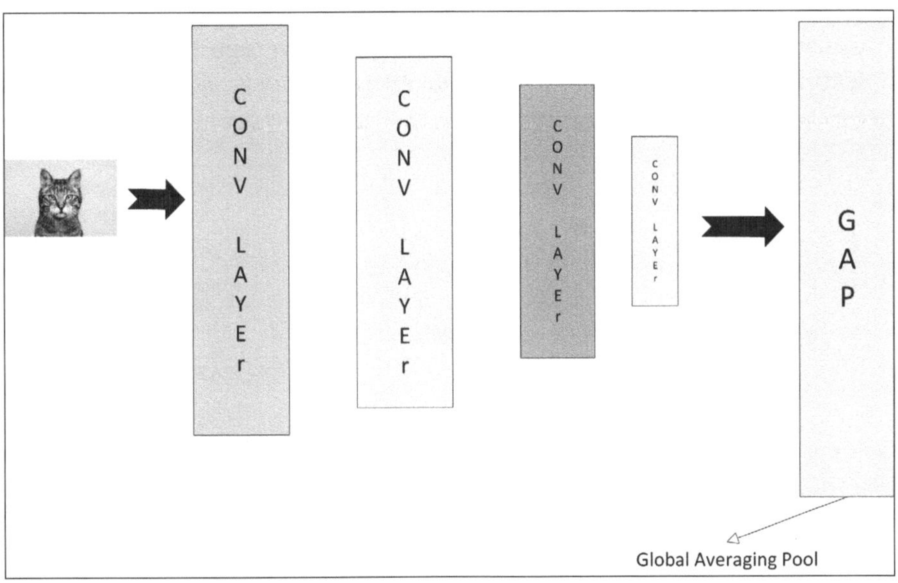

Figure 8.1: *CAM Pipeline for GAP Computation*

In the *Figure* 8.1, we have a high level representation of a CNN architecture. It is a pictorial representation and only shows the layers pertinent to understanding CAM.

In the last convolutional layer, when there are "n" filters, then there are "n" feature maps. The weighted combination of all the "n" feature maps can be considered as the activation map for a particular class. We will look at the steps that lead to the learning of the weights for CAM.

1. In the last convolutional layer, global average pooling is applied to each of the feature maps. Averaging all pixel values in a feature map is its global average. The term global in global average pooling indicates that the average is calculated on all the pixels in the feature map.

   In the following figure, we can see how global average pooling works:

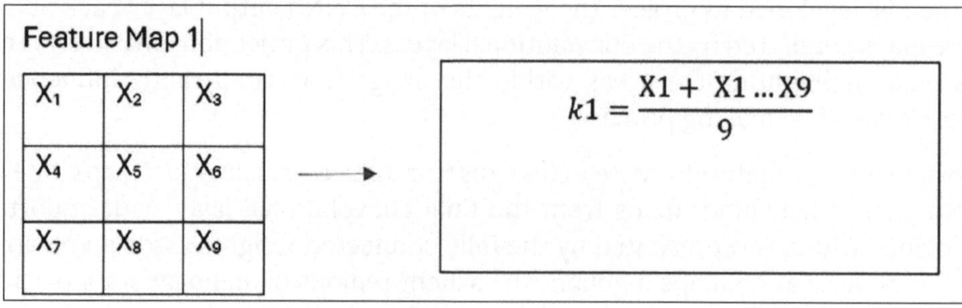

Figure 8.2: *Feature Map Calculation*

   The global average computation for each of the feature maps gives "n" scalar values.

   Consider K1, K2..., Kn as the "n" scalar global average values for each of the feature maps. Let us call them Global Average Pool (GAP) outputs.

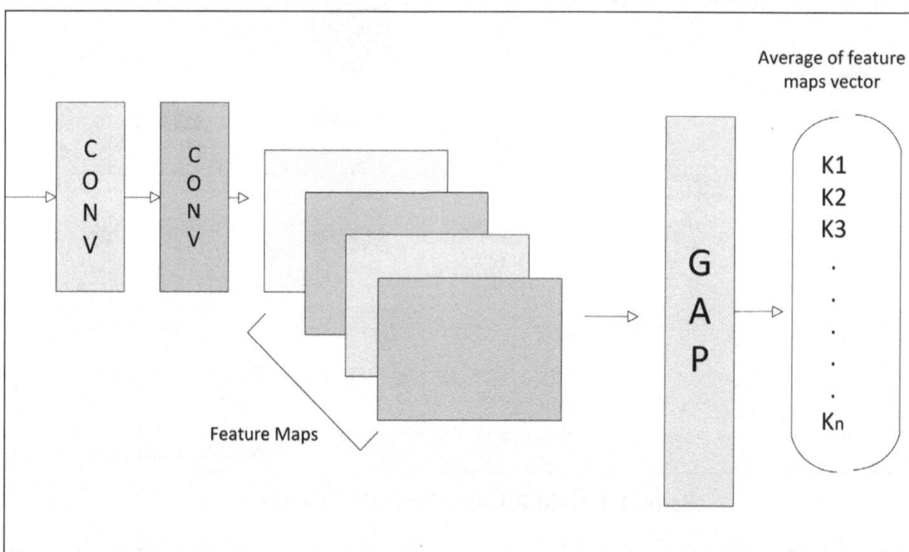

Figure 8.3: *CAM Computation Process; Averaged Feature Maps*

2. After we have "n" global average pool outputs, we have to determine a linear model from the GAP outputs for each class label. Considering we have "N" output classes, we have to learn the weights for each of the classes using a linear modeling technique. We represent the weights as w1, w2, w3..., wn.

Hence, we have to learn "N" linear models in total.

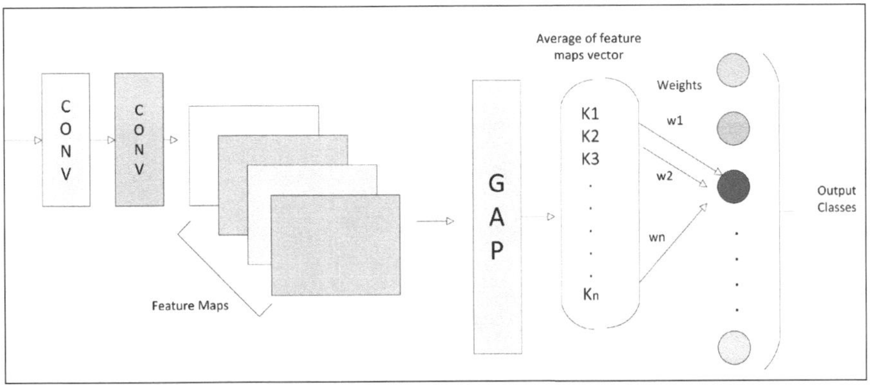

Figure 8.4: *CAM Pipeline for GAP Computation; Weights Computation*

The weights are derived for each of the "n" classes. Using the weights learned, we can get the class activation maps from the learned weights and averaged feature maps. It is important to note that the class activation maps are the weighted combination of the same set of feature maps, with the main difference being the weight value in itself for every class.

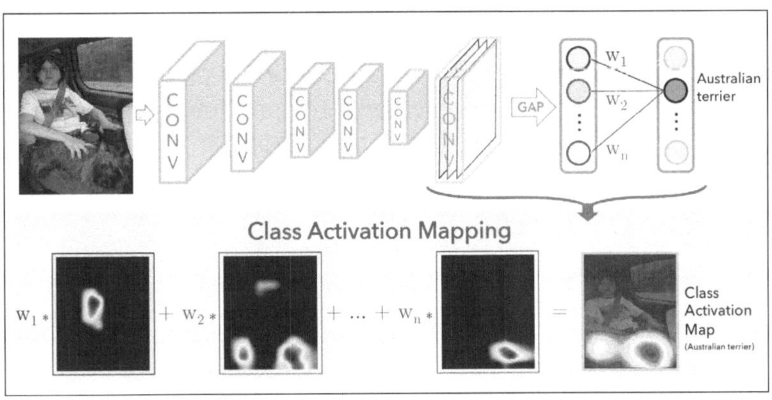

Figure 8.5: CAM Computation; *End-to- End Visual (Source: Learning Deep Features for Discriminative Localization* (2015) *Zhou et al)*

The class score for an output class c can be calculated. The mathematical formulation for the class activation map is as follows:

$$L^{(c)}_{CAM}(x, y) = ReLU\Big(\sum_k w_k^{(c)} A_k(x, y)\Big)$$

Figure 8.6: CAM *Computation*

Consider that "A" denotes the output feature map in the last convolution layer. The set of activation maps is then denoted as A1, A2, A3..., Ak.

Also, w_k^c indicates the weight for class (c) in the fully connected layer that works as a classifier. The computation of CAM requires two elements in the neural network. It relies on the fully connected layer that works as a classifier and the Global Average Pooling layer.

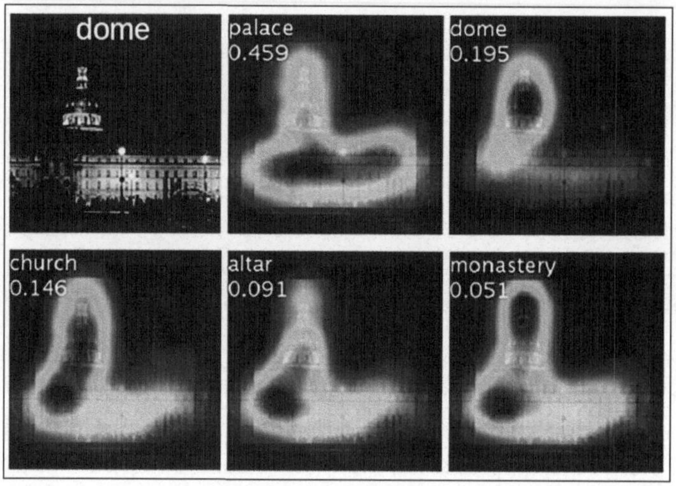

Figure 8.7: *Heatmaps of Each Class (Source: Learning Deep Features for Discriminative Localization (2015) Zhou et al)*

As evident in the preceding figure, the highlighted portion changes with each predicted class. While the ground truth is the dome, the other predicted classes are also focusing on the highlighted portions recovered from the CAMs.

Advantages of CAM

We will go through the advantages of CAM in this section.

- A backward pass is not required through the entire network for computing CAM values. A backward pass would be more expensive than learning the N linear models with weights.
- CAM benefits from the fact that convolution layers are inherently localized. As a result, the activation maps are generated without requiring any positional understanding of the target location in the image.

Limitations of CAM

The limitations of CAM are as follows:

- The learning of the N linear models with weights for each class involves some computation and increases with the number of classes. Each of the weights w1, w2, w3..., wn have to be learned. Training a CNN is computationally intensive. Learning the weights for each of the N classes adds to the computation cost of the model. This is exacerbated as the number of filters (n) and number of classes (N) increases.

- The global average pooling (GAP) is added after the last convolutional layer. This makes the architecture requirement very stringent. The outputs of the GAP layer are scalars, which are the global averages of the prior convolution layer's feature maps. This works well for image classification. However, the need for a GAP layer after the convolutional layer means that it is best suited for some tasks but cannot be used for computer vision tasks such as visual question answering (VQA).

CAM Explanations Using `pytorch` and `torchcam`

The **`torchcam`** library implements the CAM method for pytorch. We will use this library to extract a CAM from the provided image.

1. Install the libraries.

```
!pip install torchvision matplotlib
!pip install torchcam
```

2. Load an image for prediction.

```
# Download an image
#!wget https://www.woopets.fr/assets/races/000/066/big-portrait/
border-collie.jpg
# Set this to your image path if you wish to run it on your own
data
img_path = "border-collie.jpg"
```

3. Load the pretrained resnet18 model.

```
%matplotlib inline

# All imports
import matplotlib.pyplot as plt
import torch
from torch.nn.functional import softmax, interpolate
from torchvision.io.image import read_image
from torchvision.models import resnet18
from torchvision.transforms.functional import normalize,
resize, to_pil_image

from torchcam.methods import CAM
from torchcam.utils import overlay_mask
```

```
model = resnet18(pretrained=True).eval()
cam = CAM(model, 'layer4', 'fc')


# Get your input
img = read_image(img_path)
# Preprocess it for your chosen model
input_tensor = normalize(resize(img, (224, 224)) / 255., [0.485,
0.456, 0.406], [0.229, 0.224, 0.225])

# Preprocess your data and feed it to the model
#out = model(input_tensor.unsqueeze(0))
# Retrieve the CAM by passing the class index and the model out-
put
#cams = cam_extractor(out.squeeze(0).argmax().item(), out)

with torch.no_grad():
    out = model(input_tensor.unsqueeze(0))
    # Assuming you want the CAM for the class with the highest
score
    class_idx = out.argmax().item()
    activation_map = cam(class_idx)
```

4. Display the Class Activation Map.

```
import matplotlib.pyplot as plt
# Visualize the raw CAM
plt.imshow(activation_map[0].squeeze(0).numpy()); plt.axis('off');
plt.tight_layout(); plt.show()
```

Figure 8.8: *Class Activation Map Without Overlay*

5. Overlay the activation map on the original image.

```
import matplotlib.pyplot as plt
from torchcam.utils import overlay_mask

# Resize the CAM and overlay it
result = overlay_mask(to_pil_image(img), to_pil_image(activation_
map[0].squeeze(0), mode='F'), alpha=0.5)
# Display it
plt.imshow(result); plt.axis('off'); plt.tight_layout(); plt.
show()
```

Figure 8.9: *Class Activation With Overlay*

Improvements in the Basic CAM

Gradient-based techniques utilize gradients that are calculated during backpropagation to create heatmaps. These heatmaps emphasize the discriminative areas within an image for specific categories identified by Convolutional Neural Networks (CNNs). In the previous section, we looked at CAM using the GAP layers. The GAP layers are only available in certain neural networks. Thus, the original CAM method is augmented with

Grad-CAM, enabling the use of gradients from any target class flowing into the final convolutional layer. This makes it suitable for a wider variety of CNN architectures.

Grad-CAM

Grad-CAM, or Gradient-weighted Class Activation Map, relies on the gradients of neural networks. Similar to other techniques, Grad-CAM assigns a relevance score to each neuron for the decision of interest. This decision can be the class prediction found in the output layer, or it can also be any other layer in the neural network. Grad-CAM backpropagates this information to the last convolutional layer. It can be used with various CNNs, including those with fully connected layers, multi-task outputs, captioning, and reinforcement learning.

A gradient-based weighting to class activation maps is applied in this method. The gradients associated with any target concept or class computed at the last convolutional layer are used to create a coarse localization map. This map reveals regions of the image relevant to the network's prediction.

In Grad-CAM, we can get visual explanations for CNN and the predictions. Traditional gradient-based methods perform expensive backpropagation all the way back to the input image. In this method, the gradient backpropagates only to the last convolutional layer, resulting in a coarse localization map highlighting significant regions of the image.

We will take a closer look at the working of Grad-CAM and the steps used in computation. The aim of Grad-CAM is to determine the parts of the image that are the prime focus area in a convolutional layer for a specific classification. The very first convolutional layer of a CNN takes images as input and produces feature maps that encode learned features. Higher-level convolutional layers perform similarly, using the feature maps from previous layers as input. Grad-CAM examines which regions are activated in the feature maps of the last convolutional layers; that is the method employed by CNN to make the decisions.

To visualize how the convolutional neural network has made a certain classification from the feature maps, one approach is to simply display the raw values of each feature map, average them, and overlay this on the image. However, this is not useful since the feature maps contain information for all classes, while we are interested in a specific class.

Consider that there are (k) feature maps in the last convolutional layer, denoted as A1, A2 ..., Ak. Grad-CAM determines the importance of each of the (k) feature maps for the class (c) of interest by weighting each pixel of each feature map with the gradient. This is done before averaging over the feature maps. This process generates a heatmap that highlights regions positively or negatively based on the impact it has on the class of interest. The heatmap is then processed through the ReLU function, which sets all negative values to zero, as we are only interested in parts contributing to the selected class (c) and not others. Although the term "pixel" might be misleading since the feature map is smaller than the image due to pooling units, it is mapped back to the original image. Finally, the Grad-CAM map is scaled into the interval [0,1] for visualization and overlaid on the original image.

The localization map is defined as follows:

$$L^{c}_{Grad-CAM} \in \mathbb{R}^{u \times v} = \underbrace{ReLU}_{\text{Pick positive values}} \left(\sum_{k} \alpha^{c}_{k} A^{k} \right)$$

Figure 8.10: *Localization Map for Class*

Where u is the width and v is the height of the explanation. C is our class of interest. There are (k) feature maps in the last convolutional layer, denoted as A1, A2 ..., Ak.

1. The input image traverses through the CNN in the forward pass.
2. The score for class of interest is derived from the activation of the neuron before the SoftMax layer.
3. All other class activations are set to zero.
4. The gradient for the class of interest is backpropagated until the last convolutional layer before the fully connected layers: $\frac{\delta y^{c}}{\delta A^{k}}$
5. Each feature map pixel is weighted by the gradient for the class. The indices i and j represent the width and height of the feature map.

$$\alpha^{c}_{k} = \overbrace{\frac{1}{Z} \sum_{i} \sum_{j}}^{\text{global average pooling}} \underbrace{\frac{\delta y^{c}}{\delta A^{k}_{ij}}}_{\text{gradients via backprop}}$$

Figure 8.11: *Global Average Pooling of Gradients*

6. The gradients are globally pooled using the previously mentioned method.
7. An average of the feature maps is calculated, with the per-pixel weighted values determined by the gradient.
8. ReLU is then applied on the feature maps to remove the negative values.
9. This scales the values between 0 and 1, which improves the visualization.
10. The image is upscaled and overlaid on the original image.

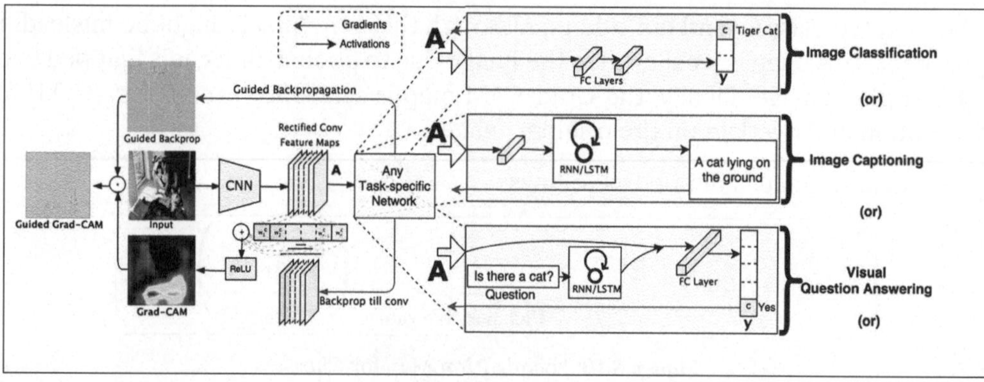

***Figure 8.12**: Grad-CAM computation Pipeline (Source: Grad-CAM: Visual Explanations from Deep Networks via Gradient-based Localization (2019))*

In the preceding figure, we have an image and a class of interest (tiger cat) or any other type of differentiable output as input. The image is forward propagated through the CNN architecture and then through task-specific computations to get a raw score for the category. The gradients of the desired class (tiger cat) are set to 1 while all the remaining classes are set to zero. This information is backpropagated into the rectified convolutional feature maps of interest, which are combined to compute the coarse Grad-CAM localization in the blue heatmap. This heatmap portrays where the model has to look to make this particular class decision. An extension on the above leads to another method called Guided Grad-CAM. The pointwise multiplication of the heatmap with the guided backpropagation leads to the Guided Grad-CAM visualizations, which are both high-resolution and concept-specific.

Advantages of Grad-CAM:

- The gradients of the output score with respect to the feature maps are used by Grad-CAM as the weights of the feature maps. Hence, we do not need to retrain N models to get the weights for explaining the ConvNets prediction as is done in CAM.
- The gradients of task-specific output with respect to the feature maps also mean that we can use Grad-CAM for all computer vision tasks, such as visual question answering and image captioning.

Limitations of Grad-CAM:

In a single image, if there are multiple instances of the target class, the spatial footprint for each of the instances is small. The smaller spatial footprint makes it difficult for Grad-CAM to give confident explanations.

Guided Grad-CAM

Guided Grad-CAM is an enhanced version of Grad-CAM. As its name suggests, it combines guided backpropagation with Grad-CAM. In our previous description of the

Grad-CAM process, we saw that there is a heatmap that portrays where the model has to look to make a particular class decision. Multiplying the heatmap with the guided backpropagation gives us Guided Grad-CAM.

Grad-CAM++

Another variant of Grad-CAM is Grad-CAM++, which improves the saliency maps for images that have multiple instances of the desired class object. Here, a linear combination of the positive derivatives of the last convolutional layer is used.

Smooth Grad

SmoothGrad aims to reduce the noise in gradient-based explanations by introducing noise and averaging the resulting noisy gradients. It is not an independent explanation method but rather an enhancement for any gradient-based explanation technique.

Here is how SmoothGrad operates:

1. Create multiple noisy versions of the target image.
2. Generate pixel attribution maps for each noisy image.
3. Average these pixel attribution maps.

This method is designed to minimize noise in Grad-CAM results. By adding noise to the image and averaging the sensitivity maps, it produces a high-fidelity saliency map and gets similar images. Neural networks are primarily concerned with classifying images correctly and have no benefits in smoothing gradients during training. The derivative fluctuates greatly at small scales, and averaging over multiple maps "smooths out" these fluctuations.

One of the limitations of Grad-CAM stems from saturation. In a neural network, gradients can be noisy and are also prone to having the vanishing phenomenon caused by the saturation problem of the Sigmoid function or the zero-gradient region of the ReLU function. As a result, the gradient of the output with respect to the input or any internal activation layer can be visually noisy.

Another limitation is false confidence. As a linear combination of activation maps, which include global pooling on the gradients, it is possible to find activation maps with higher weights that actually have lower contributions to the network's output compared to a zero baseline.

Smooth Grad-CAM++

This is a variant of Smooth Grad, which builds on the Grad-CAM++ method. The sensitivity maps are created using Grad-CAM++ as a base.

Score-CAM

Unlike Smooth Grad, Score-CAM is not reliant on gradients. In this method, the weights of each activation map is derived through its forward pass score for the target class. Score-CAM is a linear combination of weights and activation maps.

Consider a convolutional layer l in a model f. For a given class of interest (c), the Score-CAM can be defined as follows:

$$L^c_{Score-CAM} = ReLU(\sum_k \alpha^c_k A^k_l)$$

Figure 8.13: *Score-CAM for Class c*

Where,

$$\boxed{\alpha^c_k = C(A^k_l)}$$

Figure 8.14: *Weights Ccomputation in Score-CAM for Class c*

Where C (·) denotes the CIC score for activation map Ak and CIC is the Channel-wise Increase of Confidence.

The process employed to get the Score-CAM is well explained in the following figure:

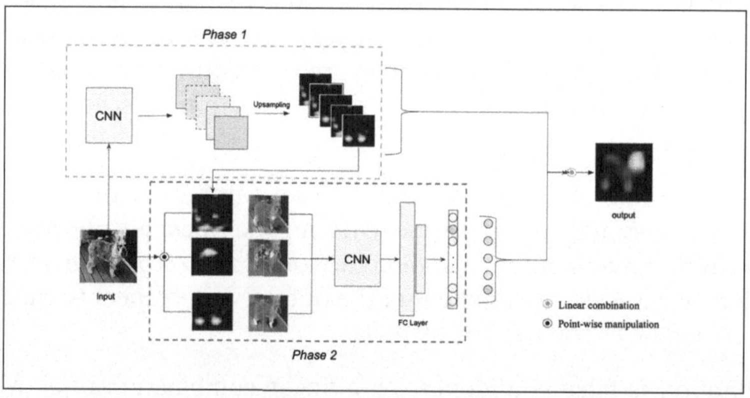

Figure 8.15: *Score-CAM pipeline (Source: Score-CAM: Score-Weighted Visual Explanations for Convolutional Neural Networks (2020) Wang et al)*

The activation maps are first extracted in phase 1. Each activation then becomes a mask on the original image. The forward-passing score on the target class is then deduced. In phase 2, the previously mentioned process is repeated N times for each of the N activation maps. The linear combination of score-based weights and activation maps gives the final value of the Score-CAM. The same feature extractor module is used in Phase 1 and Phase 2 of the CNN module.

SS-CAM

This method is a variant of Score-CAM. SS-CAM augments the Score-CAM method to provide an improved visual explanation. The explanation has visual sharpness because of a smoothing operation, which generates central localization of object features within an image.

IS-CAM

This method is a combination of IntegratedGrad within the Score-CAM pipeline. It includes an integration operation in the Score-CAM process to produce visually sharp attribution maps. The linear combination of the average scores after performing integration and the upsampled activation maps gives us the saliency map. A summation of the normalized input mask at every interval gives the average score.

XGrad-CAM

XGrad-CAM, or Axiom-based Grad-CAM, aims to achieve better visualization and an explanation of CNN model decisions using axioms. Axioms are self-explanatory properties that visualization methods satisfy. XGrad-CAM is an improved version of Grad-CAM in both sensitivity and conservation axioms.

LayerCAM

This method creates class activation maps for CNN image classifiers, enhancing object localization. It builds on the existing class activation map. Weights are assigned to the activations in the feature map according to the positive gradients. The main improvement of LayerCAM is that the class activation maps are produced from the final convolutional layer as well as the shallower layers, offering more precise localization details.

SmoothGradCAM Explanations Using `pytorch` and `torchcam`

We will be using torchcam for the class activation map functionality.

1. Install packages.

```
!pip install torchvision matplotlib
!pip install torchcam
```

2. Load the pretrained resnet18 model.

```
# Define your model
from torchvision.models import resnet18
```

```
model = resnet18(pretrained=True).eval()

# Set your CAM extractor
from torchcam.methods import SmoothGradCAMpp
cam_extractor = SmoothGradCAMpp(model)
```

3. Using the model, predict on a new image. Using the **cam_extractor**, identify the activation maps in the image.

```
from torchvision.io.image import read_image
from torchvision.transforms.functional import normalize, resize,
to_pil_image
from torchvision.models import resnet18
from torchcam.methods import SmoothGradCAMpp

model = resnet18(pretrained=True).eval()
# Get your input
img = read_image("testleaf.jpeg")
# Preprocess it for your chosen model
input_tensor = normalize(resize(img, (224, 224)) / 255., [0.485,
0.456, 0.406], [0.229, 0.224, 0.225])

with SmoothGradCAMpp(model) as cam_extractor:
  # Preprocess your data and feed it to the model
  out = model(input_tensor.unsqueeze(0))
  # Retrieve the CAM by passing the class index and the model
output
  activation_map = cam_extractor(out.squeeze(0).argmax().item(),
out)
```

4. Plot the activation areas.

```
import matplotlib.pyplot as plt
# Visualize the raw CAM
plt.imshow(activation_map[0].squeeze(0).numpy()); plt.axis('off');
plt.tight_layout(); plt.show()
```

Figure 8.16: *SmoothGrad-CAM without Overlay*

5. Overlay the activation map on the original image and display.

```
import matplotlib.pyplot as plt
from torchcam.utils import overlay_mask

# Resize the CAM and overlay it
result = overlay_mask(to_pil_image(img), to_pil_image(activation_
map[0].squeeze(0), mode='F'), alpha=0.5)
# Display it
plt.imshow(result); plt.axis('off'); plt.tight_layout(); plt.
show()
```

Figure 8.17: *SmoothGrad-CAM with Overlay*

Neural Network Explainability Approaches

Neuron Activation-Based Techniques: Various methods heavily rely on the activation values of internal neurons to explain model predictions. However, these activations may not be the only internal signals used.

Saliency Methods: These techniques compute saliency maps for inputs as visual explanations using internal neuron activations. One of the earliest methods, Class Activation Mapping (CAM), uses global average pooling neuron activations to weakly localize objects in inputs for saliency mapping. Among the many techniques for activation-based saliency mapping, GradCAM is notable for combining model gradients with neuron activations to compute saliency maps. Variants such as GradCAM++, Score-CAM, and Smooth-GradCAM++ also use neuron activation signals. Typically, there is a significant size disparity between activation maps of internal layers and the input, necessitating interpolation of activation signals, which can result in poor resolution maps. This was addressed more recently in the CAMERAS method, employing multi-scale mapping for high-resolution saliency mapping. Despite many existing methods, new techniques continue to emerge.

Classic Techniques: Methods such as Layer-wise Relevance Propagation (LRP) and DeepLift rely on activations from multiple layers to compute saliency maps. With the shift towards Transformer-based models, these classical methods are being adapted to explain Transformer models.

Neuron-Concept Association Methods: Techniques such as CBMs encourage neuron-concept association by design, while others identify such associations after the fact. Other techniques quantify the alignment between model neurons and known semantic concepts. Similarly, neuron-concept explainers use saliency maps and Shapley values. The TCAV method uses activations to identify neuron sensitivity to specific concepts.

Backpropagation-Based Methods: Gradients of a model, with respect to input, are considered analogous to coefficients in modern deep neural networks. Various methods leverage backpropagated gradients for feature relevance in explanation. Techniques such as Guided Backpropagation, SmoothGrad, and FullGrad use backpropagated gradients to estimate feature attribution scores. These gradients are sometimes used by other methods as well.

Feature Ablation

This is a perturbation-based approach to computing attribution. Each input feature is replaced with a given baseline, and the difference in output is computed. The scalar value associated with each input is taken as a feature and replaced independently. When a feature mask is passed instead, grouping features are ablated together.

For a dataset of *n* rows and *m* features:

1. Train the model on the training dataset and calculate the score on the test set using a scoring metric of choice.
2. For each of the m features, remove from the training data and train the model. Calculate the score on the test set.
3. Deduce the difference between the original score with all features and for each feature ablated score (the score for the model using all features but one). Use this value to rank the features depending on this difference.

This method is useful in images where entire segments or regions can be ablated, and the importance of the segment (feature group) can be measured.

Conclusion

In this chapter, we had primarily focused on computer vision models, but most of these methods can be used in Natural Language Processing, Genomics, and so on. This is still an evolving area, and newer techniques for explainability in neural networks are being researched. The increasing popularity of transformers has also detracted from the focus, resulting in transformers being used in most scenarios.

In the next chapter, we will delve into the latest in AI. Explainability in transformers and large language models is still largely a research topic. But there are many techniques, such as attention observation and neuron probing, or the more recent mechanistic interpretability. These form the topics for our next chapter.

References

1. Score-CAM: Score-Weighted Visual Explanations for Convolutional Neural Networks (2020) Wang et al https://arxiv.org/pdf/1910.01279
2. SS-CAM: Smoothed Score-CAM for Sharper Visual Feature Localization (2020) Wang et al https://arxiv.org/pdf/2006.14255
3. IS-CAM: Integrated Score-CAM for axiomatic-based explanations (2020) Naidu et al https://arxiv.org/pdf/2010.03023
4. Overview of Class Activation Maps for Visualization Explainability Pham Thi Minh Anh https://arxiv.org/pdf/2309.14304
5. Grad-CAM: Visual Explanations from Deep Networks via Gradient-based Localization (2019) Selvaraju et al https://arxiv.org/pdf/1610.02391

6. Efficient Saliency Maps for Explainable AI (2020) Mundhenk et al https://arxiv.org/pdf/1911.11293
7. Visualizing and Understanding Convolutional Networks (2013) Zeiler et al https://arxiv.org/pdf/1311.2901
8. STRIVING FOR SIMPLICITY: THE ALL CONVOLUTIONAL NET (2015) Springenberg et al https://arxiv.org/pdf/1412.6806
9. How to Explain ConvNet Predictions Using Class Activation Maps Bala Priya https://www.pinecone.io/learn/class-activation-maps
10. Learning Deep Features for Discriminative Localization (2015) Zhou et al https://arxiv.org/pdf/1512.04150
11. Grad-CAM: Visual Explanations from Deep Networks via Gradient-based Localization (2019) https://arxiv.org/pdf/1610.02391
12. Score-CAM: Score-Weighted Visual Explanations for Convolutional Neural Networks (2020) Wang et al https://arxiv.org/pdf/1910.01279

CHAPTER 9
Explainability in Transformers and Large Language Models

Introduction

In this chapter, we will learn about the transformer model and specifically focus on explainability in large language models. Transformer explainability ranges from leveraging attention and traditional permutation-based methods to more recently researched techniques such as Mechanistic Interpretability. Explainability techniques from the previous chapters can also be applied. We will also look at the various ways of using Large Language Models (LLMs) and the challenges around evaluation.

Structure

In this chapter, we will cover the following topics:

- Transformers
- Explainability in Large Language Models
- Explanations for Fine-tuning
- Using BertViz for Transformer Explainability
- Using Transformers-Interpret for Transformer Explainability
- Debate Over Attention
- Leveraging Explainability
- LMM Explainability

Transformers

A transformer model is a type of neural network that understands context and meaning in sequential data, such as words in a sentence, by identifying relationships between the words. Transformers are now taking over from convolutional and recurrent neural networks (CNNs and RNNs), which were the go-to deep learning models a few years back.

Previously, training neural networks required large, labeled datasets to train models that were expensive and also involved a lot of training time. Transformers, however, can find patterns mathematically, eliminating the need for such datasets and making it possible to utilize the vast amounts of images and text data available on the web and in corporate databases.

Transformers, which were first introduced in a 2017 paper by Google, are among the latest and most powerful types of models created so far. They are driving significant advancements in machine learning, with some even referring to transformers as AI. In an August 2021 paper, Stanford researchers termed transformers "foundation models" because they are leading a paradigm shift in AI. They noted that the "sheer scale and scope of foundation models over the last few years have stretched our imagination of what is possible."

Transformer models use a set of evolving mathematical techniques known as attention or self-attention to identify subtle relationships between even distant elements in a sequence. Additionally, the mathematics behind transformers supports parallel processing, allowing these models to operate quickly.

Transformers now lead popular performance benchmarks such as SuperGLUE, a standard established in 2019 for language-processing systems. Transformer models consist of large encoder and decoder blocks processing input data. The base concept is augmented with small but strategic enhancements to the blocks, making transformers exceptionally powerful.

The Transformer model is illustrated in *Figure 9.1*.

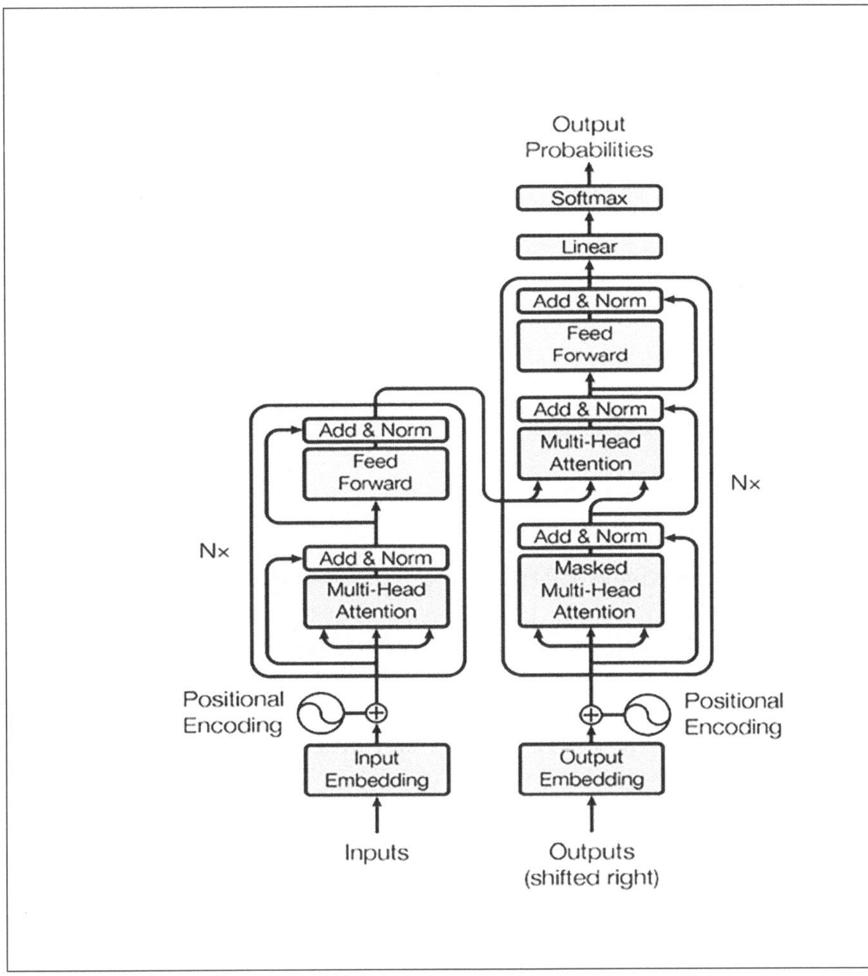

Figure 9.1: *Transformer Architecture (Source: Attention Is All You Need (2017) Vaswani et al)*

In the architecture, both the encoder and decoder contain stacked self-attention layers and pointwise, fully connected layers, as shown in the left and right halves of *Figure* 9.1, respectively.

Encoder:

There is a stack of identical layers in the encoder. There are two sub-layers in each layer. The first sublayer is a multi-head self-attention, and the second sublayer is a simple, position-wise, fully connected feedforward network.

Decoder:

The decoder also includes a stack of identical layers, and each layer has two sub-layers. The one difference in the decoder is the insertion of a third sub-layer to perform multi-head attention over the output of the encoder stack.

Self-Attention

A stacked self-attention layer is used in transformers instead of convolutions as in CNN. The self-attention layer in a Transformer model is a mechanism that allows the model to focus on different parts of the input sequence. The model understands the relationships between words in a sentence using attention.

For example, in the sentence:

She poured water from the pitcher into the cup until it was full.

We know "it" refers to the cup, while in the sentence:

She poured water from the pitcher into the cup until it was empty.

We know "it" refers to the pitcher.

This relationship between the words is captured in the self-attention layer.

The type of self-attention used in a transformer is called Scaled Dot-Product Attention, as shown in *Figure* 9.2. The self-attention layer takes in three parameters: Query, Key, and Value. Attention scores are calculated by comparing the Query vector for the current word to the Key vectors for all the words in the sequence. These values are then used to compute the weighted sum of the values.

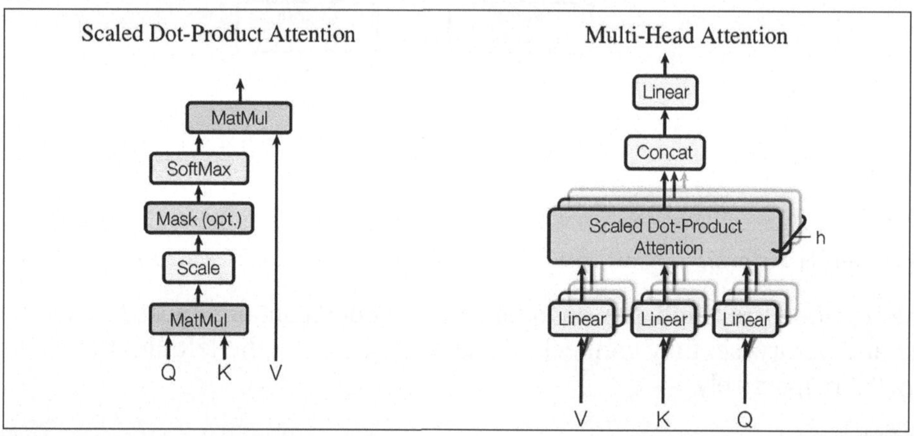

Figure 9.2: *Attention Mechanism (Source: Attention Is All You Need (2017) Vaswani et al)*

Multi-Head Attention

In addition, there is a multi-headed attention that improves performance by allowing the model to focus on different positions. This is a module that runs through the attention mechanism several times in parallel. Each of the output attention values is combined and linearly transformed. These are concatenated and once again projected, resulting in the final values.

Cross Attention

Cross attention is another element of transformers that makes it possible for a sequence to attend to information from another sequence. The decoder of transformers connects to the encoder's output, which is the cross attention. It is crucial for tasks such as translation and summarization, as it helps transformers capture the relationships between sequences.

Foundation Models

Foundation models are extensive neural networks trained on large volumes of text data to comprehend and generate human-like language. They act as a base for creating more specialized AI models. The training process involves exposing the model to a variety of language patterns and structures, allowing it to grasp the nuances of human communication.

A notable example of a foundation model is OpenAI's Generative Pre-trained Transformer (GPT) series, including GPT-4. These models have shown exceptional abilities in tasks such as language translation, question-answering, summarization, and even creative writing.

The importance of foundation models lies in their capacity to generalize knowledge from a wide range of data sources. These foundational models are trained on extensive text corpora, learning to produce clear and contextually appropriate language. As a result, they can be used in various applications either directly or fine-tuned for adaptation to specific domains or tasks.

Large Language Models (LLMs):

LLMs are a subset of foundation models and can perform a variety of natural language processing (NLP) tasks. LLMs are adept at performing a variety of text-based tasks, such as understanding context, answering questions, writing essays, summarizing texts, and generating code.

Large Multimodal Models (LMMs):

LMMs traverse beyond text and can work on images, speech, and video as well. Large multimodal models (LMMs) can be made of three components: LLMs, visual encoders, and lightweight connector modules to glue the two models.

Explainability in Large Language Models

We will now look at what explainability entails in Large Language Models or LLMs.

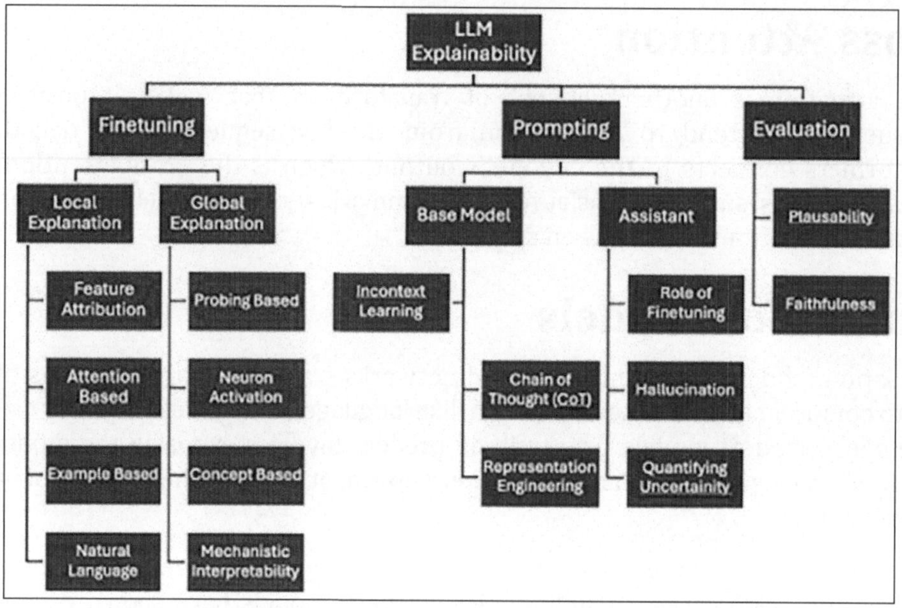

Figure 9.3: *Explainability Taxonomy in Large Language Models*

Large Language Models have become prolific in the last couple of years. Large models is an area of active research and is evidenced by the many papers being published. Explainability in large models has also seen an increased interest, and many of the works we present here could be in the early stages of research or yet to mature.

Employing LLMs

The usage of LLMs can be accomplished in two ways, that is, fine-tuning and prompting. The method employed depends on the tasks to be performed. The two approaches are very different, and the implications of the model are also distinct; hence, various types of explanations have been proposed, as shown in *Figure* 9.3.

Prompting

The prompting approach involves using natural language sentences as instructions or starting points for the model to generate completions. This method is effective for zero-shot or few-shot learning without needing additional training data. In zero-shot learning, no examples are given. In few-shot learning, a few examples with the expected response are included in the prompt that serves as guidance for the model. Models following this paradigm can be classified into two types, that is, Base model and Assistant model.

Base Model

The increasing sizes of the large language models (LLMs), which are trained on vast amounts of data, are leading to models demonstrating impressive new capabilities without requiring additional training. Few-shot learning through prompting is one instance where few examples suffice to generate responses in a required manner. These models are also alternatively known as Foundational models. This aspect typically applies to massive language models with billions of parameters, such as GPT-3, GPT-4, LLAMA-2, LLAMA-3, Claude, and Falcon. The models can respond to user queries without the need for additional alignment to human preferences. This is specifically true of the large-scale models with over 1 billion parameters. For instance, LLaMA-3 comes in sizes of 8 billion, 70 billion, and 405 billion parameters. The aim of explanations in base models is to understand how these models utilize their pre-trained knowledge in response to prompts.

In-Context Learning

In-context learning involves incorporating task demonstrations into the prompt in a natural language format. This is used by the model to leverage the relevant portions from the provided text without the need for specific examples. Explainable AI methods have been employed to clarify how prompting functions in large language models (LLMs). We explore methods that highlight the impact of in-context learning (ICL) on the model's behavior. Various studies suggest that large models can override semantic priors, or the pre-existing knowledge or assumptions learned by the models during training, and instead learn alternate input-label mappings through in-context learning. The research also seems to point to smaller models having a higher dependence on the priors.

Chain-of-Thought

Chain-of-thought (CoT) prompting involves a set of techniques for in-context learning that encourage models to generate intermediate reasoning steps or explanations before providing an answer to a question. Research has shown that for models with over 100 billion parameters, CoT explanations enhance question-answering accuracy. Chain-of-Thought (CoT) prompting alters the way models process text in few-shot in-context question-answering scenarios. Studies using techniques such as saliency scores have shown the efficacy of CoT. The saliency scores of input tokens that are semantically relevant to the question show less variation under changes in question phrasing and model output randomness compared to standard prompting. This indicates that CoT prompting helps models consider the input tokens of questions more consistently, potentially leading to more accurate answers.

Assistant Model

Base models have two main limitations. They struggle to follow user instructions because their pre-training data includes few instruction-response examples, and secondly, they often produce biased and toxic content. To overcome these issues, the base models undergo supervised fine-tuning to develop human-like abilities. The primary goal is to align the model's responses with human feedback and preferences. Instruction tuning using prompt and response pairs and Reinforcement Learning from Human Feedback (RLHF) is used to achieve that goal. These models are also trained with natural language feedback to handle complex, multi-turn conversations.

Examples of such models include ChatGPT by OpenAI, Claude by Anthropic, and open-source models such as LLaMA-2-Chat by Meta, Alpaca, and Vicuna. These models are often referred to as assistant models, chat assistants, or dialogue models. The focus here is on understanding how models learn to exhibit open-ended interactive behaviors through conversations.

The usage of base models can happen in multiple ways, as portrayed in the following figure:

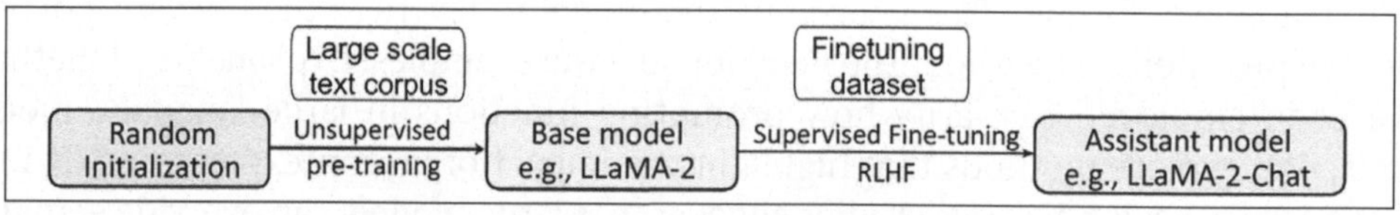

Figure 9.4: *Pretraining and Fine-tuning Process (Source: Explainability for Large Language Models: A Survey (2023) Zhao et al)*

These methods with prompting are under review and new papers are regularly being published on additional findings and techniques.

Fine-tuning

In this approach, a language model is initially pre-trained on a vast collection of unlabeled text data. This forms the base model, which is then fine-tuned on labeled data from a specific downstream domain or for a specific task. Pre-trained models, such as GPT-4 or LLAMA-3, are commonly used for this purpose. During fine-tuning, fully connected layers can be easily added above the final encoder layer of the language model, enabling it to adapt to various downstream tasks. Explanations for this approach focus on two main aspects:

- The ability of self-supervised pre-training allows models to develop a foundational grasp of language. This includes language syntax, semantics, and contextual relationships.
- Understanding the fine-tuning process in equipping pre-trained models with the ability to appropriately address downstream tasks.

Explanations for Fine-tuning

In this section, we review explanation techniques for LLMs trained with the pre-training and downstream fine-tuning. First, we introduce approaches to provide local explanations and global explanations. Here, the local explanation aims to provide an understanding of how a language model makes a prediction for a specific input instance, while the global explanation aims to provide a broad understanding of how the LLM works overall.

Local Explanations

Let us look at explanations in LLMs from a local perspective, that is, Local Explanations. In the next section, we will be discussing global explainability techniques in LLMs.

Feature Attribution:

Feature attribution is a local approach for explaining a prediction by measuring the impact of each feature on the outcome. In transformers, features correspond to tokens, and the analysis assesses the relevance of each input token to the model's prediction. For an input text x with n tokens {x1, x2, ..., xn}, a pre-trained language model f produces f(x). A relevance score $R(x_i)$ is assigned to each token x_i in attribution methods, indicating its contribution to f(x). This category encompasses perturbation-based, gradient-based, and vector-based methods.

Perturbation-Based Methods:

Perturbation-based methods, such as LIME and SHAP, modify input features to observe changes in the model's output. However, this approach assumes that input features are independent and overlooks the correlation factor among them. Moreover, models can exhibit overconfidence even when their predictions are impossible or incorrect. Efficiency and reliability are key issues encountered in such methods, which has led to a decreased focus on them in recent attribution research.

Gradient-Based Methods:

Gradient methods assess how the outcome changes when input features are adjusted. These methods compute per-token importance scores using backward gradient vectors. Backpropagation is used to calculate the gradients of the output—the logits or soft-max probabilities—with respect to the extracted features or input and is then used to estimate attribution scores. Gradients are typically noisy, resulting in attribution maps that may reflect contributions from irrelevant features. Different modification methods to the gradient-based approach have been suggested to address the noise in attribution maps.

Techniques such as integrated gradients (IG) accumulate gradients obtained as the input is interpolated between a reference point and the actual input. Although

Integrated Gradients are widely used, one major challenge of IG is its computational difficulty in arriving at high-quality integrals. The attribution scores or integrated gradients (IG) have also been found unreliable from a faithfulness lens. Additionally, their ability to explain the forward dynamics within hidden states is limited. The effect of perturbing input features is not directly factored in gradient-based methods, and assessing the validity of these methods is an ongoing challenge.

Vector-Based Methods:

In recent times, vector-based analyses focus on token representation formation, which has become extremely important and widely utilized. Global attribution from the final output layer to the more granular, layer-wise decomposition of token representations is one of the various techniques with vectors. Vector-based methods expect an accurate estimation of:

- The mixture of tokens present in each layer, that is, local-level analysis.
- The flow of attention throughout multiple layers, that is, global-level analysis.

To calculate the global impact of the inputs on the outputs, the local behavior of all layers has to be aggregated. Attention rollout and attention flow are the methodologies used for recursively aggregating the raw attention maps in each layer.

Transformer Architecture

The Transformer architecture has a series of layers, and analyzing the transformer blocks can be very insightful. The component-by-component internal processing of the transformer can be useful in understanding the intermediate processing through the stacked architecture in the encoder or decoder-based language models. The inferencing in a transformer involves the traversal of the input embeddings through a series of layers where the embeddings are transformed progressively, resulting in the prediction we see at the end. Considering the layers as denoted by "1," each of the transformer layers is composed of a multi-head self-attention (MHSA) sub-layer followed by a multi-layer perceptron (MLP) sub-layer.

We can represent x^l_i of token i at layer l as:

$$x^l_i = xi^{L-1} + a_i^l + m_i^l$$

Where a_i^l and m_i^l are the outputs from the lth MHSA and MLP sub-layers, respectively. Initially, most studies were focused on the transformer blocks, but recently there has been an increasing emphasis on trying to decipher the interactions between the internal layers.

Attention Mechanism:

The attention mechanism is presented as a way to attend to the most relevant part of inputs. Attention can be intuitive as it captures meaningful correlations between intermediate states of input within the layers in explaining the model's predictions. Multi-head self-attention is a specialized form of attention where the module for attention mechanisms runs through an attention mechanism many times in parallel.

Attention Visualization:

Bertviz is an open-source tool that is designed to visualize multi-head self-attention in transformer-based language models. It provides visualizations at three granular levels–the attention head, model, and neuron levels. Each view aids in interpreting the model, demonstrated using the BERT and OpenAI GPT-2 models.

In *Figure* 9.5 (GPT-2), the attention-head view shows the attention patterns generated by one or more attention heads in a given transformer layer.

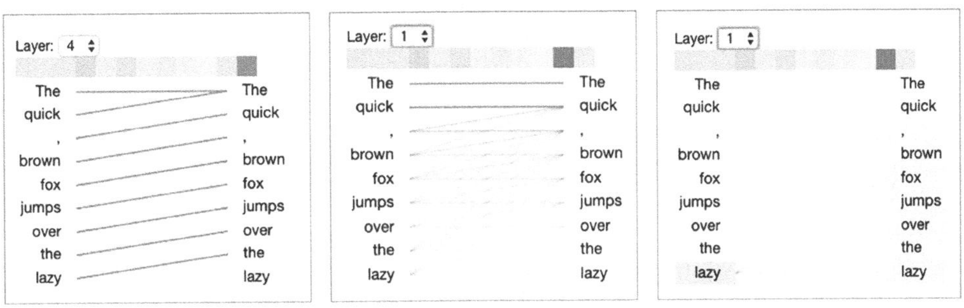

Figure 9.5: *Attention Head View for GPT2 (Source: Visualizing Attention in Transformer-Based Language Representation Models (2019) Jesse Vig)*

The self-attention focus is shown as lines connecting the tokens that are attending (on the left) with the tokens being attended to (on the right) in this view. The colors in the figures represent the corresponding attention head(s), while the line weight reflects the attention score.

In *Figure* 9.6 (BERT-3), we see the attention-head view for BERT for the inputs "The cat sat on the mat" in Sentence A and "The cat lay on the rug" in Sentence B. The left and center figures represent attention heads from different layers. The right figure shows the head of the same layer as the center figure, with the Sentence A → Sentence B filter selected.

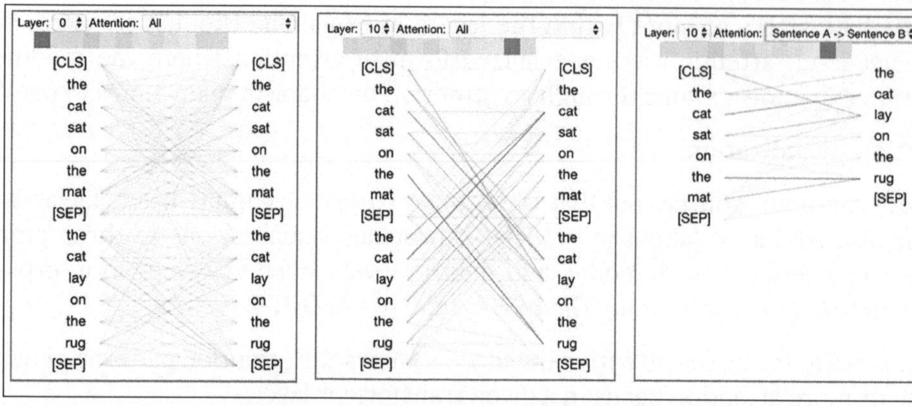

Figure 9.6: *Attention Head View for BERT-3*
(Source: Visualizing Attention in Transformer-Based Language Representation Models (2019) Jesse Vig)

The Bertviz tool works on the encoder-only BERT as well as decoder-only GPT-2 models. Attention mechanisms in MHSA sublayers play a crucial role in identifying meaningful correlations between intermediate input states, which can help explain the model's predictions. Two primary methods for analyzing these sublayers are visualizing attention weights and using gradient attribution scores.

For example, attention mechanisms often prioritize certain tokens while reducing the emphasis on common words or special tokens, a pattern observable through norm-based analysis metrics, as shown in *Figure* 9.7 (on the left).

In *Figure* 9.7 (on the right), the focus is on the outputs of the feedforward Network, demonstrating how each update within these layers can be broken down into sub-updates associated with individual parameter vectors, which often encode concepts interpretable to humans.

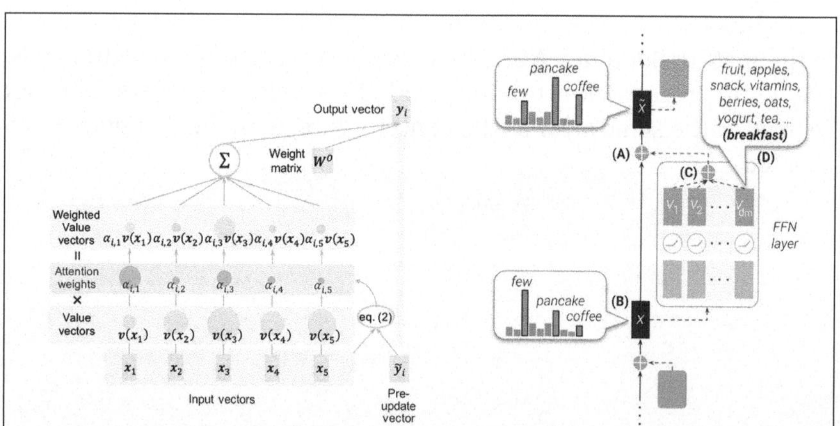

Figure 9.7: *Analysis of each Transformer Component (Source: From Understanding to Utilization: A Survey on Explainability for Large Language Models (2024) Luo et al)*

The preceding figure gives an overview of the attention mechanism in Transformers. In *Figure* 9.7 (on the left), the sizes of the colored circles indicate the value of the scalar or the norm of the corresponding vector.

Analyzing MLP Sublayers:

Feedforward layers in transformer-based language models can be considered as key-value memories where each key correlates with textual patterns in the training examples while each value adds a distribution over the output vocabulary. The lower layers mostly capture shallow patterns while the upper layers learn more semantic ones. The learned patterns are human-interpretable. Also, the output of a feedforward layer is a collection of its memories. These memories are refined throughout the model's layers via residual connections to produce the final output distribution.

Each "key" corresponds to specific textual patterns identified during training, and each "value" produces a related output vocabulary distribution. *Figure* 9.7 (on the right) highlights the FFN outputs, showing how each update can be divided into sub-updates linked to individual parameter vectors, which can be considered to denote human-interpretable concepts. Also, there is growing interest in input-independent methods that interpret model parameters directly, bypassing the need for a forward pass.

Example-Based Explanations

Explanations can also be provided through examples that will be covered in this section.

Adversarial:

Research indicates that neural models are highly sensitive to minor changes in input data. These subtle modifications can significantly alter model decisions while remaining almost imperceptible to humans. Adversarial examples are crucial for identifying model weaknesses and are often incorporated into training data to enhance robustness and accuracy. Initially, adversarial examples are created through word-level manipulations such as errors, deletions, and insertions, which are easily noticeable. Sophisticated token-level perturbation methods, such as TextFooler, prioritize important words based on ranking. Based on the word embedding similarity, part-of-speech consistency, sentence semantic similarity, and prediction shift, a potential word is selected.

However, word embeddings have limitations in representing sentences compared to contextualized representations, often resulting in unintelligible outputs. Methods using the mask-then-infill procedure have attained state-of-the-art performance, primarily focusing on contextualized representations. In these methods, pre-trained masked language models such as BERT for perturbations are used and can include replacement, insertion, and merging. A large corpus is used in training the masked language models to generate contextualized representations and learn token importance. The models are then frozen, and perturbation operations are performed on the tokens based on their ranking. In the replacement method, the generated example substitutes the masked token. Injection involves the new token being added to the left or to the right of the masked token. In merging, a consecutive pair of tokens is masked and replaced with a single token.

SemAttack, another technique, is applicable to various embedding spaces, including typo space, knowledge space, and contextualized semantic space. The input tokens are first transformed into an embedding space, generating perturbed embeddings that are iteratively optimized to achieve the target attack goals. Experiments revealed that replacing even 5% of words in the BERT model reduced its accuracy from 70.6% to 2.4%, even with defenses in a white-box setting. This highly impactful attack performance of SemAttack may be attributed to the direct manipulation of embeddings.

Counterfactual:

Counterfactual explanation is a type of causal explanation where the input is considered as the cause of the prediction. For a given observed input x and a perturbed which has some features changed, the prediction y would change as well. The perturbations are changed and with counterfactual explanations we can determine what would have happened for those particular changes in input. The perturbations are generated to meet desired requirements within business constraints by selecting specific counterfactuals. Perturbations can be achieved through paraphrasing, word replacement, or introduced by humans.

Counterfactual examples are useful in the analysis and training of NLP models. Polyjuice is a general-purpose counterfactual generator that has the ability to control the perturbation types and locations, supporting multiple permutation types for input sentences, such as deletion, negation, and shuffling. It was trained by fine-tuning GPT-2 on multiple datasets of paired sentences. Polyjuice counterfactuals are complementary to feature attribution explanations, and they tend to display information that users often miss.

Counterfactual explanation generation has been framed as a two-stage approach. The first stage is masking or selecting the important tokens, and the second stage involves infilling or editing those tokens. Minimal Contrastive Editing (MiCE) is another method for counterfactuals. In the first stage, it uses gradient attribution to choose the tokens to mask, and in the second stage, it optimizes for minimal edits while trying to find a value through binary search that is large enough to result in the contrast prediction. In contrast, CREST relaxes this hard minimality constraint of MiCE and instead leverages rationales from a selective rationalization model.

Instead, ContRastive Edits with Sparse raTionalization (CREST) combines sparse rationalization with span-level masked language modeling to produce valid, fluent, and diverse counterfactuals. Next, it decomposes a rationalizer into factual and counterfactual flows and encourages agreement between the rationales for both.

While both methods generate valid and fluent counterfactuals, there are newer counterfactual generators such as CLICK and CIEB in the works.

Global Explanations

Probing-Based Method:

Self-supervised pre-training equips models with extensive linguistic knowledge derived from large-scale training datasets. Probing-based methods are used to capture the internal representations within such networks. A classifier, known as a probe, is trained on the network's activations to differentiate between various types of inputs or outputs. We will next look at studies related to probing, categorized by their objectives, whether it be probing for semantic knowledge or analyzing learned representations.

Probing Knowledge:

LLMs trained on a vast variety of text corpora are prominent in their ability to capture context-independent semantic and factual knowledge. This can be accessed through textual prompts. Research has primarily focused on creating textual queries to extract various types of background knowledge from these models. In this context, it has been found that using methods such as probes sometimes reveals factual information even when language models may not be reliably producing truthful responses.

Probing Representations:

LLMs outshine in producing context-dependent knowledge portrayals. This can be accomplished with probing classifiers that are used in the analysis. Probing classifiers are shallow classifiers trained on the activations of attention heads for predicting specific features. Significant research in this area involved training linear classifiers to identify a select group of attention heads with high linear probing accuracy for truthfulness. A pattern of specialization across attention heads was uncovered in this work. The representation of "truthfulness" was mainly processed in the early to middle layers, with only a few heads in each layer showing striking performance. These findings are instrumental in the motivations for exploring more complex representations, such as the presence of nonlinear internal representations such as board game states, in models initially lacking explicit knowledge of the game or its rules.

Classifier-Based Probing:

The core concept of classifier-based probing involves training a shallow classifier on top of pre-trained or fine-tuned language models such as BERT and T5. During probing, the parameters of the pre-trained models are frozen, allowing the model to generate representations for input words, phrases, or sentences and learn parameters such as attention weights. The representations and model parameters are then fed into a probe classifier, which aims to identify specific linguistic properties or reasoning abilities learnt by the model. After training, the probe is evaluated on a holdout dataset, with labeled data sourced from available taggers or gold-annotated datasets. Each probe classifier is often customized for a particular task but the overall approach to training classifiers to probe different knowledge is consistent.

The following categorization is done based on the probed model components, such as vector representations and model parameters. Initially, we examine works that study vector representations to assess embedded knowledge. In this context, knowledge can refer to either low-level syntax knowledge or high-level semantic knowledge. Research shows that lower layers are more predictive of word-level syntax, while higher layers are better at capturing sentence-level syntax and semantic knowledge.

Concerns have arisen about whether probing classifiers learn syntax from representations or merely the task itself. There are arguments to the effect that only rich syntax representations allow simple classifiers to perform well. However, some studies challenge this by showing that good performance is due to encoding local neighboring words. Similarly, other works indicate that classifiers relying on semantic cues fail to extract syntax. Conversely, other research suggests that models such as BERT encode the relevant information in various ways. Thus, the validity of probing syntactic information still needs further investigation.

Sentence-level syntactic information is generally distributed across each word, predicting it is simpler with a probing classifier without needing dependency tree retrieval. Local syntax and semantics are often studied together as they examine the same elements, such as neurons, layers, and contextual representations. The differences mainly stem from their training objectives and data.

Probing work involving prompts often encounters difficulties with zero-shot and few-shot learning. Evaluating these models is more complex because the quality of the prompts significantly affects performance. The usage of well-designed datasets and prompts also does not suffice, and the results still require further scrutiny.

Parameter-Free Probing:

Another approach in data-centric probing techniques does not involve probing classifiers. This method focuses on creating datasets tailored to specific linguistic properties, such as grammar. The performance of the encoding model demonstrates its ability to capture these properties. This is measured by the probability values for positive examples being higher than that of negative examples in the language models.

Neuron Activation Method:

As against examining the entire vector space, neuron analysis focuses on individual dimensions or neurons within representations that are crucial for model performance or linked to specific linguistic properties.

This method generally involves two primary steps. The first step is identifying key neurons in an unsupervised manner, and the second step is for learning the relationships between a linguistic property and individual neurons through supervised tasks. The premise is that different models learning similar properties typically share similar neurons. Ranking of the shared neurons is accomplished through metrics such as correlation measurements and learned weights. Alternatively, simpler techniques such as supervised classification can also select important neurons in a model. The validation of the ranked neurons' significance is done using quantitative methods such as ablation experiments, masking, erasure, and visualization. Additional probing techniques, such as greedy Gaussian probing, are also capable of identifying important neurons. Balancing accuracy and selectivity is considered a challenge in existing methods.

Although examining all neurons to provide explanations is ideal, the high computational cost and the belief that only a small subset of neurons is crucial for decision-making lead to the use of ranking algorithms. The growing generalization capabilities of LLMs suggest that explaining individual neurons has become possible. In an OpenAI study, GPT-4 was used to generate natural language explanations for individual neuron activations in GPT-2 XL. GPT-4 identifies patterns in text that trigger high activation values for specific GPT-2 XL neurons, which may indicate certain references. For example, GPT-4 might describe a neuron's pattern as alluding to movies and entertainment themes. The quality of each neuron's explanation is assessed by comparing GPT-4's simulation of the neuron's behavior with its actual behavior on new text examples. The explanations are scored based on the correlation between GPT-4's simulated activation and the true activation.

A high correlation indicates an accurate explanation that captures the neuron's encoded essence. The study found that GPT-4 provided high-scoring explanations for 1,000 GPT-2 XL neurons, accounting for most of their behavior. These automatically generated natural language explanations demonstrate an inherent understanding of the inner computations and feature representations in GPT-2 XL. However, the lack of ground truth explanation annotations for individual components poses a challenge in evaluating component-level explanations in LLMs.

Concept-Based Method:

In concept-based interpretability, algorithms map inputs to sets of concepts and then measure the importance of each predefined concept in the model predictions. Models can be explained in a way that is understandable to humans by introducing abstract concepts rather than relying on low-level features. The latent space information can also be transformed into a comprehensible explanation.

A notable framework, TCAV uses directional derivatives to measure the contribution of defined concepts to model predictions. Each concept is represented with a set of examples and then a linear classifier is learned (the Concept Activation Vector (CAV)), to detect the concept of interest. This vector is used to measure prediction sensitivity to the concepts, effectively providing an important score for each concept. TCAV was initially designed to work in the computer vision domain. It has now also been adapted for NLP models such as sentiment classification.

Concept-based interpretability can also enable the manipulation of these representations, also known as representation engineering. This can potentially enhance safety by promoting concepts such as honesty, harmlessness, and morality.

Sparse Autoencoders:

Sparse autoencoders is another method to get interpretable features in LLM. Recent papers dive into the details of using SAE in Claude and GPT-4. They achieved this by matching patterns of neuron activations (calling them features) to human-interpretable concepts. The Anthropic paper describes dictionary learning as a technique to isolate the patterns of neuron activations that repeat across many different contexts. The premise is that any internal state of the model can be represented in terms of a few active features instead of many active neurons, and in turn, every feature in an AI model is made by combining neurons. A sparse autoencoder (SAE) was trained on the model activations. Once the SAE is trained, it provides us with an approximate decomposition of the model's activations into a linear combination of feature directions (SAE decoder weights) with coefficients equal to the feature activations. The sparsity penalty ensures that for multiple given inputs to the model, a very small fraction of features will have nonzero activations. Thus, for any given token in any given context, the model activations are explained by a small set of active features (out of a large pool of possible features). In their research, they cite an example of successfully extracting millions of features from the middle layer of Claude 3.0 Sonnet, with the features in the larger models being more meaningful.

Mechanistic Interpretability

Mechanistic interpretability is an emerging field, and its goal is to find the internal reasoning processes of trained neural networks. It adopts a bottom-up approach, unlike concept-based, which is top-down in its working. MI attempts to reverse engineer neural networks similar to reversing a compiled binary program into human-readable code. It can be described as a global, post-hoc, model-specific method, and it needs access to the model's internals.

Mechanistic interpretability studies the fundamental components of models through granular analysis of features, neurons, layers, and connections, offering an intimate view of operational mechanics. Unlike concept-based interpretability, it aims to uncover causal relationships and precise computations transforming inputs into outputs, often identifying specific neural circuits driving behavior. This reverse engineering approach draws from interdisciplinary fields such as physics, neuroscience, and systems biology to guide the development of transparent, value-aligned AI systems.

Mechanistic interpretability aims to understand language models by analyzing individual neurons and their connections, often viewed as circuits. This field includes several methods, mainly divided into three categories: circuit discovery, causal tracing, and vocabulary lens. Each method provides unique perspectives and insights into the workings of language models.

The core concepts in neural network interpretability are:

- Features are meaningful, isolated concepts that are encoded by a neural network. They are things that a network knows or is representing. They are usually confined to a single layer of the network.
- Circuits are the relationships between groups of features. They are the computational means by which a network combines the lower-level concepts encoded by features into more complex representations. They can span across multiple layers of a network.

Monosemantic and Polysemantic Neurons: A neuron corresponding to a single semantic concept is called monosemantic. While a neuron state resulting from varied inputs is polysemantic.

Circuit Discovery:

The circuit discovery approach in mechanistic interpretability works on the premise of mapping the learned model representations with known ground truths by reverse-engineering the model's working to fully understand its features. A notable example is the analysis of GPT-2 small, where researchers identified a human-understandable subgraph within the computational graph responsible for the indirect object identification (IOI) task. For instance, in sentences such as "When Mary and John went to the store, John gave a drink to," the expected completion is "Mary." The study found a circuit of 26 attention heads (1.1% of the total, head and token position pairs) that primarily handles this task. This circuit-based mechanistic perspective offers opportunities to extend our understanding to larger models and more complex tasks.

Causal Tracing:

Causal analysis in machine learning has progressed over the years from early methods that mapped dependencies between hidden variables using causal graphs to more advanced techniques such as causal mediation analysis. The newer approaches can quantify the impact of the intermediate activations in neural networks on their output. One study, in particular, evaluated each activation's contribution to accurate factual predictions through three phases: a clean run that generates correct predictions, a corrupted run where predictions are impaired, and a corrupted with-restoration run that assesses the ability of a single state to correct the prediction. Known as causal tracing, this method has identified key causal states mainly in the middle layers, especially at the last subject position, where MLP contributions are most significant. This highlights the importance of middle-layer MLPs in factual recall within LLMs.

Vocabulary Lens:

A model's knowledge and its retrieval may be localized into smaller parts of a language model. This can be achieved through weights and hidden states being projected onto their vocabulary space. Utilizing the preceding technique, we examine the roles of individual tokens and their contributions through attention outputs. There was an impact, and it was found to have very rich semantic information.

Along with Interpretability, these methods are a path to detecting unaligned behavior in AI models. TransformerLens is a library for doing mechanistic interpretability of GPT-style language models and is a good starting point for development.

Using BertViz for Transformer Explainability

The steps include:

1. Install the required libraries.

```
pip install bertviz
```

2. Load the pre-trained gpt2 model and visualize the attention layer.

```
from bertviz.transformers_neuron_view import GPT2Model,
GPT2Tokenizer
from bertviz.neuron_view import show

model_type = 'gpt2'
model_version = 'gpt2'
model = GPT2Model.from_pretrained(model_version)
tokenizer = GPT2Tokenizer.from_pretrained(model_version)
text = "She poured water from the pitcher to the cup until it was
full"
show(model, model_type, tokenizer, text, display_mode='dark')
```

Results from the BertViz visualizer are shown in the following figure.

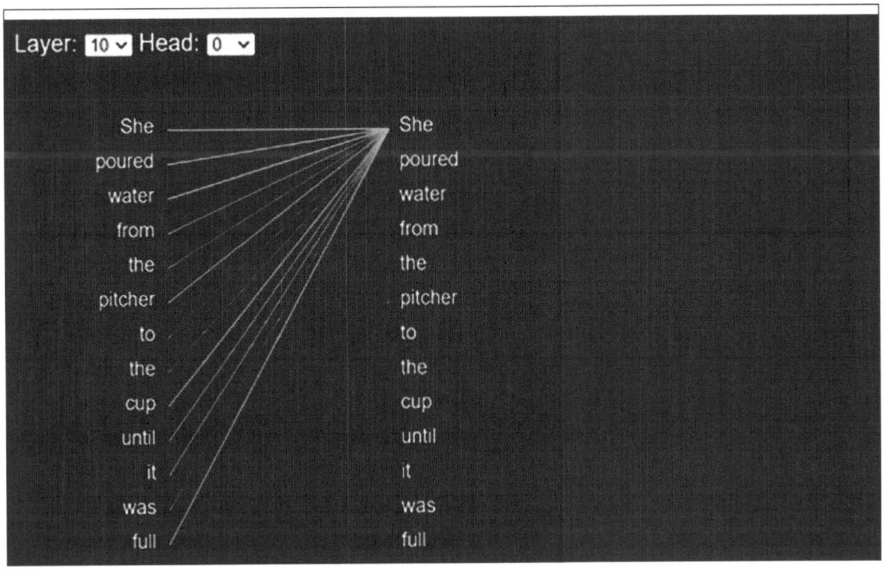

Figure 9.8: *BertViz Output*

Using Transformers-Interpret for Transformer Explainability

In this example, we will use the transformers-interpret library.

1. Install the required library.

```
pip install transformers-interpret
```

2. Load the Bert pretained model bert-large-uncased-whole-word-masking-finetuned-squad

```
from transformers import AutoModelForQuestionAnswering,
AutoTokenizer
from transformers_interpret import QuestionAnsweringExplainer

tokenizer = AutoTokenizer.from_pretrained("bert-large-uncased-
whole-word-masking-finetuned-squad")
model = AutoModelForQuestionAnswering.from_pretrained
("bert-large-uncased-whole-word-masking-finetuned-squad")

qa_explainer = QuestionAnsweringExplainer(
    model,
    tokenizer,
)

context = """
```

In Artificial Intelligence and machine learning, Natural Language Processing relates to the usage of machines to process and understand human language.

Many researchers currently work in this space.

```
"""

word_attributions = qa_explainer(
    "What is natural language processing ?",
    context,
)
qa_explainer.predicted_answer
```

```
'usage of machines to process and understand human language'
```

```
qa_explainer.visualize("bert_qa_viz.html")
```

Results from the transformer visualizer are shown in the following figure.

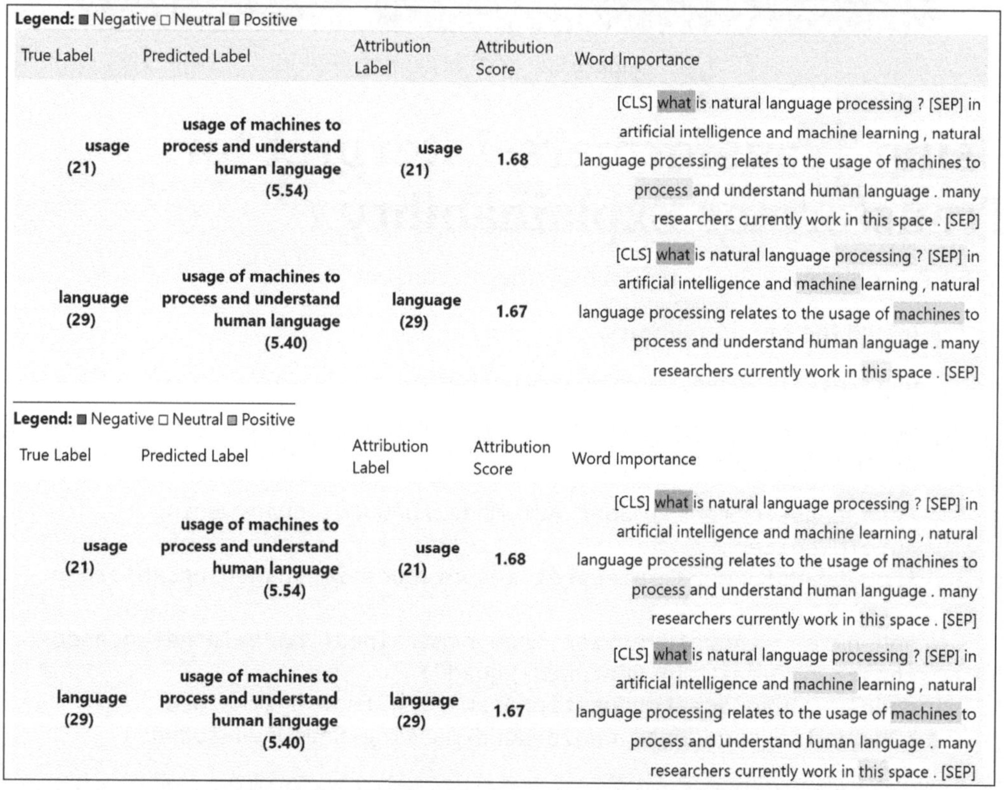

Figure 9.9: *Token Attention Map for Sentiment Analysis*

Debate Over Attention

In Transformers, attention plays an important role in determining the relationship between the words in a sequence. Attention has also been viewed as a mechanism to increase performance and enable model explanations. In contrast, there is another school of thought where attention is considered insufficient for improving performance and providing explanations. The debate over the validity of attention is ongoing and unlikely to be resolved soon.

Several key aspects fuel this debate. Some studies comparing attention-based explanations with methods such as LIME revealed that attention often fails to pinpoint the most crucial features for prediction. The studies primarily suggest that attention provides fewer effective explanations compared to alternatives or lacks correlation with other explanation methods. Secondly, some researchers are at odds over the utility of the attention mechanism in model predictions. The primary bone of contention is that raw attention does not encapsulate syntactic structures in text and hence may not be contributing to the predictions. Besides, raw attention has redundant information that diminishes its reliability in explanations.

However, there are other contradictory claims. Consistency cannot be expected while evaluating explanations and hence cannot be considered a limitation in the attention mechanism. Moreover, manipulating attention weights without retraining can bias evaluations. Furthermore, attention heads in BERT havc bccn shown to cncodc syntax effectively. Multiple technical solutions have been explored to make attention more explainable, such as optimizing input representation, regularizing learning objectives, avoiding biased learning, and incorporating human rationales.

Bringing the users into the loop is another way to make attention serve as an explanation. As user attention is used by the model during training, this method is also called supervised attention. Solutions for using attention as an explanation should consider the two key aspects–faithfulness and plausibility spectrum. When explanations need to be plausible as well as faithful, supervised attention offers a good perspective to add. The argument for supervised attention states that since attention is not an explanation, and if faithfulness alone is not enough, then making machine attention match human attention may be the solution. Studies show that using human rationale to supervise attention can produce explanations that are better accepted by users and can also lead to better performance.

Leveraging Explainability

In the previous section, we looked at the various local and global explainability methods reviewed in recent literature. In this section, we will look at how explainability can be used as a tool to debug and improve models. While approaches aimed at improving model capabilities through fine-tuning or re-training are noteworthy, we will focus on methods that specifically focus on model explainability.

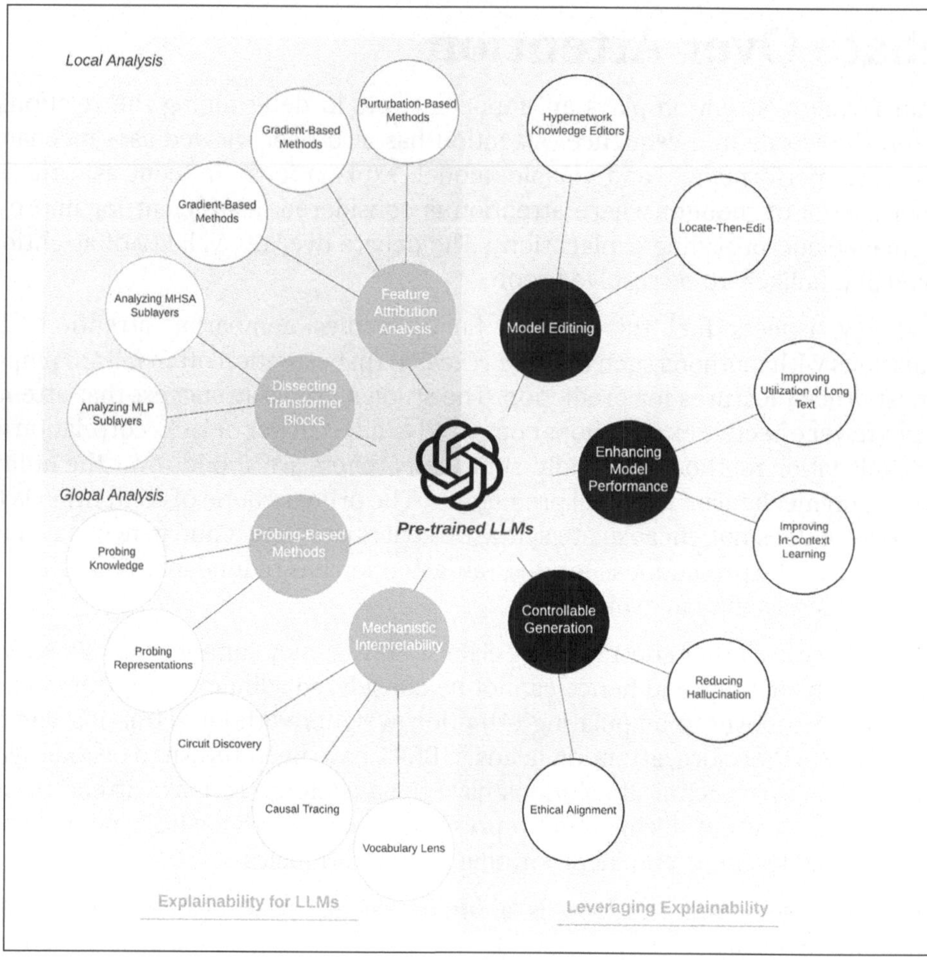

Figure 9.10: *Explainability Spectrum in LLM (Source: From Understanding to Utilization: A Survey on Explainability for Large Language Models (2024) Luo et a)*

The preceding figure captures multiple methods of Interpretability in LLMs, which we have discussed in the previous section. It also captures additional aspects, such as Evaluation and Alignment, which fit into the larger spectrum of working with LLMs. Methods such as Model Editing are also being viewed for error corrections.

Model Editing

The methodologies for making large language models provide relevant outputs, and correcting the errors is nascent. LLM editing is a technique that fits into this purview of model editing. In this method, the knowledge or behavior of LLMs is efficiently modified within specific domains without adverse effects on the performance of other inputs. Hypernetwork Knowledge Editors and Locate-Then-Edit are model editing methods.

Representation Engineering

Representation Engineering includes a set of methods to understand and control the behavior of LLMs. In this method, a specific set of activations is identified corresponding to a model's behavior. These representations can also be utilized to control the model's behavior. A linear direction in the activations related to a specific concept is identified. This could be a type of behavior, or a function, which we call the concept vector. The similarity of activations to the concept vector can help to detect the presence or absence of this concept direction during the forward pass. The concept vector can then be added to the activations during the forward pass to direct the behavior of the LLM towards the concept direction. This is an interesting approach to model transparency and exhibits a strong focus on desirable traits such as honesty.

Enhancing Model Capability

LLMs have demonstrated flexibility in various natural language processing tasks and the insights from explainability have shown to significantly enhance these capabilities. Explainability has demonstrated considerable impact in two key areas:

- Improving the utilization of long text.
- Enhancing the performance of In-Context Learning (ICL).

LLMs are shown to have trouble generalizing to sequence lengths longer than their pretrained lengths, such as the 4K limit for Llama-2. StreamingLLM, a technique that uses Multi-Head Self-Attention (MHSA) explanations, is an efficient framework that allows LLMs to handle unlimited text without fine-tuning. Similarly, mechanistic interpretability reveals that label words in the demonstration examples function as anchors and can be used to improve in-context learning performance with simple anchor reweighting methods.

Controllable Generation

Despite the exceptional performance of text generation by LLMs, they sometimes make errors when producing factual content. Hallucination is a common challenge in large language models where the model confidently produces non-factual responses. Explainability is a significantly less expensive way to reduce hallucination while being adjustable and minimally invasive. Ethical alignment and AI fairness to detect social bias is an important area of research. Interpretable techniques, such as Integrated Gap Gradient (IG2), to pinpoint social bias neurons by backpropagating have been introduced. These methods have made the applicability of explainability for ethical alignment in LLMs possible, and experiments have verified their effectiveness.

Evaluation

Large Language Models, such as GPT-4, have portrayed abilities to generate natural language explanations for their predictions. Evaluation methods that are better designed are needed to assess the performance of explainability methods such as attribution. Having evaluation datasets is important for evaluating factual editing in LLMs. Also, evaluation using GPT-judge is regularly being used for truthfulness checks. The GPT, as a judge, is commonly used to evaluate the TruthfulQA benchmark, a dataset that is widely used and was adversarially constructed for measuring the truth factor of a language model in generating answers.

LMM Explainability

This is an emerging area of interest. Similar to LLM, a dictionary learning-based extraction framework is being reviewed for multimodal explainability. It is useful in understanding the internal representations of a large multimodal model. Other methods, such as Semi-NMF, a variant of the concept dictionary learning problem, are also recommended. The prominence of large multimodal models in real-world applications is further fueling the research on multimodal explainability.

The increasing focus on LLMs and LMMs indicates the growing vitality of explainability. Explainability will become immensely important in ensuring that these models are transparent, fair and beneficial.

Conclusion

While transformers have been around for less than a decade, the Large Language Model adoptions of the transformer models have become very popular. The adoption of LLMs in applications has picked up steam. Hence, the demand for explainability is bound to increase. At this time, explainability in Large Language Models is an area of active research, and many of the techniques mentioned in this chapter are either in early stages, exploratory in nature, or not yet matured. There is also a heavy focus on making LLMs more trustworthy and aligned with human values by using explainability knowledge.

The applications of AI in the industry are growing, and many applications using traditional machine learning as well as LLMs are starting to become very mainstream, implying a growing impact on societies. In this context, ensuring alignment and ethical usage is a priority. The last concluding chapter will focus on Responsible AI, providing the guidelines and tools available in aiding adherence to RAI.

References

1. Attention Is All You Need (2017) Vaswani et al: https://arxiv.org/pdf/1706.03762
2. [MLLM Talk] Explainability for Large Language Models:
3. https://www.youtube.com/watch?v=4AGvGhVzMnI
4. From Understanding to Utilization: A Survey on Explainability for Large Language Models (2024) Luo et al: https://arxiv.org/pdf/2401.12874
5. Explainability for Large Language Models: A Survey (2023) Zhao et al: https://arxiv.org/pdf/2309.01029
6. A Concept-Based Explainability Framework for Large Multimodal Models (2024) Parekh et al: https://arxiv.org/pdf/2406.08074
7. An Introduction to Representation Engineering - an activation-based paradigm for controlling LLMs (2024) Jan Wehner:
8. https://www.alignmentforum.org/posts/3ghj8EuKzwD3MQR5G/an-introduction-to-representation-engineering-an-activation
9. Analyzing Chain-of-Thought Prompting in Large Language Models via Gradient-based Feature Attributions (2023) Wu et al: https://arxiv.org/pdf/2307.13339
10. REPRESENTATION ENGINEERING: A TOP-DOWN APPROACH TO AI TRANSPARENCY (2023) Zou et al: https://arxiv.org/pdf/2310.01405
11. The Geometry of Truth: Emergent Linear Structure in LLM Representations of True/False Datasets (2024) Marks et al: https://arxiv.org/pdf/2310.06824
12. A Survey on Natural Language Counterfactual Generation (2024) Wang et al: https://arxiv.org/pdf/2407.03993
13. Mapping the Mind of a Large Language Mode: https://www.anthropic.com/research/mapping-mind-language-model
14. Mechanistic interpretability of large language models with applications to the financial services industry (2024) Golgoon et al https://arxiv.org/html/2407.11215v1
15. Visualizing Attention in Transformer-Based Language Representation Models (2019) Jesse Vig https://arxiv.org/pdf/1904.02679
16. From Understanding to Utilization: A Survey on Explainability for Large Language Models (2024) Luo et al https://arxiv.org/pdf/2401.12874

CHAPTER 10
Explainability and Responsible AI

Introduction

Interpretability and Explainability are incomplete without a conversation on Responsible AI. In this chapter, we will have a deeper look at Responsible AI or Ethical AI. Identifying and mitigating bias is also an important aspect of Responsible AI. Finally, we will look at Causal Interpretability and Adversarial attacks in XAI.

Structure

In this chapter, the following topics will be covered:

- Responsible AI
- Explainability in Bias Mitigation
- Causal Inference
- Adversarial Machine Learning
- Adversarial attacks in Explainable AI

Responsible AI

We have discussed Responsible AI in *Chapter 1, Interpreting Interpretable Machine Learning*, as a strong reason for adopting Interpretability and Explainability. Responsible AI (RAI) is the set of principles guiding the development, deployment, and utilization of AI systems to be in compliance with legal and ethical standards.

Given the regional differences in laws and ethics, there is not a universal definition of responsible AI. However, many stakeholders have attempted to create frameworks to guide its development. Recent literature often uses Responsible AI (RAI) interchangeably with terms, such as trustworthy AI, ethical AI, and fair or equitable AI. We propose that RAI include these concepts, asserting that truly responsible AI must be trustworthy, fair, and ethical, among other qualities. In the next section, we highlight the significance of responsibility in AI and outline the six key pillars of responsible AI identified by the industry.

Importance of Responsibility AI

AI systems are becoming more common in everyday life, with applications ranging from media recommendations to self-driving cars. The risks of poorly developed AI in safety-critical areas are clear: failures in autonomous vehicles, weapon systems, or automated medication delivery can result in loss of life or severe consequences. Therefore, it is crucial that AI systems involved in safety-critical decisions are designed to be reliable, accountable, and unbiased.

The risks of irresponsible AI design, while less evident in other areas, can have equal impact and cause harm. For instance, facial recognition technology is typically used by law enforcement, retail stores, and sporting venues to identify potential offenders or wrongdoers. However, studies have shown that commercial facial recognition tools have higher error rates for women and racial or ethnic minorities compared to light-skinned men. This means that innocent people from marginalized groups are more likely to be wrongly identified as criminals. Additionally, predictive policing algorithms trained on images of previously arrested individuals have been found to exhibit racial biases. These biases are often due to data imbalances, where minority groups are underrepresented in training data for commercial facial recognition models and overrepresented in data for predictive policing models. As a result, irresponsible AI can perpetuate and amplify human biases in the justice system, leading to discriminatory arrest practices.

Facial recognition is one area of how AI systems can have significant impacts. Medical AI diagnosis systems may fail to accurately diagnose conditions in gender, racial, and ethnic minorities due to historical underrepresentation in medical data. In various studies, hiring algorithms have also been prone to exhibit biases based on gender, ethnicity, age, disability, and sexuality. In fact, the removal of traces and signs of these characteristics from resumes also did not matter; the natural language processing (NLP) approaches could still be biased against these minority groups based on sociolinguistic patterns. In the banking domain, where automated lending algorithms are used to identify potential loan defaulters, a similar bias was noticed in the approval rates and loan sizes for minority groups.

Beyond these possibly life-changing outcomes, biased AI can also potentially have the risk of physical, mental, and social harm. Generative AI systems are increasingly used across fields, such as education and psychology. Recent reports have been known to produce biased content, hate speech, misinformation, or inappropriate responses to mental health crises.

In a sense, recommendation systems that can be considered harmless also have some unintended consequences. Studies have shown that recommendation systems on some media platforms can steer users towards problematic content based on their previous interactions. This leads to the amplification of misinformation and extremism, creating 'filter bubbles' that predominantly recommend content reinforcing users' existing views, resulting in confirmation bias. Multiple research indicates that such filter bubbles can be disrupted by providing more balanced recommendations, reducing the unexpected biases.

Overall, AI can cause various types of harm–social, financial, mental, and physical. The potential for AI to cause harm underscores the importance of Responsible AI (RAI). The significant risks discussed can be mitigated by strategies that make AI systems more transparent, ensuring they are developed, deployed, and used responsibly for the benefit of society and the environment.

Pillars of Responsibility

The framework states six critical characteristics for responsible AI: fairness, robustness, transparency, accountability, privacy, and safety. Each of these pillars has been identified as critical to RAI based on the RAI policies and frameworks that have been proposed in academia, industry, and governance.

Explainability is considered foundational for each of the six pillars of Responsible AI identified.

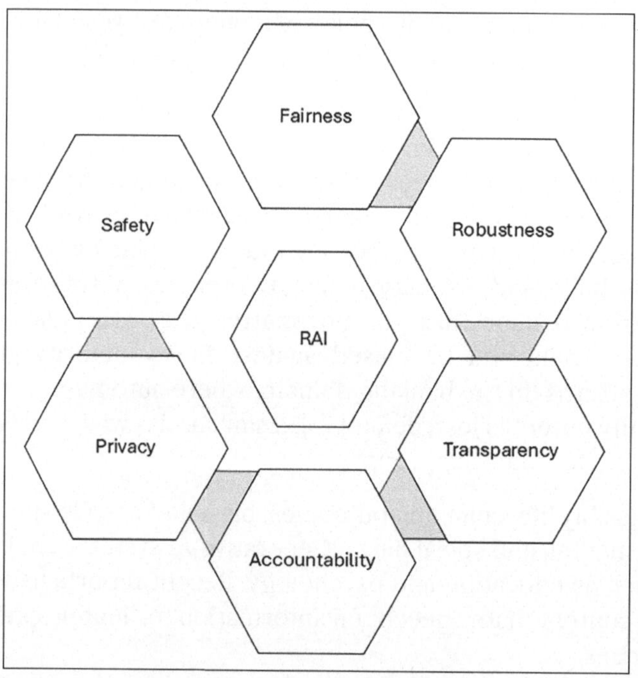

***Figure 10.1**: Pillars of Responsible AI*

Fairness

To ensure fairness in AI systems, developers must first identify instances of bias or discrimination so they can address these issues. Explainability techniques are particularly effective at uncovering a model's biases on both global and local scales. For example, in a home loan scenario, if tools such as SHAP or LIME reveal that gender was the primary factor in denying a loan application, this indicates a clear bias that needs correction. This understanding has led to the widespread consideration of explainability in the literature for developing fair AI systems.

One study examined the fairness of AI models such as Random Forest, KNN, and Decision Trees in predicting recidivism among juveniles. The analysis used LIME scoring along with accuracy and fairness metrics, comparing models trained with static inputs (unchangeable factors such as sex and nationality), dynamic inputs (changeable factors like social support and school performance), and a combination of both. LIME scoring revealed that AI models often base decisions on static variables when available, indicating learned biases. In addition, the analysis further showed increased incongruent metrics when static variables were included, with a higher incidence of incorrect recidivism identification for men and foreigners. There was a trade-off found between accuracy and fairness, with the learning fair representations (LFR) strategy identified as a potential bias mitigation method. LIME explanations were crucial in exposing biases in all AI models, enabling the application and assessment of bias mitigation strategies.

In the medical field, a recent study proposed a framework using a custom XAI tool for auditing medical diagnostic systems. Inspired by LIME and anchors, this tool generates a local 'neighborhood' of perturbations and extracts rules to provide explanations. The framework calculates disparity scores for different groups based on sex, ethnicity, and insurance status using the Wasserstein distance between predictions and ground truth. The customized XAI tool then explains system misclassifications, allowing fairness assessment at two stages: visualizing disparity scores to see if any group suffers higher disparity and inspecting local explanations of misclassifications to identify biases in predictions. This system supports fairness in a transparent and auditable manner.

Another study developed an interactive and explainable tool for loan decision-making based on a logistic regression model. This prototype explains feature importance at global and local levels using model weights and allows comparisons to similar applications. The interactive component of the prototype enables non-technical end users to label a decision as 'fair' or 'not fair' and adjust the weightings of different features to see if the decision changes. These labels and suggested weight adjustments are then used to refine the model. Previous 'fair' and 'not fair' labels are included in the explanations, allowing users to see how often the model's predictions were labeled as 'fair' or 'not fair' overall and whether similar applications were judged fairly by the model. Incorporating the suggested weight changes into the model was found to enhance fairness based on disparate impact (DI) assessment. This approach shows promise in integrating human feedback to improve model fairness, though the authors caution that users might introduce their own biases.

Another study introduced a system called Gopher, designed to enable human 'fairness debugging' by quantifying and explaining model bias. This system uses data subset removal and fairness metrics to identify which data types cause biases and suggest corrections. Explanations are provided as lists of patterns (groups of co-occurring features) responsible for biases, along with recommendations for updates or data removals to reduce bias. This method was shown to be effective on several well-known databases.

In general, the use of explainability to support fairness is well-established in the literature. Many studies use tools such as LIME and SHAP to check if specific features have an unfair spotlight by the model. Other studies propose systems that assess and explain fairness to developers and end-users, aiming to gather feedback and iterate the model to enhance fairness. It is evident from the literature that XAI significantly supports the fairness principle of Responsible AI (RAI).

Robustness

Robustness has been a central focus in many studies using explainable AI. Explainability helps determine if a model behaves consistently with similar inputs and withstands adversarial attacks. A recent study introduced a novel explainability technique called Similarity Difference and Uniqueness (SIDU) for creating heatmap explanations of image data that are robust against adversarial attacks. SIDU extracts the final layer of a CNN and calculates similarity and difference masks for various feature applications, which are then combined to produce a final heatmap. In experiments, SIDU generated explanations that closely matched human evaluations via eye tracking, outperforming models such as Grad-CAM. To test robustness, noise was added to input images, and CNN model predictions were explained using SIDU and other models. SIDU's explanations remained stable as noise levels increased, while Grad-CAM's explanations deteriorated. This work shows that explanations can assess a model's robustness to noise and that explainability tools can be improved for better robustness.

Another study explored the link between robustness and explainability from a different perspective, investigating whether robust models are inherently explainable. The study trained models with clean and adversarial data to enhance robustness and compared them to non-robust models trained only with clean data. They then evaluated how closely the salience maps from these models matched target salience maps. In a comparison of two open-access databases, the robust models' salience maps were found to be more aligned with target maps than those of non-robust models. This suggests that robust models have more interpretable salience maps and hence can reduce the requirement for a post-hoc heatmap explanation whenever robustness is achieved.

Explainability has also been employed to measure robustness, with one study introducing a robustness metric based on counterfactual explanations. Their Counterfactual Explanation-based Robustness Score (CERScore) is based on the principle that, when comparing two AI models, the model with counterfactuals further away from the input instances is considered more robust. CERScore is model-agnostic and can be utilized without understanding the underlying architecture. This makes this method noteworthy and trumps previous robustness metrics. The authors demonstrated that CERScore produced robustness scores that are consistent with literature benchmarks through various experiments on established AI models, this showing that explainability can quantify robustness.

Explainable AI (XAI) has also been used to enhance model robustness. In a recent study, a Deep Neural Network model was trained to identify malware by using adversarial training and then with XAI-based finetuning. After the initial adversarial training, SHAP scores were calculated for the input features. These scores were used to create a second adversarial database, which was then used to train the final DNN model. When testing was done on the two models, it revealed that the combination of training with XAI-based finetuning approach improved the accuracy of the model on unseen test data in comparison to only doing traditional adversarial training.

A series of recent studies shows that explainability can be used both to quantify and enhance robustness. These are both desirable and crucial characteristics for Responsible AI (RAI). Additionally, quantifying robustness provides a functional metric for comparing candidate models. Also employing XAI to develop more robust models ensures resilience against adversarial attacks and invalid inputs.

Transparency

Transparency is arguably the most obvious benefit that XAI brings to Responsible AI (RAI); the main goal of XAI is to demystify AI systems to enhance transparency and comprehensibility. Models must offer explanations that are interpretable and understandable to end-users to attain transparency. This can involve clarifying the inner workings of a black box model or explaining a model's decisions in a way that users find meaningful and acceptable.

Several recent studies have explored the claim of XAI explanations being transparent, interpretable, and understandable to end-users. A counterfactual-based explanation strategy was devised in one study for explaining decisions made by a chest X-ray CNN classifier to expert radiologists. Survey questions and free-text responses were used to evaluate the transparency of this approach. The survey sought to determine if the explanations improved understandability and trust in their XAI system, compared to no explanation, saliency maps, and cycleGAN. On a 5-point Likert scale, experts rated the counterfactual explanations highest on understandability and justifiability. Also, all explainability tools tested were rated significantly higher for understandability than in the case of no explanations. Free-text comments also confirmed that experts had a better understanding of the AI model through counterfactual explanations.

Another research sought to assess behavioral anomalies and cognitive status in a smart home residential care setting using text-based explanations that were generated by analyzing the decision pathways of a trained Decision Tree model. On a Likert scale survey, clinicians had to rate their experience with the provided explanations. The questions about transparency received high ratings, and all clinicians agreed that the explanations were easily understandable as well as crucial for understanding the basis for the model classification of anomalies for individual patients. Most of the clinicians were in consensus that the explanations would help them determine whether the model's assessments were correct.

In another study focused on the education sector, a Random Forest model was developed to make decisions on graduate school admissions, with explanations provided using LIME, local SHAP, global SHAP, and Partial Dependence Plots (PDP). A survey of university students with varying levels of AI experience on a Likert scale was used to determine if these explanations improved their understanding of the model. Both PDP and LIME markedly enhanced understandability for AI newbies as well as for those with some AI experience. SHAP also improved understandability, but to a lesser extent, possibly due to the unclear graphical format used to present SHAP scores.

A study was conducted to identify the level of transparency that gives users the most confidence in an autonomous vehicle's driving decisions. A confidence metric based on case-based reasoning was developed where past situations were used to determine the vehicle's confidence in current scenarios. This confidence level was presented to a non-expert group using various text structures. Survey participants ranked the text structures based on usefulness. The most well-received explanation included the confidence level along with general information about past situations. Explanations that combined confidence with current or future situation information were also well-received. The least favored explanation provided only the confidence level without explaining how it was determined. These findings suggest that text explanations of model confidence are crucial for improving the acceptability of AI systems.

In essence, multiple recent studies indicate a strong link between explanations and transparency in AI systems. Various explanation methods, including text-based, visual, and feature-based explanations, have been shown to enhance transparency to some degree. These explanations support transparency for a wide range of users with different levels of domain and AI expertise.

Accountability

Accountability in AI requires models to justify their decisions, ensuring they can be audited and assessed for compliance with legal and governance standards. This requirement is closely tied to transparency since models must explain their decisions to be considered accountable. In the finance sector, accountability is particularly crucial. A recent study proposed an auditable pipeline using various XAI techniques to provide transparent and accountable credit scoring. The authors noted that logistic regression is popular in credit risk scoring due to its inherent explainability, which has gained acceptance among regulators. However, as we have discussed in previous chapters, logistic regression does not perform as well as advanced AI techniques for this task. A pipeline starting with global explanations was proposed. The pipeline also used feature permutation importance, followed by assessing the most important features with PDP and ICE plots. Local instances are then explained using LIME, SHAP, and another SHAP variant. This pipeline aims to explain advanced AI algorithms in a way that meets regulatory and legal requirements for transparency, accountability, and privacy.

Accountable AI systems are also needed to establish liability in legal cases. Another study identified XAI as highly suitable for providing a 'forensic toolset' to help establish AI system liability in various settings. They illustrated a case study where an autonomous vehicle changes lanes to avoid a collision with car A, ultimately causing a collision with car B. XAI tools could help in demonstrating why the AI model made the particular decision, thus establishing factual and legal causation as required by many common law systems. This enables legal systems to hold AI systems accountable for their actions and determine whether the AI system or another party is at fault for an accident. The study suggests that LIME, ICE, and PDP are important XAI tools in understanding the global model, while SHAP was crucial in deciphering the individual decisions, consistent with the credit scoring study's suggestions.

In the medical field, an auditable pipeline was developed to predict oxygen requirements in COVID-19 patients using GradCAM explanations of features identified in chest x-ray images. This technique involved creating model-derived atlases for similar feature patches and overall predictions based on areas highlighted by GradCAM. After a prediction is made, clinicians are shown eight similar patches from the atlas alongside the test patch, a GradCAM heatmap of the entire x-ray. There was also a table comparing the test x-ray with multiple similar x-rays, both visually and with feature-based similarity scores, and a table displaying the model's confidence in each detected feature. In addition, clinicians can also select feature labels to receive further characterization of the disease.

The usage of example-based explanations and numerical confidence scores makes AI decisions highly auditable and accountable to both expert clinicians and regulatory bodies. It is evident that accountability is crucial in various sectors to establish that AI models meet the same standards as humans. The literature review also suggests that XAI can produce the necessary level of accountability and auditability across several important sectors, significantly contributing to the development of Responsible AI (RAI) systems.

Privacy

Privacy is crucial for AI systems, ensuring that no sensitive information is accessible to users. Balancing privacy with transparency has been identified as a key challenge in developing responsible AI systems. Generally, most techniques for global and local explanations are inherently privacy-preserving, as they do not explicitly reveal identifiable information from the training data. However, recent studies have shown that targeted adversarial attacks on CAM-based XAI models have a slightly higher chance of breaching privacy through training image reconstruction or model duplication compared to models without explanations. Importantly, these attacks were successful against both explainable and unexplainable models, highlighting the need for data protection and privacy-preserving techniques in responsible AI development.

However, these techniques can make AI opaque, conflicting with transparency and accountability principles. This is where XAI comes in: several recent studies have shown that XAI techniques can still provide robust and meaningful explanations even when data protection and privacy-preserving techniques are applied, thus supporting privacy without compromising other RAI principles.

For instance, one study applied federated learning to develop a model for heart arrhythmia classification from electrocardiogram (ECG) signals before applying explainability. Federated learning preserves privacy by allowing individual institutions to train local models, which are then shared with a central node for aggregation. The aggregated model is returned to the institutions for use, enabling the development of more robust models without direct data sharing and protecting against data inversion attacks. In this particular study, it was found that federated learning improved accuracy in detecting key ECG features and classifying arrhythmia in comparison to local models. This was the case even with noisy signals. GradCAM was used to build the explanations where heatmaps of the most important regions in a signal were generated. While model duplication is still possible, reconstructing local models is unlikely if weight sharing is protected.

In another study, swarm learning was used to develop a model for cancer diagnosis from histopathology slides. Swarm learning is similar to federated learning, where models are trained locally first, but it aggregates models by sharing trained local models in a peer-to-peer structure. This decentralized architecture ensures that the failure of a single node does not compromise the entire network. The study showed that swarm models outperformed local models across all criteria. Model predictions were explained with heatmaps. The generated heatmap highlighted the regions of interest leading to a prediction. Like federated learning, this approach is robust against data inversion attacks since the final aggregate model has no knowledge of the training data. Swarm learning being decentralized, this aspect also enhances robustness in case of node failure.

Another approach to privacy preservation is differential privacy, which anonymizes data by injecting noise. A recent study examined the impact of this approach on SHAP values using various open-access databases, data perturbation methods, and AI models. The findings showed that SHAP values were minimally affected by data protection techniques. While simple linear models were more affected than advanced models such as support vector regression, they still provided meaningful explanations. The authors concluded that data protection and explanation are not mutually exclusive.

Differential privacy was also explored in an image context using image compression to remove spatial and edge information, thus privatizing data before training. This study considered three image-based use cases: chest x-ray classification, cervix type classification, and glaucoma detection. The results indicated that high accuracy could still be achieved with compressed images. Salience map explanations provided meaningful information about relevant areas of an image even without access to the original uncompressed image, improving privacy as original images were not used for model training.

In summary, we can state that XAI indirectly supports privacy. AI systems are vulnerable to adversarial attacks, and privacy-preserving techniques can conflict with transparency and accountability principles. XAI helps by enabling privacy-preserving learning and data protection techniques without compromising other key RAI requirements.

Safety

Ensuring the safety of humans, environments, and societies is crucial for AI systems, especially in high-risk areas such as autonomous driving and healthcare. XAI can help uncover the inner workings of an AI model, thereby identifying potential safety risks. Additionally, XAI systems can be integrated with existing AI systems to enhance safety by detecting network intrusions or other attacks, protecting the overall pipeline from adversarial threats and supporting Responsible AI (RAI).

A recent study examined the role of XAI in ensuring safety in healthcare through a case study on predicting when a patient should be extubated from mechanical ventilation in intensive care. In this context, safety is paramount because early extubation can lead to emergency re-intubation, while late extubation increases the risk of complications such as pneumonia. The study found that XAI techniques are valuable for verifying safety at various stages of AI development. Specifically, feature importance and counterfactual example methods were highlighted as supporting safety in AI. Feature importance allows clinicians to verify that the model uses features that align with clinical expectations, boosting confidence that the model's decisions will benefit the patient. Counterfactual explanations can show how many features need to change and by how much so as to alter the decision. This helps clinicians assess the model's confidence in its decision, which in turn supports patient safety. Clinicians are thus empowered with the additional tools to make informed decisions about whether to trust the model in the particular case or if additional investigation is needed.

In the autonomous driving domain, XAI has been used to compare the performance of three models in classifying traffic signs under various conditions, including camera failures, such as broken lenses, ice coverage, or dead pixels. The study found that the AlexNet-based model performed best across most lens failure modes. LIME heatmaps were applied to understand this further, showing that AlexNet's predictions used features spread over a larger section of the input image compared to other models. This likely contributes to AlexNet's higher tolerance to camera failures, as widely distributed features are less likely to be obscured by defects. Thus, XAI supports safe autonomous driving by identifying the most reliable traffic sign model under adverse conditions.

Another study reviewed goal-driven AI systems (GDAIs), which include robots and other agents operating independently to achieve their goals. They emphasized the need for explainable GDAIs in safety-critical applications to prevent harm to humans or environments. The study highlighted that explanations via CAM, SHAP, and textual descriptions are essential for communicating GDAI decisions. These explanations support human-computer interaction, enabling early detection of problems and intervention to prevent failures, which is crucial for safety-critical applications.

XAI can also protect against adversarial attacks on digital systems using AI. One study used explainability techniques in an intrusion detection system for IoT networks. The system, which included rule-based explanations, LIME, and SHAP, accurately detected intruders or compromised nodes, providing global and local explanations to help human experts decide on a response. This use of XAI helps protect AI models operating on IoT network data from attacks, as rapid and interpretable detection of intruders reduces the risk of malicious data injection.

In summary, we can state that explainability strongly supports safety across various AI applications. XAI techniques enhance safety by allowing human experts to review decisions and determine their reasonableness. Additionally, XAI can be integrated with other AI systems to detect security risks such as network intrusions, reducing the risk of adversarial attacks. Thus, XAI is a crucial tool for ensuring the RAI principle of safety is met.

Explainability in Bias Mitigation

A very important pillar of Responsible AI is the handling of bias. As we have seen in previous chapters, explainability plays a crucial role in identifying bias.

Bias Detection

Explainability can be approached in various ways. We can distinguish between local and global explainability methods. Local approaches explain model behavior in the vicinity of a specific instance, while global methods aim to explain the model's behavior at a higher level. The explainability techniques can be categorized into model-agnostic methods and model-specific methods that utilize model internals such as gradients. Explanations based on counterfactuals is also a growing trend. Techniques such as KernelSHAP can also be used to detect bias in models.

Bias Mitigation

The techniques to mitigate bias can involve modifying the model itself by adjusting its optimization process or post-processing its predictions. Several open-source repositories provide bias management approaches, such as fairness-comparison2, Aequitas3, Themis4, responsibly5, and LiFT. Additionally, products such as IBM's AI Fairness 3606, Microsoft's Fairlearn7, and TensorFlow's What-If-Tool are designed around bias metrics and mitigation strategies.

Bias Mitigation Using Fairlearn

Here we will look at a bias mitigation example using the Fairlearn package. Fairlearn package has two aspects:

- **Metrics**: This is for analyzing the groups that are negatively impacted by a model and in comparing multiple models across various fairness and accuracy metrics.
- **Algorithms**: This is for mitigating the unfairness in a variety of AI tasks and also along a variety of fairness definitions.

It is important to note that fairness is a fundamental sociotechnical challenge and cannot be addressed solely with technical tools. Additionally, fairness has different definitions in different contexts, and it may not be possible to represent it quantitatively at all. But in many scenarios, it may be helpful for tasks such as assessing unfairness through various metrics or mitigating the observed unfairness while training a model.

1. Install required Fairlearn package.

   ```
   !pip install fairlearn
   ```

2. Load the diabetes dataset, check the feature race to understand the different races in the dataset and the data distribution.

   ```
   from fairlearn.datasets import fetch_diabetes_hospital
   from sklearn.model_selection import train_test_split
   from sklearn.tree import DecisionTreeClassifier
   ```

```
from sklearn.metrics import accuracy_score
import pandas as pd

# Fetch the dataset
data = fetch_diabetes_hospital(as_frame=True)

# Extract features and target
X = data['data'].copy()
y = data['target']

X.drop(columns=["readmitted"], inplace=True)
y = data.target
X_frame = pd.get_dummies(X)
race_values = X['race']
print(race_values.value_counts())

X_frame = pd.get_dummies(X)
```

```
race
Caucasian          76099
AfricanAmerican    19210
Unknown             2273
Hispanic            2037
Other               1506
Asian                641
Name: count, dtype: int64
```

Figure 10.2: *Dataset grouped on feature race*

3. Train the dataset, run predictions on the test set, and check the accuracy score. We are using a decision threshold for positive predictions that is 0.1.

```
# Split the data into training and testing sets
import numpy as np

X_train, X_test, y_train, y_test, A_train, A_test = train_test_
split(X_frame, y, race_values, random_state=123)

# Initialize the DecisionTreeClassifier
clf = DecisionTreeClassifier(min_samples_leaf=10, max_depth=4)

# Train the classifier
clf.fit(X_train, y_train)
```

```
# Make predictions
#y_pred = clf.predict(X_test)
y_pred = (clf.predict_proba(X_test)[:,1] >= 0.1)

# Calculate accuracy
accuracy = accuracy_score(y_test, y_pred)
print(f'Accuracy: {accuracy}')

Accuracy: 0.6475119880512539
```

4. Using the MetricsFrame, we compare the false positive rates across races.

```
from fairlearn.metrics import MetricFrame, false_negative_rate,
false_positive_rate, selection_rate, count

mf = MetricFrame(metrics=false_positive_rate, y_true=y_test, y_
pred=y_pred, sensitive_features=A_test)
print(mf.overall.item())

mf.by_group
```

```
0.39662111361726593

race
AfricanAmerican    0.389325
Asian              0.235294
Caucasian          0.406423
Hispanic           0.370370
Other              0.344937
Unknown            0.248148
Name: false_positive_rate, dtype: float64
```

Figure 10.3: *False Positivity Rate grouped by feature race*

5. A plot of the various metrics such as accuracy, **false_positive** rates across the races is then visualized. The plot shows that the races Asian and Other do have a lower false positive rate in comparison.

```
metrics = {
    "accuracy": accuracy_score,
    "false positive rate": false_positive_rate,
    "false negative rate": false_negative_rate,
    "selection rate": selection_rate,
    "count": count,
}
metric_frame = MetricFrame(
```

```
    metrics=metrics, y_true=y_test, y_pred=y_pred, sensitive_
features=A_test
)
metric_frame.by_group.plot.bar(
    subplots=True,
    layout=[3, 3],
    legend=False,
    figsize=[12, 8],
    title="Show all metrics",
)
```

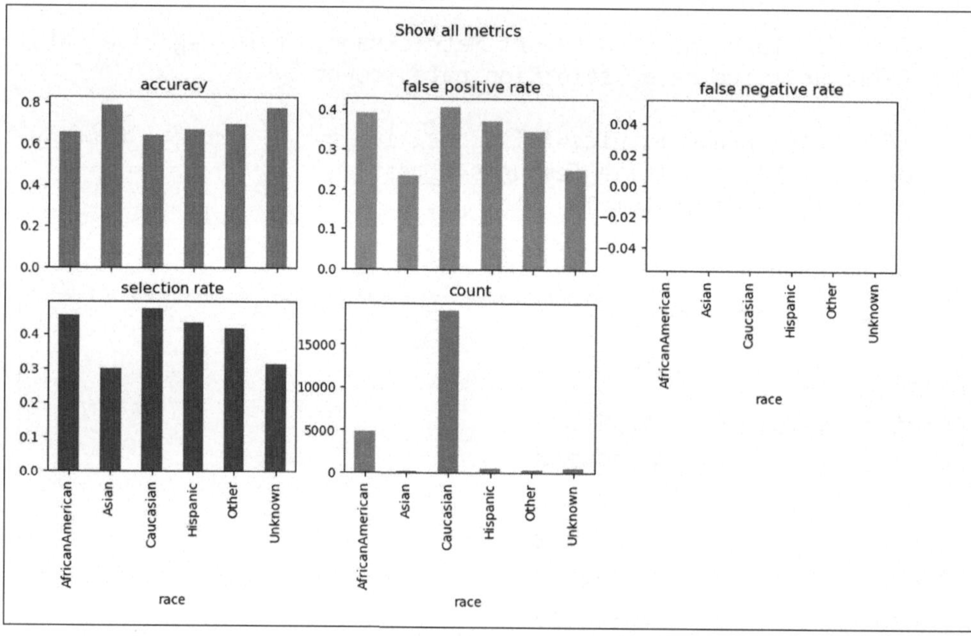

***Figure 10.4**: Metrics display using Fairlearn library*

6. Run the mitigation on the model. Since we are concerned with both the false positive and false negative rate, we use the **EqualizedOdds** constraint. Also, the **ExponentiatedGradient** method is used as the mitigation technique, with an appropriately weighted Error rate as the objective.

```
from fairlearn.reductions import ErrorRate, EqualizedOdds,
ExponentiatedGradient
objective = ErrorRate(costs={'fp': 0.1, 'fn': 0.9})
constraint = EqualizedOdds(difference_bound=0.01)
classifier = DecisionTreeClassifier(min_samples_leaf=10, max_
depth=4)
mitigator = ExponentiatedGradient(classifier, constraint,
objective=objective)
mitigator.fit(X_train, y_train, sensitive_features=A_train)
y_pred_mitigated = mitigator.predict(X_test)
```

```
mf_mitigated = MetricFrame(metrics=accuracy_score, y_true=y_test,
y_pred=y_pred_mitigated, sensitive_features=A_test)
print(mf_mitigated.overall.item())

mf_mitigated.by_group
```

```
0.6428739878940335

race
AfricanAmerican    0.653649
Asian              0.682635
Caucasian          0.639443
Hispanic           0.636008
Other              0.645070
Unknown            0.657627
Name: accuracy_score, dtype: float64
```

Figure 10.5: *Model Accuracy grouped by races*

7. Display the new mitigated model metrics.

```
from fairlearn.metrics import MetricFrame

mf = MetricFrame(metrics=false_positive_rate, y_true=y_test, y_
pred=y_pred_mitigated, sensitive_features=A_test)
print(mf.overall.item())

mf.by_group
```

```
0.40183981248065104

race
AfricanAmerican    0.389325
Asian              0.346405
Caucasian          0.406423
Hispanic           0.405229
Other              0.398734
Unknown            0.374074
Name: false_positive_rate, dtype: float64
```

Figure 10.6: *Model Accuracy after bias mitigation*

8. Validate the plot of metrics using the mitigated model.

```
metrics = {
    "accuracy": accuracy_score,
    "false positive rate": false_positive_rate,
    "false negative rate": false_negative_rate,
    "selection rate": selection_rate,
    "count": count,
}
metric_frame = MetricFrame(
    metrics=metrics, y_true=y_test, y_pred=y_pred_mitigated,
sensitive_features=A_test
)
metric_frame.by_group.plot.bar(
    subplots=True,
    layout=[3, 3],
    legend=False,
    figsize=[12, 8],
    title="Show all metrics",
)
```

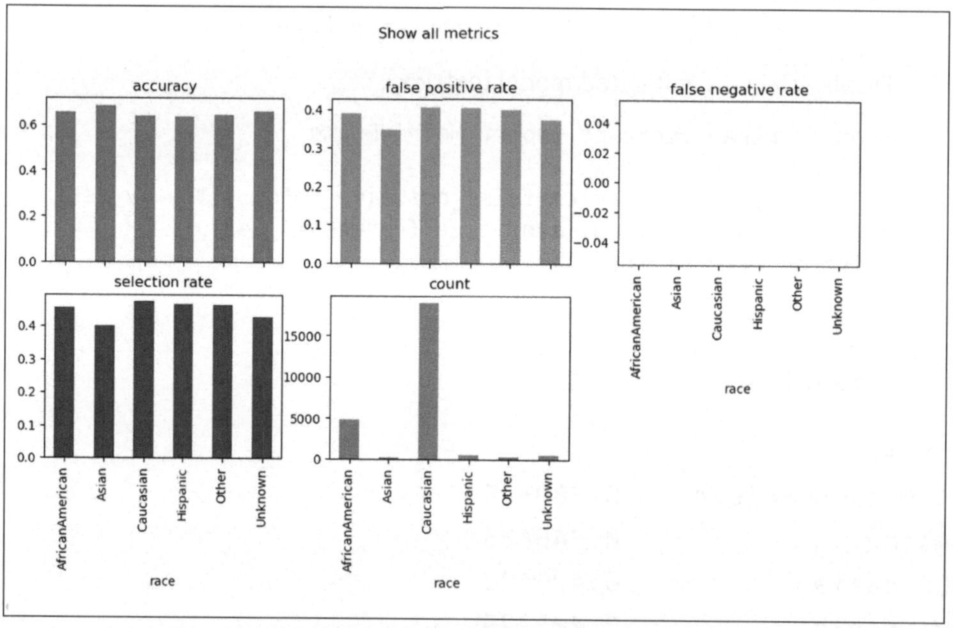

***Figure 10.7**: Metrics display for mitigated model*

These are the strategies for mitigating the performance disparities:

- **Postprocessing**: The outputs of a trained classifier are transformed so as to meet a fairness criterion in the postprocessing approach.
- **Reductions**: In the reductions approach, a model class is considered and

iteratively creates a sequence of models to optimize a fairness constraint. In comparison to the postprocessing approach, the fairness constraint is addressed during the model training time instead of posttraining.

Here is a rephrased version:

Postprocessing mitigation is provided by the ThresholdOptimizer algorithm, which uses an existing (possibly pre-trained) machine learning model's predictions as a scoring function to identify separate thresholds for each sensitive feature group. The ThresholdOptimizer method optimizes a specified objective metric and also conforms to a fairness constraint. This results in a threshold-bound version of the underlying model. A key limitation of the ThresholdOptimizer is that it needs access to the sensitive feature during prediction.

The reductions approach, on the other hand, produces models that satisfy fairness constraints without requiring access to sensitive features at deployment time. The primary reduction algorithm in Fairlearn is ExponentiatedGradient. A sequence of re-weighted datasets is created, and then the wrapped classifier is retrained on each dataset. This process ensures the resulting model meets fairness constraints while optimizing the performance metric.

The ExponentiatedGradient model has multiple inner models, which are returned in the wrapper estimator. To instantiate an ExponentiatedGradient model, two parameters are needed:

- A base estimator (an object that supports training)
- Fairness constraints

Causal Inference

Causal inference focuses on determining the causal impact of a specific variable or treatment on a particular outcome of interest. As humans, we are exceptionally skilled at forming mental decision models from limited data samples. We are well-versed in generalizing data and thinking in terms of cause and effect. Therefore, incorporating causal knowledge into Explainable AI (XAI) is crucial to achieving greater interpretability and preventing unexpected failures. To this end, Causal Discovery (CD) methods can identify all causal pathways to a variable and deduce how different variables are interconnected. Partial knowledge of the causal structure of observational data also suffices and can enhance the understanding of the input features that the black box models have used in making their predictions. This leads to higher interpretability and more robust explanations.

Causal Interpretability

In the following sections, we provide an extensive review of existing work on causal interpretability. This is specifically required as the objective functions of machine learning models only capture the correlations and not the real causes. Consequently, these models might cause problems in real-world decision making, such as making policies related to smoking and cancer. Besides, the training data that is used to train these models might not be an appropriate representation of the real environment. Also, the train and test sets might also have different distributions. A causal interpretable model helps understand the real causes of the decisions made by machine learning algorithms, thus improving the model performance and avoiding failures in unforeseen circumstances.

Traditionally, the main focus of interpretability was on statistical interpretability, while the causal interpretability aims to answer questions associated with causal interventional interpretability and counterfactual interpretability. Judea Pearl has stated the following levels of interpretability and definitions:

- **Statistical or associational interpretability**: This is primarily concerned with uncovering statistical associations for asking questions such as "How would seeing x change my belief in y?"
- **Causal interventional interpretability**: This is concerned with answering "What if" questions.
- **Counterfactual interpretability**: This is the highest level of interpretability with an objective to answer "Why" questions.

There are four main categories of classification in this domain:

- Causal interpretability for model-based interpretations: Methods in this category aim to explain the causal effect of a model's component on the final outcome.
- Counterfactual explanation generators: In this method, the primary concern is to generate counterfactual explanations for alternative situations and outcomes.
- Causal interpretability and fairness: Interpretable models are considered crucial in ensuring fairness. In this context, this is a method with a strong focus on causal fairness.
- Causal interpretability and its role in verifying the causal relationships discovered from data: These are methods that utilize interpretability as a mechanism for verifying causal assumptions and relationships. There are also scenarios where causal inference can be considered as a guarantee for the interpretability of a machine learning model.

Causal Inference in Neural Network Interpretation

Causality has garnered increasing attention in explaining deep learning models. These methods are typically designed to elucidate the role and importance of each component of a machine learning model on its decisions using concepts from causality. Consider the explanation for the role of a neuron in the decision of a neural network; this can be achieved by estimating the Average Causal Effect (ACE) of the neuron on the output. We have discussed many interpretable model techniques in previous chapters, but these methods cannot answer crucial questions for understanding machine learning models. For example, they are not capable of answering causal questions such as "*What is the impact of the n-th filter of the m-th layer of a deep neural network on the model's predictions*?" These answers are essential for understanding a neural network model. Additionally, techniques such as performing ablation testing, which involves removing a component of the model and retraining it to measure performance for a fixed dataset while being simple and intuitive, are computationally expensive and impractical.

This gap is handled with causal interpretability frameworks. The frameworks are mainly geared to explain the importance of a component in a deep neural network on the predictions by answering counterfactual questions such as "What would have happened to the model's output if we had a different component in the model?" The answers to such questions are possible through concepts of causal inference literature. The central theme is to model the structure of the Deep Neural Network (DNN) as a Structural Causal Model (SCM) and then estimate the causal effect of each component on the output through causal reasoning.

Some methods consider the DNN as an SCM and then apply a function on each filter of the model to obtain targeted values, such as variance or expected value, and then reason on the obtained SCM. Further enhancements for effective interpretability include having a human understandable causal model of DNN, which allows different kinds of causal interventions. Based on this premise, an interpretability framework is proposed to extract human understandable concepts such as the eyes and ears of a cat from deep neural networks. It then learns the causal structure between the input, output, and concepts in an SCM, finally performing causal reasoning to gain more insights into the model.

Attribution methods have also been proposed based on the first principles of causality, specifically SCMs and do-calculus. Similar to other proposed methods in this category, their framework models the structure of the machine learning algorithm as an SCM and proposes a scalable causal inference approach to estimate the individual treatment effect of a desired component on the decision made by the algorithm.

Causal Inference and Example-based Interpretation

As discussed in the previous chapter on Counterfactuals, we seek data instances that can explain the model or the underlying data distribution. Counterfactual explanations, a type of example-based explanation, are widely used to interpret a model's decisions. They aim to answer "Why" questions, such as "Why did the model decide Y?" or "Did input X cause the model to predict Y?" Counterfactuals typically address hypothetical questions such as "What would have happened to Y if I hadn't done X?". They are based on a new type of conditional probability, P(yx|x′ , y′) which indicates the likelihood that the outcome (label) of an observed instance, y′ would change to yx if x′ is set to x. These questions can be answered using Structural Causal Models (SCMs).

Causal Inference and Fairness

Today, politicians, journalists, and researchers are increasingly concerned about the interpretability of model decisions and their adherence to ethical standards. Algorithmic decision-making is widely used for tasks, such as approving credit lines, filtering job applicants, and predicting the risk of recidivism. The prediction of recidivism, which determines whether to detain or release a person, must ensure it does not discriminate against any group. Conventional evaluation metrics such as accuracy do not account for this, necessitating interpretable models to meet fairness criteria.

Recently, there has been a significant focus on integrating fairness into decision-making methods and its relationship with causal inference. A new metric was proposed for assessing the fairness of decisions based on counterfactuals. In this paper, a decision is considered fair for an individual if the outcome remains the same in both the actual world and a counterfactual world where the individual belongs to a different demographic group. Alternatively, the issue can be tackled from a data generation perspective, moving beyond observational data. They suggest using causal reasoning to address fairness by asking, "What assumptions must we make about the causal data-generating process?" instead of "What should the fairness criterion be?".

In another technique, causal inference model where the sensitive attribute confounds both the treatment and the outcome, deep learning techniques are then used to learn the model parameters. Similarly, a metric was proposed to quantitatively measure algorithmic fairness through causal explanations, based on three measures of transmission from cause to effect: counterfactual direct (Ctf-DE), indirect (Ctf-IE), and spurious (Ctf-SE) effects.

Causal Inference as Guarantee for Interpretability

Machine learning has achieved significant success in medical, legal, and economic decision-making. Frameworks for these applications must meet two criteria: they must be causal and interpretable. For instance, to determine a drug's efficacy on a patient's health, one must estimate the causal effect of the drug on the patient's health status. Additionally, to ensure the results are reliable for doctors and experts, an explanation of the background for the decision is required.

Despite recent advancements in these fields individually, few works address both requirements simultaneously. Moreover, the state-of-the-art approaches in each field are often incompatible and cannot be combined. A framework was proposed to bridge the gap between causal and interpretable models by transforming any algorithm into an interpretable individual treatment effect estimation framework. Specifically, their work leverages an algorithm to learn a predictive function f that estimates the causal effect of a treatment for any observed instance and then learns an interpretable function f' to estimate f. They also provide a bound for the error produced by their framework.

In another line of research, causal interpretability has been used to verify causal relationships in data. The two case studies conducted to identify rules, where generalized additive models with pairwise interactions (GA2Ms) learn rules based only on correlations in the data, which may conflict with causal rules. They propose fixing the learned rules based on domain experts' knowledge. Alternatively, a simple decision tree-based explanation method can be used to generate global explanations for a black box model. Their framework offers powerful insights into the data, such as causal issues previously confirmed by physicians.

Performance Evaluation

Evaluating interpretability is challenging due to the lack of agreement on the definition and the complexity of human understanding. Evaluating causal interpretability is even more difficult because of the absence of ground truth data for causal explanations and the verification of causal relationships. Therefore, a unified guideline for evaluating proposed models is essential.

Datasets: The type of data (text, image, or tabular) determines the datasets used to assess interpretability. Commonly used datasets are not particularly drafted for causal interpretability. They do not contain the ground truth to capture the causal aspect of the model. However, there are benchmark datasets specifically designed for evaluating tasks in causal inference.

Evaluation Metrics: The interpretability of generated explanations can be evaluated from two perspectives: (1) the quality of the explanations–are they interpretable to humans? and (2) the causality of the explanations–are they causal?

Evaluation metrics for traditional machine learning can be classified into two types:

- **Human Subject-Based Evaluation Metrics:** These determine how well explanations align with human expectations from various aspects.
- **Non-human Based Evaluation Metrics:** These assess the quality of generated explanations without human subjects. For example, how well does an interpretable model recover important features of the data for a specific prediction task?

Causal Evaluation Metrics can be classified into the following types:

- **Counterfactual Explanations Evaluation Metrics:** Causal interpretability is often measured by the quality of generated counterfactual explanations.
- **Model-based Evaluation Metrics:** These report the most important components of a model by measuring their causal effects on the model's outcome.
- **Causal Fairness Evaluation:** This assesses the model's performance in detecting discrimination.

The techniques mentioned while useful in causal interpretability evaluation are not entirely sufficient, and this area needs more exploratory analysis.

Implementation frameworks are available for causal Interpretability. Opensource frameworks such as CALIME and Causal SHAP add causality to traditional Interpretability techniques such as LIME and SHAP.

Adversarial Machine Learning

There has been significant development in adversarial methods within (deep) machine learning in the past decade. These algorithms aim to attack a model's behavior, impacting the security, safety, and robustness of AI systems. The most extensively studied class of attacks in machine learning is adversarial examples, particularly in computer vision tasks, where minimal modifications to input data can fool a model into misclassification.

A study demonstrated that a model can be misled by perturbing just a single pixel in an image. While image data is often the most illustrative, adversarial examples were initially studied for machine learning models predicting tabular and text data. Adversarial perturbations of text inputs can include misspellings, punctuation errors, and swapping words or characters. This threat of model manipulation impacting predictions using adversarial inputs makes it risky to deploy and use AI systems in real-world scenarios. Defense algorithms, such as data augmentation, model regularization, and distillation, aim to counter these attacks by making it harder for an attacker to deceive the model's behavior, thereby minimizing potential risks.

Backdoor attacks are another commonly adopted adversarial method in machine learning models. In this attack, it is assumed that the adversary has access to the model, such as in outsourced training scenarios. The goal is to make the model predict incorrectly for new inputs with a specific trigger pattern that is only known to the adversary. A commonly used method in backdoor attacks is poisoning the training data so that the adversarial model remains very similar to the desired one.

Adversarial Attacks in Explainable AI

A common critique of Explainable AI (XAI) is its inability to faithfully explain black box predictive functions, favoring inherently interpretable models instead. However, explanations have proven successful in applications such as autonomous driving and drug discovery, helping to better understand the reasoning of large models.

Recently, adversarial machine learning (AdvML) has become more rampant in XAI research, revealing vulnerabilities in explanation methods and raising concerns about trustworthiness and security. Adversarial attacks such as data poisoning, model manipulation, and backdoors have emerged as significant failure modes for XAI methods. To counter these attacks, defense strategies such as focused data sampling and model regularization have been proposed.

Figure 10.8 illustrates common failure modes caused by data and models influencing the outputs of explanation methods. The primary goal of an attacker is to manipulate the model's explanation by altering data or the model itself, misleading reviewers of the explanations. This poses a real threat in sensitive applications, such as decision-making systems that assist judges in making bail decisions. Attacks on explanations differ depending on the machine learning task at hand, the model architecture as well as the class of XAI methods, which are not yet well regularized.

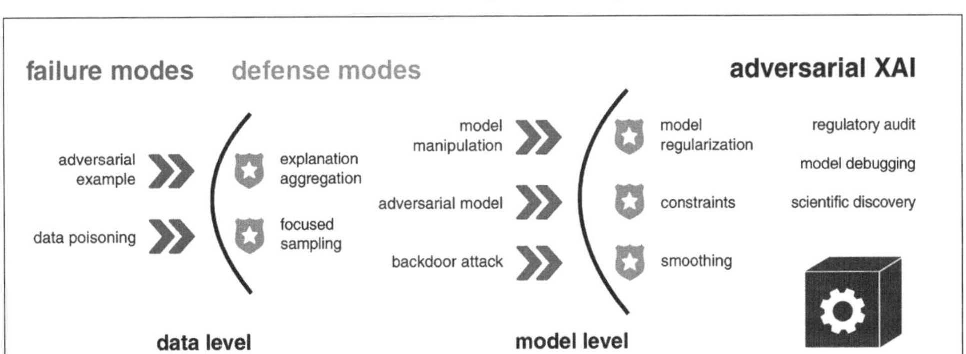

Figure 10.8: *Adversarial attack (Source: Adversarial attacks and defenses in explainable artificial intelligence: A survey (2024) Baniecki et al)*

Figure 10.8 illustrates a common attack mechanism known as adversarial examples. This involves applying a slight perturbation to an input image, which drastically changes the explanation for the "dog" class predicted by a model. By accessing the model, one can use differentiation to optimize input perturbations that significantly affect the explanations without altering the model's predictive performance. More advanced attacks involve poisoning the training data to manipulate explanations for a specific set of inputs, such as those from a particular class. Different optimization methods that do not require model access have also been developed to perform such manipulations.

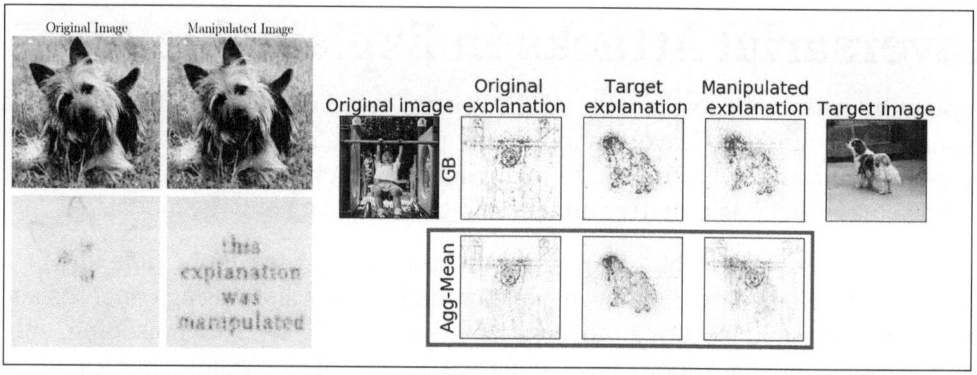

Figure 10.9: *Misclassification after image perturbation (Source: Adversarial attacks and defenses in explainable artificial intelligence: A survey (2024) Baniecki et al)*

Figure 10.9 also shows a simple defense mechanism against adversarial examples. Aggregating explanations obtained from different algorithms make them less susceptible to input manipulation, as the attacker typically targets a single explanation method, and their ensemble is more robust. There is an ongoing debate about whether the most effective defense is to patch explanation methods or to improve model algorithms, such as through regularization during training.

Defense Against the Attacks on Explanations

Whenever a new attack algorithm is introduced in adversarial machine learning, various methods are proposed to address the limitations and insecurities of explanations. A common defense against adversarial examples is by regularizing a neural network. The robust attribution regularization ensures that the integrated gradient explanations remain stable even under perturbation attacks. An alternative defense strategy is the aggregation of multiple explanations generated by different algorithms. The feature importance scores derived using various heuristics are averaged to create a more robust explanation. Since the attack targets only a single explanation method, the ensemble of explanations will remain close to the original explanation.

These are some of the defensive mechanisms in Adversarial machine learning. There is a new set of threats in the large language space that involves techniques, such as jailbreaks, prompt injections, and even the models feigning alignment. While some security measures are underway to address these concerns, there is more active research and tools required to build the required moats for such models.

Conclusion

There is still a lack of universal consensus on the set of principles for Responsible AI (RAI). There has been concentrated effort across the industry to outline various guidelines and standards for ensuring safe and responsible AI applications across development and deployment phases. The methods and tools covered in this chapter are a subset of the techniques available at this point. The entry of transformers and large language models has only increased the laser focus on Responsible AI with the hope of seeing the agreed-upon global standards and advanced tooling to achieve RAI adherence.

References

1. Explainable AI is Responsible AI: How Explainability Creates Trustworthy and Socially Responsible Artificial Intelligence (2023) Baker et al: https://arxiv.org/pdf/2312.01555
2. Amazon SageMaker Clarify: Machine Learning Bias Detection and Explainability in the Cloud (2021) Hardt et al: Amazon SageMaker Clarify: Machine Learning Bias Detection and Explainability in the Cloud
3. Data augmentation and explainability for bias discovery and mitigation in deep learning (2023) Agnieszka Mikołajczyk-Bareła: https://arxiv.org/abs/2308.09464
4. Fairlearn open source: Fairlearn (https://fairlearn.org/)
5. Causal Interpretability for Machine Learning - Problems, Methods and Evaluation (2020) Moraffah et al: https://arxiv.org/pdf/2003.03934
6. The role of causality in explainable artificial intelligence (2023) Carlonia et al: https://arxiv.org/pdf/2309.09901
7. Adversarial attacks and defenses in explainable artificial intelligence: A survey (2024) Baniecki et al: https://arxiv.org/pdf/2306.06123

Index

N

P

R

S